I0834168

PROLEGOMENA LOGICA:

AN INQUIRY

INTO

THE PSYCHOLOGICAL CHARACTER OF LOGICAL PROCESSES.

BY

HENRY LONGUEVILLE MANSEL, B.D., LL.D.

WAYNFLETE PROFESSOR OF MORAL AND METAPHYSICAL PHILOSOPHY, OXFORD;
EDITOR OF SIR WILLIAM HAMILTON'S LECTURES; AUTHOR OF
"LIMITS OF RELIGIOUS THOUGHT," ETC. ETC.

La Logique n'est qu'un retour de la Psychologie sur elle-même.

COUSIN.

FIRST AMERICAN, FROM THE SECOND ENGLISH EDITION,

CORRECTED AND ENLARGED.

BOSTON:
GOULD AND LINCOLN,
59 WASHINGTON STREET.
NEW YORK: SHELDON AND COMPANY.
CINCINNATI: GEORGE S. BLANCHARD.
1860.

Andover:
Electrotyped and Printed by W. F. Draper.

PREFACE.

A PORTION of the following pages has already appeared in two Articles contributed by the Author to the *North British Review*.[1] The present Work is an attempt to exhibit more fully the relations there intimated as existing between Logic and Psychology, with some additional matters, which could not be included within the limits of a Review. The title of the work is not meant to imply that it contains an introduction to Logic, or is designed for the use of those unacquainted with its rudiments. On the contrary, without some previous knowledge of the elementary portion of that science, the greater part of the present volume will not be intelligible. But it is intended as an inquiry into that which in the order of nature is prior to Logic; though in the order of time it is of later scientific development, and in the order of study should be postponed till after an acquaintance at least with the elements of logical science; — an inquiry into a subject which is indicated by every page of Logic in which mind and

[1] No. 27: Art. *Philosophy of Language.* No. 29: Art. *Recent Extensions of Formal Logic.*

its operations are mentioned, and which is the touchstone by which the whole truth and scientific value of Logic must ultimately be tested; — an inquiry into the constitution and laws of the thinking faculty, such as they are assumed by the Logician as the basis of his deductions. It may, therefore, be regarded as an attempt to prosecute, in relation to Logic, the inquiry instituted by the Prolegomena of Kant in relation to Metaphysics; namely, What are the psychological conditions under which a scientific system is possible; and what, in conformity to those conditions, are the characteristic features which such a system must exhibit? It is not intended as a complete treatise, either on Psychology alone, or on Logic alone; but as an exposition of Psychology in relation to Logic, containing such portions of the former as are absolutely necessary to the vindication and even to the understanding of the latter.

That something of the kind is not altogether unneeded, will be acknowledged by those who are acquainted with the literature of the subject. During the last and present century, under the influence of the Critical Philosophy of Kant, Formal Logic, in itself and in its relations to Psychology, has been elaborated by numbers of eminent writers in Germany, from whose labors the English student has, as yet, derived hardly any benefit. Misconceptions are still allowed to prevail concerning the nature and office of Logic, which the slightest acquaintance with the actual constitution of human thought and its laws would suffice to dissipate forever. Matters treated of by different logicians are alternately expelled from and restored to the province of the science, without the appearance of anything like a sound canon of criticism to determine what is logical and what is not. Attack and defence of the study have been conducted on grounds equally untenable; and a conception of Logic as it might be were the human mind constituted as it is not, is frequently tossed to and fro between contending parties, to the exclusion of Logic as it must be while the human mind is constituted as it is.

But if an exposition of Psychology in relation to Logic is thus needed for a distinct conception of the latter science in itself, it is not less needed when we look to the conditions under which that science may be most profitably employed as a branch of academical study. Few who are acquainted with the various logical systems of modern times will hesitate to give a decided preference over all others to the formal view of the science, which from the days of Kant has gradually been advancing to perfection. Whether we regard the unity and scientific completeness of the system itself, the great names by which it is supported, the valuable works that might easily be made available for its communication, or the facility with which it might be introduced into the existing course of study, in all it possesses unquestionable advantages, as the basis of logical instruction. But, on the other hand, its compass is small; and its contents, though clear and definite, are, taken by themselves, too meagre to be an adequate substitute for the miscellaneous reading which is so often misnamed Logical. To supply this defect, two courses are open. The study of Formal Logic may be combined either with its objective or with its subjective applications. We may treat, that is to say, a system of Logic, either in connection with some of the various objects of thought to which it may in practice be applied, or in relation to the thinking mind, and to that mental philosophy of which it forms a portion. The former method has been abundantly tried, and has abundantly failed in the trial. A system of Logic treated in its objective application has no alternative between an impossible universality or an arbitrary exclusiveness. By whatever right one iota of the matter of thought can claim admission into the system, by the same right the whole universe of human knowledge is entitled to follow. Such a method can only be employed as a bad means of collecting desultory information on unconnected subjects. As a system, it postulates its own failure.

It is in connection, not in confusion, with cognate sciences, as a branch of mental philosophy, that Logic may and ought to be studied. One of the objects of the present work is to show that Logic as a science cannot be rightly understood and appreciated, except in relation to Psychology. The neglect of this relation has been acknowledged as the weak side of the Kantian Philosophy;[1] its recognition has been imperatively demanded by the ablest modern writers on the subject.

[1] See Fries, *System der Logik*, p. 22.

"Selon moi," says M. Duval-Jouve, "l'objet de la logique n'est pas seulement *la direction* de l'intelligence, mais encore *l'étude* de l'intelligence; la direction après l'étude; et un traité de logique doit comprendre la description du fait intellectuel, la théorie de ses lois, l'exposé des règles qu'il doit reconnaître, soit dans son état psychologique et de pure pensée, soit dans sa manifestation par la parole."[1] The propriety of including these psychological matters in a *Treatise on Logic* may be questioned; but to the necessity of including them in a philosophical course, of which Logic should form a portion, the whole history of the science bears witness. The alliance established of old between Logic and Metaphysics was dissolved by the Critical Philosophy of Kant, and cannot be restored, except by identifying the two, with Hegel. To those who reject this alternative a blank is made in philosophical study, which can only be adequately supplied by a well-connected course of Mental Science, embracing, as its constituent portions, the three cognate subjects of Logic, Ethics, and Psychology.

To Ethics, as well as to Logic, Psychology is an indispensable supplement. The science of man as he ought to be must be based on that of man as he is. In Moral Philosophy, as in Logic, questions of a psychological character meet us at every stage of our course; and the value of every ethical system must ultimately be tested on psychological grounds. Perhaps

[1] *Traité de Logique*, Préface, p. viii.

it is not too much to say, that half the ethical systems which have been at different times in vogue, have started from a psychological assumption, which, consistently carried out, would make Ethical Philosophy impossible.

May I be allowed to suggest a still higher application of the same criterion? In the very conception of Revealed Religion, as a communication from an Infinite to a finite Intelligence, is implied the existence of certain ideas of a purely negative character, the purpose of which is not speculative but regulative truth; which are designed, not to satisfy our reason, but to guide our practice. These, from their very nature, are beyond the criticism of reason. But in order to discriminate accurately between the provinces of reason and faith, to determine what we may and what we may not seek to comprehend as a speculative truth, an examination of the limits of man's mental powers is indispensable. The ground of many a controversy might be considerably narrowed were we to inquire at the outset what are the mental powers that can be brought to the solution of the question, and how are they related to the data on which they must operate. Fichte made his earliest attempt, as a disciple of the Kantian philosophy, by an Essay towards a Critique of every Revelation. The positive portion of his principles of criticism (for many of them have a negative character only) might be better applied to a Critique of every Critique of Revelation; — an inquiry, that is to say, what portion of the contents of Revelation, as addressed to human minds, can be wrought by human interpretation into the form of speculative dogmas.

"La psychologie," says M. Cousin, "n'est assurément pas toute la philosophie, mais elle en est le fondement." If there be any truth in this saying of one of the highest philosophical authorities of our own or of any age, it will follow of necessity that a course of instruction in this fundamental branch must be an integral and indispensable portion of any system of philosophical teaching.

The psychological criticisms of the present work are mainly limited to logical questions, and are designed to throw some light on matters which, almost from the commencement of my logical studies, have appeared to me to stand in especial need of elucidation. Much of what has been acquired from foreign sources, with much labor and little guidance in the search, might have been learned in an easier and more direct manner, had the course which I have ventured to recommend been adopted in relation to my own early studies. The numerous obligations which the work is under to previous writers are most of them acknowledged as they occur. One or two, however, demand an express mention here. The reader who is familiar with Kant's writings will probably discern obligations to the Critical Philosophy in almost every page; even where the language of Kant has been departed from, and the difference in detail is such as would not justify a direct reference to his works. The method and material for thinking derived from the study of the Kantian philosophy is in many respects far more valuable than the direct information communicated. This is especially the case with a student who views that philosophy from the psychological rather than the metaphysical side, in its relation to Hume and Locke rather than to Wolf and Leibnitz, and who endeavors to combine the materials thence obtained with the most valuable results of the Scottish philosophy, which owes its rise, like the Kantian, to the skepticism of Hume.

To two other eminent philosophers a similar acknowledgment is due. The German side of M. Cousin's Eclecticism approaches, in aim at least, if not in method, nearer to the philosophy of Schelling and Hegel than to that of Kant. It is natural, therefore, that his view of the limits of human thought, and consequently of the province of Logic and of its relation to Psychology, should contain much which cannot be directly transferred to the pages of a work which advocates a strictly formal view of Logic, and which would rather contract than enlarge the limits assigned by Kant to the Understanding and the Reason. But the writings of M. Cousin are indispensable to all who would gain a true estimate of the importance of Psychology and its position in a philosophical course; and the benefits which I am conscious of having derived from their study are far more than can be adequately expressed by a direct acknowledgment of passages borrowed from them. From the author's view of the office of Logic I have departed widely; which makes it the more necessary to confess the numberless advantages derived from his writings, in relation to almost every point treated of in the following pages.

In many points in which I have departed from the doctrines of the great Eclectic, I am much indebted to the writings of his illustrious critic, Sir William Hamilton. The same acknowledgment may indeed be made in relation to nearly the whole contents of the present volume, partly by way of direct obligation, and still more by way of hints and suggestions of questions to be solved, and the method of their solution. I cannot, indeed, claim the sanction of this eminent authority for any statement which is here advanced, except where direct reference is made to his writings; yet probably even where I have differed from him in opinion, there is much that would never have been written at all but for the valuable aid furnished by him. To say that I have occasionally ventured to dissent from the positions of each and all of the philosophers to whom I am so much indebted, is only to say that I have endeavored to study their works in the spirit in which they would wish to be studied — with the respect and gratitude of a disciple, but, it is hoped, without the servility of a copyist.

For the phraseology which I have occasionally been compelled to employ in the course of the following remarks, no apology will be required by those acquainted with the history of mental science. In no branch of study is it so necessary to observe the Aristotelian precept, ὀνοματοποιεῖν σαφηνείας ἕνεκεν. Nine-tenths of the confusion and controversy that have existed in this department are owing to that unwillingness to innovate in matters of language, which leads to the employment of the same term in various shades of meaning, and with reference to various phenomena of consciousness. In this respect philosophy is under deep obligations to the purism of German writers, which has enabled subsequent thinkers to examine the most important problems of Psychology apart from the old associations of language. A new phraseology may occasion some little difficulty at the outset of a work; but to adhere to an inadequate vocabulary merely because its expressions are established, is to involve the whole of the subject in hopeless confusion and obscurity. In this respect, however, I trust I shall not be found to have departed from authorized language in a greater degree than is absolutely necessary for the purpose of communicating to English readers some of the most valuable results of German thought, and of carrying into effect the main design of the present Essay,—that of testing the received processes of Logic, by reference to the facts of human consciousness.

CONTENTS.

CHAPTER V.

CHAPTER VI.

CHAPTER VII.

CHAPTER VIII.

CHAPTER IX.

PROLEGOMENA LOGICA.

CHAPTER I.

ON THOUGHT, AS DISTINGUISHED FROM OTHER FACTS OF CONSCIOUSNESS.

WITHOUT entering into the countless disputes which have taken place concerning the nature and definition of Logic,[1] it is sufficient to observe that it will be treated in the following pages, in accordance principally with the views of Kant, as the Science of the Laws of Formal Thinking. In the wide sense, indeed, in which the term is used by Archbishop Whately, it may be admitted that Logic, as furnishing rules to secure the mind from error in its deductions, is also an Art, or, to speak more correctly, a Practical Science.[2] Still, it may be questioned whether the practical service thus performed by Logic can with propriety be allowed to influence its definition. The

[1] For a summary of various opinions on this question, see Zabarella, *de Natura Logicæ*, lib. i.; Smiglecii *Logica*, Disp. ii. Qu. v.; Burgersdicii *Inst. Log.* lib. i. cap. 1, and Sir W. Hamilton, *Edinburgh Review*, No. 115, p. 203.

[2] For the distinction between these terms, see Wolf, *Phil. Rat.* Proleg., § 10. "Omnis Logica utens est habitus, qui proprio exercitio comparatur, minime autem discendo acquiritur, adeoque et ipsa doceri nequit. Quamobrem, cum Logica omnis vel sit docens vel utens, neque enim præter regularum notitiam atque habitum eas ad praxin transferendi tertium

benefits performed by Logic as a medicine of the mind, however highly we may be disposed to rate them, are accidental only, and arise from causes external to the Science itself: its speculative character, as an inquiry into the laws of thought, is internal and essential. To the twofold character of Logic two conditions are necessary. Firstly, that there exist certain mental laws to which every sound thinker is bound to conform. Secondly, that it is possible to transgress those laws, or to think unsoundly. On the former of these conditions depends the possibility of Logic as a speculative Science; on the latter, its possibility as a practical Science or Art. Now, if we look at these two conditions with reference to the actual contents of pure Logic, it is manifest that the abrogation of the first would utterly annihilate the whole Science; whereas the abrogation of the second would at most only necessitate the removal of a few excrescences, leaving the main body of Logical doctrine substantially as it is at present. Suppose, for example, that the difference between sound and unsound reasoning could be discerned in individual cases as a matter of fact, but that we had no power of classifying the several instances of each and referring them to certain common principles. It is clear that, under such a supposition, the present contents of Logic, speculative and practical, could have no existence. The number of sound and unsound thinkers in the world might remain much as it is now, but the impossibility of investigating the principles of the one and applying them to the correction of the other would make an Art or Science of Logic unattainable.

concipi potest; sola Logica artificialis docens ea est, quæ doceri adeoque in numerum disciplinarum philosophicarum referri potest. Atque ideo quoque Logicam definivimus per scientiam, minime autem per artem vel habitum in genere, quod genus convenit Logicæ utenti."

But let us imagine, on the other hand, a race of intelligent beings, subject to the same laws of thought as mankind, but incapable of transgressing them in practice. The elements of existing Logic, the Concept, the Judgment, the Syllogism, would remain unaltered. The Science of Logic would investigate the laws of unerring Reason, as the Science of Astronomy investigates the unvarying laws of the heavenly phenomena; but an Art of Logic, to preserve the mind from error, would be as absurd as an Art of Astronomy proposing to control and regulate the planets in their courses. From these considerations it follows that, even granting Logic to be, under existing circumstances, both Science and Art, yet the former is an essential, the latter an accidental, feature; the one is necessarily interwoven with the elements of the system, the other a contingent result of the infirmities of those who possess it. In this respect, pure Logic may not unfairly be compared to Mechanics treated as a branch of Mathematics. As Sciences, both proceed deductively from assumptions more or less inconsistent with the actual state of things. As Arts, neither can be put in practice without making allowance for contingencies neglected in the scientific theory. The assumed logical perfection of thought bears about the same relation to the ordinary state of the human mind as the assumption of perfectly rigid levers and perfectly flexible cords bears to the action of those instruments in practice. But, on the other hand, the possibility of making such allowances implies that the difference between practice and theory is one of degree only, and not of kind. The instrument as used may not be identical with the instrument as contemplated, but it must be supposed capable of approximation to it. A Science of the Laws of Thought is only valuable in so far as its laws are acknowledged to be those to which actual thinking ought, as far as possible, to conform, and which, if fully complied with, would represent only the better performance of existing obligations, not the imposition of new ones. The same may be said of Ethical Philosophy likewise. In describing the perfection of moral and intellectual virtue, we describe a standard to which, in the existing state of human nature, no man does or can attain; but the whole value of the portrait is derived from its being a more or less accurate representation of man as he ought to be, not the imaginary sketch of a being of a totally distinct kind.[1]

In order therefore to the right appreciation of any given system of Logic, it becomes necessary to ask, What is the actual nature of Thought as an operation, to what laws is it subject, and to what extent are they efficient? This inquiry does not, strictly speaking, fall within the province of *Logic* itself. No Science is competent to criticise its own principles. That there is such an operation as thinking, and certain laws to which it is bound to conform, the Logician does not question, but assumes. Whether there are other mental operations besides thinking, and whether these must act in combination with Thought for the attainment of any special class of truths; — these and such like questions it is beyond his province to investigate. His own branch of inquiry is twofold, partly constructive, and partly critical. In the former capacity, he inquires, what are the several forms, legitimate or illegitimate, which

[1] "*Beide, Logik und Ethik, haben Vorschriften aufzustellen,* nach welchen sich, hier das Denken, dort das Handeln richten *soll,* obgleich es sich eins wie das andere, aus psychologischen Gründen gar oft in der Wirklichkeit nicht darnach richtet, und nicht darnach richten *kann.*"—Herbart. *Psychologie als Wissenschaft,* Th. ii. § 119.

Thought as a product will assume, according as the act of thinking is or is not conducted in conformity to its given laws. In the latter capacity, he sifts and examines the special products of this or that thinker, and pronounces them, according to the features which they exhibit, to be legitimately produced or otherwise.[1]

Beyond the boundaries of pure Logic there is thus another and important field of inquiry. Is the mind capable of other operations besides those of Thought; and are there other kinds of mental rectitude besides that which results from the conformity of Thought to its own laws? Do the several mental faculties act in the pursuit of truth conjointly or separately? Does each process guarantee the complete attainment of a limited class of truths, or the attainment of a single element which becomes truth only in combination? Do the Laws of Thought, as assumed by Logic, exhibit those features which, from the general constitution of the human mind and the peculiar character of the thinking faculty, they might be expected to exhibit? In relation to these and similar questions, Logic is subordinate to Psychology.

To Psychology we must look for the explanation and justification of the peculiar features of Logic. Logic, says one antagonist, furnishes no criterion of material truth and falsehood. It may be that, from the constitution of the human mind, such a criterion is impossible. Its principles, says another, are mere frivolous tautologies. It may be that this very tautology has a psychological significance, that it is the necessary consequence of a mind gazing upon its own laws. It is barren in the production

[1] See Clauberg, *Logica*, Proleg. § viii. Drobisch, *Neue Darstellung der Logik*, § 9. Fries, *System der Logik*, § 1.

of positive science. It may be that Thought alone was never designed by man's Maker to be otherwise. As an instrument, it has attempted much and accomplished little. The fault may lie, not in the tool, but in the workman. Before we condemn Logic for what it does not perform, or despise it for what it does, it may be as well to ask, what we may learn elsewhere of the nature of the thinking faculty, and what it may reasonably be expected to accomplish.

In order, therefore, to determine accurately the province and capabilities of Logic, it will be necessary to examine the psychological distinction between Thought, properly so called, and other phenomena of mind. This being ascertained, there will remain the inquiry, in what manner our consciousness itself and the several objects submitted to it may be regarded as subject to *law;* what are the different classes of laws, whether of the subject or of the object, the characteristic features of each, their mode of determining the several operations subject to them, and the consequent character of the respective products.

Every state of consciousness necessarily implies two elements at least: a conscious subject, and an object of which he is conscious. In every exercise, for example, of the senses, we may distinguish the object seen, heard, smelt, touched, tasted, from the subject seeing, hearing, smelling, touching, tasting. In every emotion of pleasure or of pain, there is a certain affection, agreeable or disagreeable, existing within me, and of this affection I am conscious. In every act of volition, there takes place a certain exercise of my will, and I am conscious that it takes place. In this point of view, it is not necessary to enter on the often disputed question, whether such states of consciousness furnish immediate evidence of the existence of a world external to ourselves. That of which I am directly conscious may be an object numerically distinct from myself, or it may be a modification of my own mind. All that need be insisted upon here is, that there is present an individual object, whether thing, act, or state of mind, and that we are conscious of such an object as existing within or without ourselves. A psychological dualism is implied in the very notion of consciousness: whether this necessarily involves an ontological dualism, is beyond our present purpose to inquire.[1]

But to constitute an act of *Thought*, more is required than the immediate relation of subject to object in consciousness. Every one of the above states might exist in a mind totally incapable of thought. Let us suppose, for example, a being, in whose mind every successive state of consciousness was forgotten as soon as it had taken place. Every individual object might be presented to him precisely as it is to us. Animals, men, trees, and stones, might be successively placed before his eyes; pleasure, and pain, and anger, and fear, might alternate within him; but, as each departed, he would retain no knowledge that it had ever existed, and consequently no power of comparison with similar or dissimilar objects of an earlier or later consciousness. He would have no knowledge of such objects *as referred to separate notions;* he could not say, this which I see is a man, or a horse; this which I feel is fear, or anger. He would be deficient in the distinctive feature of Thought, the concept or general notion resulting from the comparison of objects. Hence arises

[1] This point has been already argued fully and satisfactorily by the great modern advocate of Natural Dualism, Sir William Hamilton. The reader is referred to his edition of Reid's works, especially to his notes B and C, for a masterly dissertation on this important question.

the important distinction between *Intuitions*,[1] in which the object is immediately related to the conscious mind, and *Thoughts*, in which the object is mediately related through a concept[2] gained by comparison. The former contains two elements only, the subject and the object standing in present relation to each other. The latter contains three elements, the thinking subject, the object about which he thinks, and the concept mediating between the two.[3] Thus even the exercise of the senses upon present objects, in the manner in which it is ordinarily performed by a man of mature faculties, does not consist of mere intuition, but is accompanied by an act of thought. In mere intuition, all that is simultaneously presented to the sense appears as one whole; but mere intuition does not distinguish its several parts from each other under this

[1] Here, and throughout the following pages, the word *Intuition* is used in the extent of the German *Anschauung*, to include all the products of the perceptive (external or internal) and imaginative faculties ; every act of consciousness, in short, of which the immediate object is an *individual*, thing, act, or state of mind, presented under the condition of distinct existence in space or time.

[2] The revival of this term, unfortunately, till very recently, suffered to grow obsolete in philosophy, will need no apology with those who are acquainted with the writings of Sir W. Hamilton. It is absolutely necessary to distinguish in language between the act of thought and its product, a distinction expressed in Greek by νόησις and νόημα, and in the following remarks by *conception* and *concept*. The latter term has been fully sanctioned by the usage of French philosophers, as well as of the eminent writer above mentioned.

[3] "In apprehending an individual thing, either itself through sense or its representation in the phantasy, we have, in a certain sort, an absolute or irrespective cognition, which is justly denominated *immediate*, by contrast to the more relative and *mediate* knowledge which, subsequently, we compass of the same object, when, by a comparative act of the understanding, we refer it to a class, that is, think or recognize it, by relation to other things, under a certain notion or general term."— Sir W. Hamilton, *Reid's Works*, p. 804.

or that notion. I may see at once, in a single panorama, a ship upon the sea, an island lying behind it, and the sky above it. To mere intuition this is presented only in confusion, as a single object. To distinguish its constituent portions, as sea and land, ship and sky, requires a comparison and classification of them relatively to so many separate concepts existing in the mind; and such classification is an act of Thought.[1]

In every act of Consciousness the ultimate object is an *individual*. But in intuition this object is *presented* to the mind directly, and does not imply the existence, past or present, of anything but itself and the mind to which it is presented. In thought, on the other hand, the individual is *represented* by means of a concept, which contains certain attributes applicable to other individuals of the same kind.[2] This implies that there have been presented to the mind prior objects of intuition, originating the concept or general notion to which subsequent objects are referred. Hence arises another important distinction. All intuition is direct and presentative; all thought is indirect and representative.

This distinction necessitates a further remark on the characteristic feature of thought, as compared with one special class of intuitions. That sensitive perception

[1] Hoffbauer, *Logik*, § 10.

[2] The terms *represent*, *representation*, etc., are, here and throughout the present work, used in a wider sense than that to which they are confined by Sir W. Hamilton. With that philosopher, the representative faculty is synonymous with the imagination proper, and the above terms are used exclusively with reference to individual objects. See *Reid's Works*, pp. 805, 809; *Discussions*, p. 13. In the following pages the term *representation* and its cognates are extended so as to include the concept, which is representative of many individuals, as well as the image, which is representative of one.

takes place through the medium of a representative idea, is a hypothesis which was made more than questionable by the philosophy of Reid, and may be regarded as completely overthrown by the recent labors of his illustrious editor, Sir William Hamilton. But there still remains the faculty of Imagination, whose office is the production of images representative of the several phenomena of Perception,[1] internal as well as external. In relation to this

[1] The term *Perception* requires a few words in explanation. In modern philosophy, from Descartes to Reid, this term was used widely, as coëxtensive with Apprehension or Consciousness in general, with some minor modifications, for an account of which the reader is referred to Sir W. Hamilton's Reid, p. 876. By Reid and his followers it was used for the consciousness of an external object presented to the mind through the organs of sense, as distinguished from *Sensation*, the consciousness of an affection of the subject through the same organs. In this sense they are clearly distinguished by M. Royer Collard, Jouffroy's Reid, iii. p. 329. "Il y a dans l'opération du toucher sensation et perception tout ensemble: changement d'état ou modification intérieure, c'est la sensation; connaissance d'un objet extérieur, c'est la perception." Cf. Reid, Intell. Powers, Essay i. ch. i. Stewart, Outlines of Moral Philosophy, § 15. According to M. Royer Collard, the senses of smell, hearing, and taste, give rise to sensations only; touch is in every case a union of sensation and perception; while sight holds an intermediate and doubtful position, as informing us of the existence of extension, but only in two dimensions of space. Sir W. Hamilton, on the other hand, holds that the general consciousness of the locality of a sensorial affection ought to be regarded as a Perception proper; and, in accordance with this view, he has announced the important law, that Sensation and Perception, though always coëxistent, are, as regards their intensity, always in an inverse ratio to each other. Some recent French philosophers, influenced by the union of physiological with psychological researches, have employed the term *Perception* in another sense, to denote Sensation with Consciousness, *Sensation* being extended to those affections of the nervous organism of which we are not conscious. This occurs in the writings of Maine de Biran, and appears to have misled M. Ravaisson into imagining that that philosopher had anticipated the above-mentioned law of Sir W. Hamilton. The passage alluded to is apparently one in the *Essai sur la décomposition de la Pensée*, p. 116, but

faculty, the criterion above given as characteristic of Thought requires a few words of explanation.

Imagination, regarded as a product, may be defined, the consciousness of an image in the mind resembling and representing an object of intuition.[1] It is thus at the same time *presentative* and *representative*. It is presentative of the image which has its own distinct existence in consciousness, irrespective of its relation to the object which it is supposed to represent. It is representative of the object which that image resembles; and such resemblance is only possible on the condition that the image be, like the object, *individual*. If we try to form in our minds the

the resemblance is merely verbal. A nearer anticipation may perhaps be found in Kant, *Anthropologie*, § 20.

In the text, Perception is employed to denote all those states of Consciousness which are presentative only, not representative. It will thus include all intuitions except those of Imagination, and may be divided into external or sensitive, and internal; the former corresponding to the Perception of Reid. This use of the term, allowance being made for a different theory of external Perception, accords with that of Kant.

[1] This is the ordinary psychological sense of Imagination; however variously the term may have been employed in reference to poetry, and generally to the philosophy of taste. It corresponds with the definition given by Descartes (*Meditatio Secunda*), "*imaginari nihil aliud est quam rei corporeæ figuram seu imaginem contemplari;*" except that the latter is incorrectly limited to the reproduction of objects of sight only. The beautiful lines of Shelley furnish an exact description of imagination relatively to two other senses:

> "Music, when soft voices die,
> Vibrates in the memory;
> Odors, when sweet violets sicken,
> Live within the sense they quicken."

But the operation of the imaginative faculty must not be confined even to the general field of sensations. The important question, How many presentative faculties has man? will be referred to again. The province of imagination will be determined by the answer to this question, as every original presentation may be represented in a phantasm.

image of a triangle, it must be of some individual figure, equilateral, isosceles, or scalene. It is impossible that it should be at the same time all of these, or none. It may bear more or less resemblance to the object which it represents; but it can attain resemblance at all only by being, like the object itself, individual. I may recall to mind, with more or less vividness, the features of an absent friend, as I may paint his portrait with more or less accuracy; but the likeness in neither case ceases to be the individual representation of an individual man. But my notion of *Man* in general can attain universality only by surrendering resemblance. It becomes the indifferent representative of all mankind only in so far as it has no special likeness to any one. It is thus not the adequate and actual representative of any single object, but an inadequate and potential representative of many; that is, it may *in different acts of thought* be employed in relation to distinct, and in some respects dissimilar, individuals of the same class. From this neglect of individual characteristics arises the first distinguishing feature of a concept; viz. *that it cannot in itself be depicted to sense or imagination.*[1] It is not the sensible image of one object, but an intelligible relation between many.

A second important characteristic of all concepts is, that *they require to be fixed in a representative sign.* This characteristic cannot indeed be determined *à priori*, from the mere notion of the concept as universal, but it may be proved to a moral certainty *à posteriori*, by the inability of which in practice every man is conscious, of advancing, without the aid of symbols, beyond the individual objects of sense or imagination. In the presence of several individuals of the same species, the eye may observe points of

[1] Cf. Hamilton on Reid, p. 360.

similarity between them; and in this no symbol is needed; but every feature thus observed is the distinct attribute of a distinct individual, and, however similar, cannot be regarded as identical. For example: I see lying on the table before me a number of shillings of the same coinage. Examined severally, the image and superscription of each is undistinguishable from that of its fellow; but, in viewing them side by side, *space* is a necessary condition of my perception; and the difference of locality is sufficient to make them distinct, though similar, individuals.[1] The same is the case with any representative image, whether in a mirror, in a painting, or in the imagination, waking or dreaming. It can only be depicted as occupying a certain place; and thus as an individual and the representative of an individual. It is true that I cannot say that it represents this particular coin rather than that; and consequently it may be considered as the representative of all, *successively but not simultaneously.* To find a representative which shall embrace all at once, I must divest it of the condition of occupying space;[2] and this, experience assures us, can only be done by means of *symbols*, verbal or other, by which the concept is fixed in the understanding. Such, for example, is a verbal description of the coin in question, which contains a collection of attributes freed from the condition of locality, and hence from all resemblance to an object of sense. If we substitute Time for Space, the same remarks will be equally applicable to the objects of our internal consciousness. Every appetite and desire, every affection and volition, as *presented*, is an in-

[1] On this ground Kant refutes Leibnitz's principle of the *identity of indiscernables*, a principle applicable to concepts, but not to objects of intuition.

[2] Compare Herbart, *Psychologie als Wissenschaft*, § 120. *Werke*, vi. p. 163.

dividual state of consciousness, distinguished from every other by its relation to a different period of time. States in other respects exactly similar may succeed one another at regular intervals; but the hunger which I feel to-day is an individual feeling, as numerically distinct from that which I felt yesterday, or that which I shall feel to-morrow, as a shilling lying in my pocket is from a similar shilling lying at the bank. Whereas my *notion* of hunger, or fear, or volition, is a general concept, having no relation to one period of time rather than to another, and, as such, requires, like other concepts, a representative sign.

Language, taking the word in its widest sense, is thus indispensable, not merely to the communication, but to the formation of Thought. This doctrine is not unfrequently estimated as the correlative or consequent of that which derives all knowledge from sensation; an estimate apparently warranted by the association of the two theories in the philosophy of Condillac. But it would not be difficult to show that the ultra-sensational philosophy is that which could most easily dispense with the necessity of introducing language at all. Ideas, says Condillac, are but transformed sensations; and his disciple, Destutt de Tracy, has carried the doctrine to its fullest development in the aphorism *penser c'est sentir*. But who imagines language to be essential to sensation? Or who does not see that the introduction of such an instrument for the purpose of transforming our sensations implies the existence of a mental power which mere sensation can never confer? It is only on the supposition that the concept is something distinct from and unlike all the products of the senses, that the representative symbol becomes necessary. Sensation, imagination, and memory, so far as the latter is distinct from thought,[1] may dispense with its assistance. As for the crowning extravagance of Horne Tooke, who tells us that what are called operations of mind are merely operations of language, we have only to ask, what makes language operate? It might as reasonably be maintained that a coat is not the work of the tailor, but merely of his needle. But it is the perpetual error of the sensational school to confound the indispensable condition of a thing with the thing itself. Thought is not sensation, though the exercise of the senses is a necessary preliminary to that of the understanding. Science is not a well-constructed language, as the skill of the painter is not indentical with the goodness of his brushes and colors; yet we must acknowledge that the power of the artist could neither have been acquired nor exhibited, had these necessary implements been withheld.

The above view of the relation of thought to language is sometimes met by the following dilemma. "Language, you say, is essential to thought; yet language itself, if not of divine origin, must have been thought out by man. You must, therefore, be prepared to defend in its utmost rigor the hypothesis of a supernatural origin of speech; or you must allow that its inventor, at least, was a man capable of thinking without its aid."[2] To solve this

[1] So far, namely, as it corresponds to the *μνήμη*, not to the *ἀνάμνησις* of Aristotle. The neglect of this distinction led Condillac to deny that brutes have any memory, since they are destitute of language. Aristotle, with more accuracy, allows that memory is common to men and brutes, but reminiscence peculiar to the former. See *De Memoria*, ch. 2, § 25.

[2] See Rousseau, *Discours sur l'origine de l'inégalité parmi les hommes*, Première Partie. "Franchissons pour un moment l'espace immense qui dut se trouver entre le pur état de nature et le besoin des langues; et cherchons, en les supposant nécessaires, comment elles purent commencer à s'établir. Nouvelle difficulté pire encore que la précédente: car si les

3*

dilemma, we need not call in aid the curious hypothesis of Condillac, who held that the dependence of thought on sensation (and by implication on language) was a consequence of the fall of Adam; we need only observe what actually takes place in the formation of language and thought among ourselves. To the child learning to speak, words are not the signs of thoughts, but of intuitions; the words *man* and *horse* do not represent a collection of attributes, but are only the name of the individual now before him. It is not until the name has been successively appropriated to various individuals, that reflection begins to inquire into the common features of the class.[1] Language, therefore, as taught to the infant, is chronologically prior to thought and posterior to sensation. In inquiring how far the same process can account for the invention of language, which now takes place in the learning it, the real question at issue is simply this: Is the act of giving names to *individual objects of sense* a thing so completely beyond the power of man, created in the full maturity of his faculties, that we must suppose a divine Instructor performing precisely the same office as is now performed for the infant by his mother or his nurse; teaching him, that is, to associate *this sound* with *this sight?* This question may be answered affirmatively or negatively, but in either case it has nothing to do with the relation of language to thought, properly so called.[2]

hommes ont eu besoin de la parole pour apprendre à penser, ils ont eu bien plus besoin encore de savoir penser pour trouver l'art de la parole."

1 See Adam Smith's *Considerations concerning the first Formation of Languages*, appended to his *Theory of Moral Sentiments*.

2 On this subject, the following remarks of Maine de Biran are well worthy of attention: "Pour que ces premiers signes donnés deviennent quelque chose pour l'individu qui s'en sert, il faut qu'il les institue lui-même une seconde fois par son activité propre, ou qu'il y attache un sens.

In relation to this question, the reader must be careful not to confuse *Language* with *Articulations*. The case of the deaf and dumb, so often quoted as an instance of thought without language, is in this respect utterly irrelevant. The education of these persons consists in the substitution of a system of signs addressed to the eye or the hand in the place of one addressed to the ear. This system performs precisely the same office in relation to them that speech performs in the ordinary mental development of children: it constitutes, in fact, their language. They are thus in no respect an exceptional case; and the whole question has to be considered on general, not on special data. I cannot perceive any other man's thoughts as they pass in his mind: I can only infer their existence by perceptible signs; and this presupposes an established system of communication. The only valid method of investigating the relation between thought and speech is to examine the only instances in which both

Ceux qui pensent que l'homme n'eût pu jamais inventer le langage, si Dieu même ne le lui eût donné ou révélé, ne me semblent pas bien entendre la question de l'institution du langage: ils confondent sans cesse le fond avec les formes. Supposé que Dieu eût donné à l'homme une langue toute faite ou un système parfait de signes articulés ou écrits propres à exprimer toutes ses idées: il s'agissait toujours pour l'homme, d'attribuer à chaque signe sa valeur ou son sens propre, c'est-à-dire d'instituer véritablement ce signe avec une intention et dans un but conçu par l'être intelligent, de même que l'enfant institue les premiers signes quand il transforme les cris qui lui sont donnés par la nature en véritables signes de réclame.

"La difficulté du problème psychologique, qui consiste à déterminer les facultés qui ont dû concourir à l'institution du premier langage, subsiste donc la même, soit que les signes qui sont la forme et comme le matériel de ce langage aient été donnés ou révélés par la suprême intelligence, soit qu'ils aient été inventés par l'homme ou suggérés par les idées ou les sentimens dont ils sont l'expression."—*Nouvelles Considerations sur les rapports du physique et du moral de l'homme*, p. 93.

elements are *presented*, the operations of my own consciousness. Accepting what is there given in combination, I must endeavor by analysis to ascertain how much of the compound phenomenon is necessary, and how much accidental.

The concept, as thus described, is the characteristic feature of Thought proper, as distinguished from other facts of consciousness: and the thinking process may be adequately defined as *the act of knowing or judging of things by means of concepts.*[1] It remains to inquire what, according to this definition, must be the limits within which Thought is operative, and what, consequently, will be the distinguishing character of its laws.

Thought is only operative within the field of possible experience; *i. e.*, upon such objects as can be presented in an actual intuition or represented in an imaginary one. For the concept is the result of data furnished by intuition; and its legitimacy, as an object of thought, must be tested by reference to the same data. It is true that the concept itself, as such, cannot be presented intuitively; but it must contain no attribute which is incompatible with the intuitive presentation of its object. The concept is not itself individual, but it must comprehend such attributes as are capable of individualization, such as can coëxist in an object of intuition. The notion of a triangle,

[1] "Der Verstand überhaupt kann als ein Vermögen zu urtheilen vorgestellt werden. Denn er ist nach dem Obigen ein Vermögen zu denken. Denken ist das Erkenntniss durch Begriffe." Kant, *Kritik der rein. Vern.* (p. 70). An exact adherent of Kant would regard the definition given in the text as tautological; for with him the provinces of Thought and Judgment are coëxtensive, and all judgment requires concepts. But as in the following remarks the province of judgment is extended beyond that of thought, the limitation becomes necessary.

as a rectilinear figure of three sides, does not itself contain the attributes of equilateral, isosceles, or scalene; but it is capable of being combined with any one of the three in a perceived or imagined figure. But a rectilinear figure of two sides is, by the application of the same test, shown to be no concept at all. So long as we merely unite the attributes in speech, without attempting to combine them in an individual object, we may not be aware that we are talking nonsense; the attempt to imagine the figure shows at once the incompatibility of the attributes. This, then, is the criterion of positive thinking. A form of words, uniting attributes not presentable in an intuition, is not the sign of a thought, but of the negation of all thinking. Conception must thus be carefully distinguished, as well from mere imagination, as from a mere understanding of the meaning of words.[1] Combinations of attributes logically impossible may be expressed in language perfectly intelligible. There is no difficulty in understanding the meaning of the phrase *bilinear figure*, or *iron-gold*. The language is intelligible, though the object is inconceivable. On the other hand, though all conception implies imagination, yet all imagination does not imply conception. To have a valid conception of a horse, I must not only know the meaning of the several attributes constituting the definition of the animal, but I must also be able to combine those attributes in a representative

[1] These have been confounded by others besides Reid. Thus Aldrich, after defining Simple Apprehension as *nudus rei conceptus intellectivus*, proceeds: "Si quis dixerit *Triangulum æquilaterum esse æquiangulum*, possum Apprehensione Simplici incomplexa intelligere quid sibi velint singula Orationis hujus vocabula." Apprehension in this sense is not a logical process at all, and is not governed by any of the laws of logical thinking. — Cf. Hamilton on Reid, p. 377.

image; that is, to *individualize* them. This, however, is not mere imagination, it is imagination relatively to a concept. I not only see as it were the image with the mind's eye, but I also think of it as *a horse*, as possessing the attributes of a given concept, and called by a name expressive of them. But mere imagination is possible without any such relation. Without any effort to recall an object by means of its distinctive attributes, I may be passively conscious of the continuance, in a weaker state, of a sensible or otherwise intuitive impression, when the object which gave rise to it is no longer present. This is the Imagination which is described by Aristotle as a *kind of weak sensation*,[1] and as *sensitive imagination*.[2] When coupled with a consciousness of the past existence of the impression which it represents, it forms the *Memory*, as distinguished from the *Reminiscence*, of Aristotle.[3] This kind of imagination does not in itself involve a distinction or comparison of presentations: it is compatible with an ignorance or forgetfulness of the existence of any presentations, save the one represented by the image. Conception, on the other hand, in its lowest degree, implies at least a comparison and distinction of *this* from *that*. When exhibited, as for its ultimate verification it must be, in the construction of an individual image answering to the general notion, it is still an act of thought, rather than of intuition; and when coupled with the conscious effort to recall a past impression, it answers in some degree to the *Reminiscence* of Aristotle.[4]

[1] *Rhet.* I. 11. [2] *De Anima*, III. 11. [3] *De Memoria*, c. 1.

[4] "The Understanding, thought proper, notion, concept, etc., may coincide or not with Imagination, representation proper, image, etc. The two faculties do not coincide in a general notion; for we cannot represent Man or Horse in an actual image without individualizing the universal; and

Conception, where it does not coincide with imagination, implies imagination as the test of its validity. To form the notion of a class as distinguished from an individual, I must emancipate the attributes of which I am conscious from their connection with a definite time and place, and this, as has been already observed, requires the intervention of language. The consciousness of a general notion is thus an instance of *symbolical* as distinguished from *intuitive* knowledge;[1] and the act of Conception, viewed apart from Imagination, could only consist in the enumeration, by means of verbal or other symbols, of the different parts constituting a given notion.[2] But the symbol, though in-

thus contradiction emerges. But in the individual, say Socrates or Bucephalus, they do coincide; for I see no valid ground why we should not *think*, in the strict sense of the word, or *conceive* the individuals which we *represent*."— Sir W. Hamilton, *Discussions*, p. 13. The Reminiscence of Aristotle will include this kind of imagination under it, as the last step of the process.

[1] This distinction is due to Leibnitz. See his *Meditationes de Cognitione, Veritate, et Ideis, Opera*, ed. Erdmann, p. 79.

[2] "*In cognitione symbolica prima mentis operatio absolvitur recensione vocabulorum, vel aliorum signorum, quibus ea indigitantur quæ notionem rei distinctam ingrediuntur.* Etenim in cognitione symbolica tantummodo verbis enunciamus quæ in ideis continentur, vel aliis signis eadem repræsentamus, ideas vero ipsas verbis aut signis aliis indigitatas non intuemur. Quare cum in cognitione intuitiva prima mentis operatio absolvatur si attentionem successive in idea rei ad ea dirigimus quæ notionem distinctam generis vel speciei ingrediuntur, singula autem hæc enunciabilia sint, adeoque vocabulis vel signis aliis indigitari possint; in cognitione symbolica prima mentis operatio absolvi debet recensione vocabulorum, vel repræsentatione aliorum signorum, quibus ea denotantur, quæ notionem rei distinctam ingrediuntur. Ita prima mentis operatio in cognitione symbolica arboris absolvitur, si dicimus vegitabile, quod ex trunco, ramis, surculis et foliis constat; etenim sigillatim recensemus verba quibus ea indigitantur quæ in arboribus tanquam communia distinguimus, consequenter quæ notionem arboris in genere, quatenus distincta est, ingrediuntur. Non autem jam nobis quæstio est, utrum notio distincta sit completa

dispensable as an instrument of thought, lends itself with equal facility to every combination, and thus furnishes no criterion by which we can distinguish between sense and nonsense, between the conceivable and the inconceivable. *A round square*, or *a bilinear figure*, is, as a form of speech, quite as possible as *a straight line*, or *an equilateral triangle*. The mere juxtaposition of words does not indicate the possibility or impossibility of the corresponding notion, until we attempt to construct in imagination an individual object in accordance with it. Till this criterion is applied, the act of conception is rather a substitute for consciousness than a mode of consciousness itself. The sign is substituted for the thing signified; a step which considerably facilitates the performance of complex operations of thought, but in the same proportion endangers the logical accuracy of each successive step; since we do not, in each, stop to verify our signs. Words, as thus employed, resemble algebraical symbols, which, during the process of a long calculation, we combine in various relations to each other, without at the moment thinking of the original signification assigned to each. But those who, on this account, would reduce the whole of thought to an algebraical computation, overlook the most important feature, the verification, namely, of the result, according to the logical conditions of conception, after the algebraical process is finished. It may be convenient, in the course of a complicated reasoning, to assume the logical accuracy of the sub-

atque determinata, atque oratione ista talis notio significetur, ut hæc definitionis loco inservire possit. Sufficit enim hic ea sigillatim enunciari quæ mente ab idea rei separantur, dum distincte nobis genus vel speciem repræsentare conamur. Pendet enim cognitio symbolica ab intuitiva, quam supponit et ad quam refertur. Quicquid igitur huic deest, idem etiam illi deesse debet."— Wolf, *Psychologia Empirica*, § 328.

ordinate parts, and to employ their respective symbols on this assumption. But what the concept gains in flexibility it loses in distinctness; and the logical and algebraical perfections are thus in an inverse ratio to each other. It therefore becomes necessary, at the end of the process, to submit the result to the logical test, to which each step has been tacitly supposed to conform; that of the possible co-existence of the several attributes in an individual object.[1]

The above remarks will necessitate some modification of the doctrines ordinarily taught in logical treatises concerning general notions, or, as they are commonly though not very happily called, abstract ideas. We are told that the mind examines a number of individual objects, agreeing in some features and differing in others, that it separates the points in which they agree from those in which they differ, and makes, of the former only, an abstract idea or general notion, which is indifferently applicable to all the individuals from which it was derived, and by virtue of which they are all called by a common name.

The reality of this process of Abstraction,[2] and of the

[1] "Plerumque, præsertim in analysi longiore, non totam simul naturam rei intuemur, sed rerum loco signis utimur, quorum explicationem in præsenti aliqua cogitatione compendii causa solemus prætermittere, scientes, aut credentes nos eam habere in potestate: ita cum chiliogonum, seu polygonum mille æqualium laterum cogito, non semper naturam lateris, et æqualitatis, et millenarii (seu cubi a denario) considero, sed vocabulis istis (quorum sensu obscure saltem, atque imperfecte menti obversatur) in animo utor loco idearum, quas de iis habeo, quoniam memini me significationem istorum vocabulorum habere, explicationem autem nunc judico necessariam non esse; qualem cogitationem cæcam, vel etiam symbolicam appellare soleo, qua et in Algebra, et in Arithmetica utimur, imo fere ubique."— Leibnitz, *Meditationes de Cognitione, Veritate et Ideis.*

[2] Drobisch observes that the term *Abstraction* is used sometimes in a psychological, sometimes in a logical sense. In the former, we are said to abstract the attention from certain distinctive features of objects pre-

4

idea to which it is supposed to give rise, has been matter of considerable controversy among modern philosophers. Bishop Berkeley, and subsequently Hume, denied altogether the possibility of such an operation, on the following grounds. The general idea of a triangle, it was argued by Locke,[1] is an imperfect idea, wherein parts of several different and inconsistent ideas are put together. As limited to no particular kind of triangle, but comprehending all, it must be neither oblique, nor rectangle, neither equilateral, equicrural, nor scalene, but all and none of these at once. The abstract idea, as thus described, Berkeley easily perceived to be self-contradictory, and the doctrine suicidal. "I have a faculty," he says, "of imagining or representing to myself the ideas of those particular things I have perceived, and of variously compounding and dividing them. I can imagine a man with two heads, or the upper parts of a man joined to the body of a horse. I can consider the hand, the eye, the nose, each by itself, abstracted or separated from the rest of the body. But then, whatever hand or eye I imagine, it must have some particular shape and color. Likewise the idea of man that I frame to myself, must be either of a white, or a black, or a tawny, a straight or a crooked, a tall or a low, or a middle-sized man. To be plain, I own myself able to abstract *in one sense*, as when I consider some particular parts or qualities separated from others, with which though they are united in some object, yet it is possible they may really exist without

sented (*abstrahere a differentiis*). In the latter, we are said to abstract certain portions of a given concept from the remainder (*abstrahere differentias*). The former sense must be understood here, where we are considering the mental process by which concepts are formed. To the latter, as a conscious process of thought, the following remarks do not apply.

[1] *Essay*, book iv. ch. 7, § 9.

them. But I deny that I can abstract one from another, or conceive separately, those qualities which it is impossible should exist so separated; or that I can frame a general notion by abstracting from particulars in the manner aforesaid."[1]

"It is, I know," continues the Bishop, "a point much insisted on, that all knowledge and demonstration are about universal notions, to which I fully agree: but then it doth not appear to me that those notions are formed by *abstraction* in the manner premised; universality, so far as I can comprehend, not consisting in the absolute, *positive* nature or conception of anything, but in the *relation* it bears to the particulars signified or represented by it: by virtue whereof it is that things, names, or notions, being in their own nature *particular*, are rendered *universal*. Thus when I demonstrate any proposition concerning triangles, it is to be supposed that I have in view the universal idea of a triangle; which ought not to be understood as if I could frame an idea of a triangle which was neither equilateral, nor scalene, nor equicrural. But only that the particular triangle I consider, whether of this or that sort it matters not, doth equally stand for and represent all rectilinear triangles whatever, and is in that sense *universal*. . . . . Though the idea I have in view whilst I make the demonstration be, for instance, that of an isosceles rectangular triangle, whose sides are of a determinate length, I may nevertheless be certain it extends to all other rectilinear triangles, of what sort or bigness soever; and that, because neither the right angle, nor the equality, nor determinate length of the sides, are at all concerned in the demonstration. It is true, the diagram I have in view includes all these particulars; but then there is not the least

[1] *Principles of Human Knowledge*, Introduction, § x.

mention made of them in the proof of the proposition. . . . And here it must be acknowledged, that a man may consider a figure merely as triangular, without attending to the particular qualities of the angles or relations of the sides. So far he may abstract: but this will never prove that he can frame an abstract general inconsistent idea of a triangle."[1] On the other hand, it was argued by Reid, that if a man may consider a figure simply as triangular, without attending to the particular qualities of the angles or relations of the sides, he must have some conception of this object of his consideration; for no man can consider a thing which he does not conceive. He has a conception, therefore, of a triangular figure, merely as such; and this is all that is meant by an abstract general conception of a triangle.[2]

In this controversy, the question has been needlessly confused by the vague and inaccurate use of terms. *Idea* has been indifferently employed, by modern philosophers, to denote the object of thought, of imagination, and even (under the representative hypothesis) of perception.[3] Conception, again, has not been sufficiently distinguished, on the one side, from imagination, and, on the other, from a mere understanding of the meaning of words; and too little attention has been paid to the office of language, both as a substitute for consciousness, and as contributing to the distinctness of consciousness itself. It is not strictly

1 *Principles of Human Knowledge*, Introduction, §§ xv. xvi.

2 *Intellectual Powers*, Essay v. ch. 6.

3 As it is sometimes convenient to have a general term indifferently applicable to any object of internal consciousness, I have in the present work occasionally availed myself in this extent of the term *Idea*, rejecting, however, the representative idea of perception. But the term has been avoided wherever it is necessary to distinguish between two different states of consciousness.

correct to say that the individual alone is perceived first, and the general notion formed from it by abstraction; for, without the assistance of the general notion, the individuals themselves and their several parts could not be distinguished from each other. If I am to form a general notion of *man* by examining the individuals Peter, James, and John, and separating the accidents in which they differ from the essential points in which they agree, it is clear that I must previously have formed general notions of the parts thus separated from each other. In order to separate, by an act of thought, the figure common to a number of men from the accidents of stature, complexion, etc., peculiar to each, I must first be able to form distinct notions of the human figure on the one side, and of the several statures, complexions, etc., on the other. Abstraction thus presupposes conception, no less than conception presupposes abstraction; and we have still to learn how either process can be a preliminary condition to the other.

The fact is, that our earliest consciousness is neither of the individual discerned as an individual, nor of the universal discerned as an universal, but of a confused mixture of the two, which it requires a further development of thought to analyze into the one or the other.[1] Whatever we perceive occupies a definite position in time and space; it is seen *now* and *here;* so far it is an individual. But position in time and space does not constitute a mark by which this individual can be distinguished from that; I cannot by these relations alone determine whether the object seen now and here is or is not the same individual that was formerly seen elsewhere. To discern the individual as such or the universal as such, I must by an

[1] See Sir W. Hamilton's *Lectures on Metaphysics*, p. 497.

act of thought discern certain attributes as characteristic of one, and certain others as common to many; and this power of discernment is gradually imparted to each of us in practice by the use of language, in which our earliest abstractions are given to us already made. In this gradual formation of distinct thought from confused intuition, it may in one sense indeed be said that our knowledge of the class is prior to that of the individual. For resemblances are noticed earlier than differences;[1] and the names distinctive of individuals are at first associated only with their general features. "Children," says Aristotle, "at first call all men *father*, and all women *mother*, but afterwards they distinguish one person from another."[2] By degrees the individual attributes are discerned and separated from the generic; but in the first instance the name is applied to different objects before we have learned to analyze the growing powers of speech and thought, to ask what we mean by each several use of this or that appellation, and to correct and fix the signification of words at first used vaguely and obscurely. Such is the actual service performed by language in the education of mankind under the existing conditions of social intercourse. What was the origin of language itself, and how far the same description will apply to the mental development of the first man, is matter rather of ingenious conjecture than of scientific explanation.

Berkeley, therefore, was clearly right in denying the existence of any such process of Abstraction as that described by Locke. The error of the latter consisted

[1] A contrary theory on this point is the source of most of the difficulties which Rousseau professes to find in accounting for the origin of general language from the names given to individuals.

[2] *Phys. Ausc.* I. 1.

in regarding Abstraction as a positive act of thought, instead of the mere negation of thought. Abstraction is nothing more than non-attention to certain parts of an object: we do not positively think of a triangle as neither equilateral, isosceles, nor scalene; but we think of the figure as composed of three sides, without asking the question whether those sides are equal or unequal. But, on the other hand, Berkeley, in maintaining that all notions are in their own nature particular, has overlooked the fact that thought, and language as the instrument of thought, is necessary to distinguish the particular as particular, no less than the universal as universal; and that we are thus enabled, partially in intuitive and wholly in symbolical cognition, to discern generic attributes, and to constitute them an object of conception, without being conscious of the particulars by which they are accompanied. Berkeley is right in denying that we can *imagine* the universal entirely apart from the particular, but, owing to the vague significance of the word *idea*, he seems to speak of imagination as if it were coëxtensive with conception. In symbolical cognition, the latter process may be carried on apart from the former, subject, however, as has been already observed, to the condition of being tested as valid or invalid by the power of imagining a corresponding object. This distinction has been clearly indicated by Berkeley in another of his works;[1] and perhaps his whole discussion needs only a more exact distinction between the perception of individuals in time and space and the recognition of them by their peculiar attributes, to render it philosophically unexceptionable.

In speaking of Imagination as the test of Conception, we do not accede to the ultra-sensationalism of Condillac,

[1] *Minute Philosopher*, Dial. vii. § 8.

nor even to the modified doctrine of Laromiguière, who derives from the senses the whole *matter* of our knowledge. *Individualize your concepts*, does not mean *sensationalize them*, unless the senses are the only sources of presentation. If I am immediately conscious, for example, of an exercise of will, as an individual act taking place within me, the phenomena of volition become a distinct class of presentations, coördinate with, not subordinate to, those of the senses, and capable, like them, of being represented by the imagination and thought upon by the understanding. If I am conscious of emotions of joy or sorrow, of anger or fear, existing as present individual states of mind, distinct from sensible impressions, these, in like manner, must be considered as data for thought, furnished by intuition. If, on the perception of certain individual acts performed by myself or by another, I am immediately conscious of an idea of *right* or *wrong;* I have again a distinct class of intuitions, simple and undefinable, the laws and common features of which may furnish matter of further reflection, but the existence of which, as individual facts, is the indispensable condition of all moral speculation.

The possibility, therefore, of any branch of scientific inquiry depends upon the psychological question, *How many presentative faculties has man?*[1] Every such faculty may

[1] In speaking of the human mind as possessing a plurality of faculties, it is perhaps hardly necessary to protest against the misinterpretation of this language, as if it implied that these faculties were distinct and independent portions of the mind, like the separate members of the body. Sir W. Hamilton (*Lectures on Metaphysics*, Lect. xx.) has shown that the contrary opinion has been the one generally prevalent, that the vast majority of philosophers have either openly asserted or silently assumed that the faculties of mind are nothing more than modes in which the simple indivisible principle of thought may act and exist. As thus explained,

furnish distinct materials for thought. Physical Science is possible, if the senses present us with material phenomena whose relations and laws thought may investigate. Moral Science is possible, if we are presented with the fact of moral approbation and disapprobation of this or that action, in itself, and for its own sake; and the question for thought to investigate is, Whence do these feelings arise, and on what laws are they dependent? Æsthetical Science is again possible as a distinct branch of inquiry, if the emotions arising from the contemplation of beauty in the works of nature or of art can be shown to be distinct from any communicated by their mere relation to the senses. And Metaphysics must submit to the same criterion. Rational Cosmology and Rational Psychology are possible, only if Matter and Mind, as distinct from their several phenomena, can be shown to be in any way *presented*, as the object of an immediate intuition.

This distinction between the presentations of intuition and the representations of thought, which is thus the key to all the most valuable applications of Psychology, is intimated with more or less accuracy in the writings of several modern philosophers. The often-quoted passage of Locke, in which the operations of thought are com-

the term is unobjectionable. It may be that in mental, as in physical mechanics, we know force only from its effects; but the consciousness of distinct effects will then form the real basis of Psychology. The faculties may then be retained as a convenient method of classification, provided the language is properly explained, and no more is attributed to them than is warranted by consciousness. The same consciousness which tells me that seeing is distinct from hearing, tells me also that volition is distinct from both; and to speak of the faculty of will does not necessarily imply more than the consciousness of a distinct class of mental phenomena. No one but an advocate of the grossest materialism could understand such an expression as implying numerically distinct organs of mind, as of body.

pared to the productions of art, furnishes in this respect, when understood in its proper latitude, an unexceptionable description of the respective provinces of the intuitive and discursive faculties. "It is not in the power of the most exalted wit, or enlarged understanding, by any quickness or variety of thought, to invent or frame one new simple idea in the mind. The dominion of man, in this little world of his own understanding, being much the same as it is in the great world of visible things; wherein his power, however managed by art and skill, reaches no farther than to compound or divide the materials that are made to his hand; but can do nothing towards the making the least particle of new matter, or destroying one atom of what is already in being."[1] The *Ideas of Sensation* and *Ideas of Reflection* of the same philosopher, however unfortunate may be the original choice of terms, and however inconsistent their subsequent employment, point correctly enough to the two great sources of external and internal intuition.[2] A further step in accuracy is gained in the *Impressions* and *Ideas* of Hume, though the distinction loses most of its value in his hands by the absurd ground of distinction which he has laid down between them, and by the unfortunate metaphor which declares every idea to be an *image* of an impression.[3] Kant, who

[1] *Essay*, b. ii. ch. 2 § 2.

[2] *Reflection*, in consistency with etymology, ought to have been limited to the operations of thought; in which sense we can reflect upon sensible objects as upon all other things. Locke only escapes from Reid's criticism on this point by using reflection improperly, as Stewart has observed, as synonymous with [internal] consciousness. This use of the term, however, is not peculiar to Locke. See Sir W. Hamilton's *Lectures on Metaphysics*, pp. 162, 406.

[3] According to Hume, Ideas and Impressions differ from each other only in their different degrees of force and vivacity; and belief he defines as

took up the discussion where Hume left it, with the advantage of a new philosophical language, unencumbered with the associations of earlier systems, is the earliest philosopher whose writings have disentangled the confusion universally following on the use of the term *idea*, and exhibited this most important distinction with any degree of accuracy and precision.[1] It is one of the most valuable principles of the Critical Philosophy, that *the understanding has no power of intuition;* a principle which does not, however, necessitate the adoption of the Kantian division of the mental faculties, nor even the determination of the question, whether the mind possesses numerically distinct faculties at all. It simply means, that the act of Thought cannot create its own object: that, being mediate and representative, it requires to be based on an immediate and presentative fact of consciousness.

It cannot therefore be maintained that the senses are the sole criteria of truth and of reality, unless we assume,

"a lively idea associated with a present impression;" a doctrine which almost justifies the sarcastic application of Reid, "it will follow, that the idea of a lion is a lion of less strength and vivacity. And hence may arise a very important question, whether the idea of a lion may not tear in pieces and devour the ideas of sheep, oxen, and horses, and even of men, women, and children."

[1] In this respect, nothing can be more unfair than Stewart's sneers at the obscurity and new technical language of Kant. The philosophical terms of English and French writers are derived from the same source, and subject to the same varieties of application. The purism of German writers has given to all subsequent thinkers the inestimable advantage of contemplating the same thoughts under a new phraseology, and with new associations of etymology and metaphor; an advantage which no one has appreciated more highly, or explained more happily, than Stewart himself, on another occasion. As it is impossible to comply exactly with the precept of Locke, to judge of ideas in themselves, their names being wholly laid aside, the next best course is, to examine them, as far as possible, through the medium of two independent languages.

in defiance of all consciousness, that there exist no immediate mental phenomena, but those communicated by sensation. Any one presentation is as true and as real as any other. Falsehood and unreality can only begin with thought. The immediate judgment of presentation, that I am at this moment conscious of a certain object, is equally true as regards any class of presentations. Unreality, in this case, can only consist in the distinctness of one class of presentations from another, which latter we have arbitrarily selected as the test of reality; and falsehood, in the assertion of the identity of distinct classes, or of the distinctness of identical ones. But such a selection or assertion involves an act of thought; it is a judgment concerning intuitions as classified under certain concepts. If I choose arbitrarily to select the senses as the sole test of reality, the phantasms of imagination are so far unreal; but their unreality implies no more than that they are not perceived by the senses. If I say, "A centaur exists as an image in my mind, therefore it exists in nature," the assertion is false, because, by an act of thought, I judge that to be an object of possible sense, which is only given to me as an object of imagination: its reality in relation to the latter faculty remains undisturbed.

This view of the reality of all presentations, as such, could not indeed be consistently held by the advocates of a representative theory of perception. If, in all intuition, I am immediately conscious only of certain ideas or modifications of my own mind, I am reduced to the alternative, either of disbelieving the existence of an external world altogether, or of drawing a distinction between such ideas as are representative and indicate the existence of objects without my mind, and such as are purely imaginary and have no objective reality corresponding.[1] The former will then be distinguished as real, the latter as unreal presentations. But if, in perception, I am immediately and presentatively conscious of a *non-ego* (and such is the soundest view, both in common sense and in philosophy), the representative idea and its supposed claim to superior reality vanishes altogether. Every presentation is real in itself, some as immediately informing me of the existence of states of my own mind, others as immediately informing me of the existence of objects without; and my judgment about each is equally true when I assert it to be what it is, and equally false when I assert it to be what it is not. In this respect, the philosophers of the school of Common Sense have not always consistently adhered to their fundamental principle, in the distinction which they have drawn between perception and imagination.[2]

But though it is not true that the whole matter of knowledge is furnished by the senses, it cannot be denied that it is entirely furnished by the *presentative faculties.* And this may throw some light on a distinction, concerning which there frequently exists considerable confusion, the distinction between what are, vaguely enough, termed *positive* and *negative ideas.* A positive intuition is one which has been presented to us in actual consciousness, real or imaginary: a positive concept is one whose component parts are capable of being so presented in combination. A negative concept, on the other hand, which is in fact no concept at all, is the attempt to realize in

[1] See Locke, *Essay,* b. iv. ch. 4, §§ 3—12.

[2] See Reid, *Inquiry,* ch. ii. § 3, and the antagonist remarks of Stewart, *Elements,* vol. i. ch. 3. Both discussions might have been cleared of some confusion by determining accurately what is meant by reality in *Presentations.*

thought those combinations of attributes of which no corresponding intuition is possible. The inability may be absolute or relative, owing to the general limitations of all human consciousness, or to peculiar deficiencies in the experience of this or that individual. Thus a blind man may be said to have a negative idea of color, when he attempts to supply the defects of his experience by analogy from other sensations; as in the case mentioned by Locke, of the man who supposed the color of scarlet to resemble the sound of a trumpet.[1] But in like manner any man, though in the full possession of his faculties, can only negatively conceive those simple ideas[2] which have never been actually presented in their proper intuition. The nature of the presentation will of course depend upon the faculty to which that class of intuitions belongs. If I have never seen objects of any other color than white and red, I have a positive idea of these, a negative idea of blue and yellow. If I had all my lifetime been subject to coercion, and had never performed an act of volition, I should have a negative idea of free agency. If I had never in my life found my volition opposed, I should have a negative idea of coercion. As it is, I have a positive idea of both. I desire to thrust my arm out in open space, and my desire is carried into effect. Here is the positive consciousness of freedom. I try to thrust it through a wall, and am resisted. Here is the positive consciousness

[1] *Essay*, b. iii. ch. 4, § 11.

[2] By *simple ideas* are meant the immediate objects of sensation or reflection in Locke's sense of the terms, such as color and sound, which can be apprehended only by actual sight or hearing; perception and volition, which can be known only by the actual experience of self-consciousness. Complex notions may be formed from these by an act of pure imagination, but the elements must be given beforehand. Compare Locke, *l. c.*

of coercion.[1] When Locke declared infinite space and infinite duration to be negative ideas, he was right, if we grant his hypothesis of their origin. The former he derived from sensation; and all the space which we can actually perceive by the senses is finite: the latter he derived from reflection; and every duration which we have personally experienced is finite also. Those who do not accede to his conclusion ground their dissent on a denial of his premises.[2] The language in which the concept is expressed is in this respect altogether indifferent. We may speak of the same act as *voluntary*, or *not constrained*, as *compulsory*, or *not voluntary*. The test of its positive or negative character is to be found in the question, Has it ever been realized in an intuitive presentation?

Those ideas whose negative character depends merely on the deficiences of individual experience, and which may therefore be described as *accidentally or relatively negative*, are beyond the consideration of pure Logic, or

[1] Some philosophers represent the idea of freedom as a negative one. Thus Kant (*Rechtslehre*, p. 28, ed. Schubert) and Fichte (*Kritik aller Offenbarung*, § 2) describe it as merely an absence of the feeling of compulsion. This description would be correct, if we had never performed an act in our lives except under coercion. As it is, the idea of freedom is as positive as that of restraint, both being at different times presented in actual consciousness. The same is the case with heat and cold, good and evil, and other pairs of contraries, each of which, as a phenomenon of consciousness, is as positive as the other. What may be their respective relations to a transcendental cause beyond the sphere of consciousness, we have no means of determining.

[2] See Cousin, *Histoire de la Philosophie*, leçon xviii. On the other hand, Locke's conclusion is supported, though on different grounds, by Sir W. Hamilton, *Discussions*, p. 605, who shows that an absolutely first unit of Space or Time, and an infinite extent of either, are both equally inconceivable.

pure Metaphysics, which deal only with those conditions of thought which are common to all mankind. Hence the only negative ideas with which the logician or metaphysician as such is concerned, are those which arise from an attempt to transcend the conditions of all human thought. If the human mind is subject to laws and limitations which it is unable to transgress by any effort of thought (and that this is the case will be shown at a further stage of our inquiry), there will arise in relation to these a class of notions which may be distinguished as *essentially or absolutely negative.* Such negative notions, however, must not be confounded with the absence of all mental activity. They imply at once an attempt to think, and a failure in that attempt.[1] The language by which such notions are indicated is not like a word in an unknown tongue, which excites no corresponding affection in the mind of the hearer: it indicates a relation, if only of difference, to that of which we are positively conscious, and a consequent effort to pass from one to the other. Thus, if it be true that the infinite is not a positive object of human thought, it will not follow that the word is to us wholly unmeaning. We may attempt to separate the condition of finiteness from our conception of a given object, though the result may ultimately involve a self-contradiction. We may attempt in like manner to conceive a space enclosed by two straight lines, and it is not till after the attempt has been made that we become aware that the expression *bilinear figure* admits of no corresponding notion. And it may frequently happen, owing to the use of language as a substitute for positive thought, that a process of reasoning may be carried on to a considerable length, without the reasoner being aware of the essentially inconceivable

[1] See Sir W. Hamilton's *Discussions*, p. 602.

character of the terms which he is employing. If we assume without inquiry the possible existence of a circular square, we may demonstrate of it in succession all the properties of the circle and all those of the square, without at the moment perceiving their incompatibility with each other. Such a self-deception is still easier when the negative character depends, not on the union of attributes which cannot be conceived in conjunction, but on the separation of those which cannot be conceived apart. We may easily analyze in language that which it is impossible to analyze in thought. Thus we can neither perceive nor imagine color without extension; an unextended color is therefore a purely negative notion. Yet many philosophers of eminence have maintained that the connection between these two ideas is merely one of association, and have reasoned concerning color apart from extension with as much confidence as if their language represented a positive thought. The speculations concerning the seat of the soul may be cited as another instance of the same kind. Position in space and occupation of space are correlative notions; neither is conceivable apart from the other. Yet the above speculations for the most part proceed on the tacit assumption that it is possible to assign a local habitation to an unextended substance. Such is the influence of language, even when representing, not thought, but its negation.

If thought is operative only within the field of possible experience, it follows, that we are not entitled, in any act of thought, to add to the data given in the concept, without a fresh appeal to intuition. I have in my mind the notion of a centaur, as a creature with the upper parts of a man and the lower parts of a horse. But this concept does not in itself contain the attribute of existence in space as an object of possible perception. I am therefore not warranted in thinking of the centaur as so existing, until the attribute is supplied from its proper source of presentation, which in this case is sensible experience. If my notion of man does not contain the attribute of mortality, I may think of man as mortal or as immortal, but I cannot determine which of these judgments is true, *i. e.*, is in accordance with the corresponding intuition, without comparing them with the fact as presented by experience. In the mere notion of two straight lines, it is not contained that they cannot inclose a space; and in the mere notions of the numbers 7 and 5, it is not contained that their sum is 12. Neither of these judgments, therefore, can be determined to be true without an appeal to some fact or other of intuition. This limitation of the province of thought implies some important consequences, which will appear when we come to consider the character of the laws of pure thinking recognized by Logic.

Before taking leave of this part of our subject, it may be useful to point out one or two questions of controversy, to which the distinction between Thought and other facts of consciousness may be applied with advantage.

It has been remarked by Sir William Hamilton,[1] that the whole controversy of Nominalism and Conceptualism is founded on the ambiguity of the terms employed; on the want, that is, of an accurate distinction, such as is furnished by the German *Anschauung* and *Begriff*, between the individual intuitions of sense and imagination, and the general concepts of the understanding. We may observe further, that the controversy between Nominalism and Realism may be, if not absolutely decided, at least considerably simplified, by attending to the same distinc-

[1] *Reid's Works*, p. 412.

tion. Some recent critics, in examining this question, have managed to introduce additional confusion into what was sufficiently confused before. It is asked, for example, whether the great division of animal, vegetable, and mineral is not to be regarded as the work of nature, rather than as the arbitrary product of man's classification. Undoubtedly: but what has that to do with the question of the existence of Universals out of the mind? We admit, that is, that nature has stamped on certain locally distinct individuals a number of prominent features of resemblance, which cannot fail to strike the eye of an observer. But has she thereby produced anything more than one set of attributes existing in one individual in one place, and another similar set existing in another individual in another place? But when, by an act of mind, we have abstracted from the existence in space under which all objects of sense are presented, and, by virtue of that abstraction, have advanced from individual similarity to specific unity, from the similar attributes of several objects to the mutual relation of all, the results of the process can only be regarded as the offspring of our minds. This consideration does not indeed prove decisively the impossibility of universals *à parte rei*, but it shows that no argument in favor of their existence can be drawn from the observed uniformities of nature.[1]

Another subject of dispute between different schools of philosophy is, What are the limits of definition? The Scholastic Logicians, holding that definition was by genus and differentia, very consistently laid it down as a canon,

[1] Since the publication of the first edition of this work, I have been gratified at finding the same view maintained in an able discussion by M. de Rémusat, *Abelard*, vol. ii. p. 125.

that no object was definable which could not be regarded as a Species. *Summa genera* and *individuals* were by this rule incapable of definition. On the other hand, Descartes and Locke, rejecting this restriction, maintain that *simple ideas* alone cannot be defined. Both are right, according to their different meanings of definition. With the former, it signifies the resolution of a complex *general concept* into the simpler concepts which it comprehends. With the latter, it is the resolution of a complex *individual object of sense* into the simpler objects of which it is composed. The one is a mental analysis of notions, the other a sensible analysis of intuitions. No definition, as Locke truly observes, will convey the *idea* of whiteness to a blind man; *i. e.*, it will not enable him to form a sensible image of the color. But no definition (in the scholastic sense) was ever intended to accomplish this object. The far-famed *animal rationale* does not do it for man; and for the very sufficient reason, that concepts, as such, are not capable of being presented in sense or imagination. If the purpose of logical definition were to enable us to form an *idea*, *i. e.*, a representative image of an object, pointing it out with the finger would be a far more satisfactory definition than any verbal analysis.[1] But ideas, in this sense, have no connection with logical definition. Locke's ideas of sensation, simple or complex, are all excluded from the province of definition, as being individuals, *i. e.*, as not being concepts at all. On the other hand, the *concept* whiteness, as a species of color, is capable of definition by its optical differentia, as a color produced by equal mixture of the simple rays. An example adduced

[1] Arist. Anal. Post. II. 7. *οὐ γὰρ δὴ δείξει γε τῇ αἰσθήσει ἢ τῷ δακτύλῳ.* Cf. Mill's Logic, vol. i. p. 183.

by Descartes, as well as by Locke and Leibnitz,[1] will illustrate the distinction still more clearly. The concept of a chiliogon is a regular polygon of 1000 sides. As addressed to the sense, this definition would not enable any man to distinguish an individual figure of the kind by sight from another which had 999 sides; but, as addressed to the understanding, it is sufficient for the demonstration of the mathematical properties of the figure. Yet even here, intuition, though not directly applied, is the virtual test of the possibility of the conception. I may not be able distinctly to represent in an image or construct in a figure a thousand sides at once; but it is from my intuitive consciousness of the same attributes as existing on a more limited scale, that I know that there is nothing incompatible between the number of a thousand sides and the property of enclosing a space. Under this conviction the symbolical takes the place of the intuitive cognition; and we are enabled, by the aid of language, to think of the figure in certain relations, without actually constructing it with the hand or in the mind.

The same distinction will furnish a ground for criticizing certain popular systems of logical notation. If Logic is exclusively concerned with Thought, and Thought is exclusively concerned with Concepts, it is impossible to approve of a practice, sanctioned by some eminent Logicians, of representing the relation of terms in a syllogism by that of figures in a diagram. To illustrate, for example, the position of the terms in Barbara, by a diagram of three circles, one within another, is to lose sight of the distinctive mark of a concept, that it cannot be presented to the sense, and tends to confuse the mental inclusion of one

[1] See Descartes, *Meditatio Sexta;* Locke, *Essay,* ii. 29, 13; Leibnitz, *Nouveaux Essais,* ii. 29, 13.

notion in the sphere of another, with the local inclusion of a smaller portion of space in a larger.[1] The diagrams of Geometry in this respect furnish no precedent; for they do not illustrate the *form* of the thought, but the *matter*, not the general character of the demonstration as a reasoning process, but its special application as a reasoning about magnitudes in space. Still less is such a practice justified by the test of conceivability which has been mentioned above, the possibility, namely, of individualizing the attributes comprehended in a concept. For, whereas that test is employed to determine the conceivability of the actual contents of each separate concept, the logical diagrams are designed to represent the universal relations in which all concepts, whatever be their several contents, formally stand towards each other. The contrast between these two, as legitimate and illegitimate appeals to intuition, will more fully appear in the sequel.

[1] "Da der Mensch die Sprache hat," says Hegel, "als das der Vernunft eigenthümliche Bezeichnungsmittel, so ist es müssiger Einfall, sich nach einer unvollkommnern Darstellungsweise umsehen und damit quälen zu wollen. Der Begriff kann als solcher wesentlich nur mit dem Geiste aufgefasst werden. Es ist vergeblich, ihn durch Raumfiguren und algebraische Zeichen zum Behufe des *aüsserlichen Auges* und einer *begrifflosen, mechanischen Behandlungsweise*, eines *Calculs*, festhalten zu wollen." While dissenting totally from the Hegelian view of Logic, I cannot resist quoting the above passage, as applicable to every view of the Science which recognizes the essential distinction between thought and intuition.

CHAPTER II.

ON THE THREE OPERATIONS OF THOUGHT.

CONCERNING the threefold division of the mental operations usually acknowledged by Logicians, it has been questioned whether they are properly to be regarded as distinct acts of Thought or not. The question may be considerably simplified, by discriminating between different principles of identity or distinctness, as applicable severally to mental and material objects. The only natural and necessary principle of distinction between objects is the numerical diversity of individuals. In this respect, not only the several acts of Simple Apprehension, Judgment, and Reasoning, but every single act of each class, is distinct from every other. An act of reasoning which I perform to-day is numerically distinct from any act performed yesterday, though both may be governed by the same laws and applied to the same objects. Beyond this, any principle of *specific* identity or diversity is to a certain extent arbitrary and artificial. The only ground of distinction between a natural and an unnatural classification of individuals depends upon the frequency with which we have occasion to view them in this or that relation; in other words, on the respective utility of different points of view for certain given purposes. On this ground, Apprehension, Judgment, and Reasoning are rightly and necessarily regarded as distinct classes of mental operations, relatively to Logic, inasmuch as their several products, the Concept, the Judgment, and the Syllogism, exhibit distinct logical forms, and require a distinct logical treatment.

Psychologically, the question must be examined on somewhat different grounds. It may be urged, for example, on the one side, that the several operations are the product of the simple faculty of Comparison; that they are not in act ever separable from each other, Apprehension being always accompanied by Judgment, and Judgment by Apprehension, and Reasoning by both; that the mind, one and indivisible, is wholly employed in each. On the other side, it may be answered, that acts of Comparison may be regarded as specifically distinct, as engaged on distinct objects; that the comparison of attributes with each other, of concepts, immediately in themselves, or mediately with a common third concept, are *pro tanto* distinct acts; that the same mind is not always equally skilful in all three; and other arguments of the like kind. Both these opposite opinions may be accepted as true, if we attend to the different points of view which render the decision of all such matters of controversy in some degree arbitrary.

The distinction between the faculties and parts of the mind is based on a principle exactly the reverse of that by which a similar distinction is made relatively to the body. The members of the latter are given as logically and numerically distinct, and thus furnish a preëxisting basis for the classification of their several operations. Thus, seeing and hearing are distinguished from each other, as the operations of the eye and the ear respectively; and the use of the pen, the brush, and the chisel, may in this point of view be classified together, as operations of the hand; whereas, in the mind, the distinctness of the operations is itself the ground on which, for mere convenience of discussion, we classify and distinguish different parts and faculties, as belonging to the mind itself.[1] The acts, therefore, must, on independent grounds, be determined to be identical or distinct, before we unite or separate them, as related to the same or diverse mental powers.

Hence it appears that the classification of operations, relatively to distinct mental faculties, is contingent upon the adoption of some independent principle for classifying the same operations in themselves. In the present state of Psychology, much must be left to the discretion of individual inquirers; no one division having been so universally adopted by philosophers, or having led to such important results, as to render imperative its adoption as the division κατ' ἐξοχήν of psychologers. But to suppose a distinct mental faculty for each of the three logical operations, solely on the ground of the distinct objects compared in each, is, to say the least, to make Psychology unnecessarily complicated, and to offend against a rule of great weight in all systems of classification, *Entia non sunt multiplicanda præter necessitatem.* Indeed, the several phenomena of conception, judgment, and reasoning, viewed merely as mental acts, and without reference to the diversity of the data from which the act commences and with which it deals, appear to furnish far more promi-

[1] "Nous ne savons que l'âme humaine possède certaines facultés, que parce que nous voyons en elle certains phénomènes se produire. Ainsi, parce que nous observons qu'elle sent, qu'elle pense, qu'elle se souvient, nous en concluons qu'elle a la capacité de sentir, la capacité de penser, la capacité de se souvenir; et ce sont ces capacités que nous appelons ses facultés."— Jouffroy, *Des facultés de l'âme humaine,* (*Mélanges Philosophiques,* p. 313, 2d ed.)

nent features of similarity than of difference. They are effected by the same means; they are governed by the same laws; they are confined within the same limits; they admit of the same distinctions of material and formal validity. The psychological analysis of any one may be applied, almost in the same words, to the others; and so far as thought alone is concerned (though not always in the possession and management of the materials upon which thought is exercised), the same mental qualities are manifested in the right performance of each. In a psychological point of view, to enumerate separate mental faculties, as giving rise to the various products of thought, is, to say the least, to encumber the science with unnecessary and perplexing distinctions. It will be sufficient to refer them to the single faculty of *Thought*, the operation of which is in all cases *Comparison*.[1]

But the faculty of *Thought*, though uniform in its own nature and in the manner of its operation, may yet give rise to different products, according to the diversity of the materials upon which it operates; and this difference, as has already been observed, forms the basis of the classification usually adopted in Logic. Hence, from the different points of view in which thought is contemplated by the two sciences, there arises some diversity of detail, which it is desirable to point out more particularly.

Extending the terms Apprehension and Judgment beyond the region of Thought proper,[2] it may be laid down,

[1] See Sir W. Hamilton's *Lectures on Metaphysics*, Lect. xxxiv.

[2] The division into Simple Apprehension, Judgment, and Reasoning, is usually given as one of the discursive faculties. Yet even Logicians have extended it to the powers of perception and imagination. Indeed, these several faculties have shared in the confusion arising from the vague use, in modern philosophy, of the term *idea*. A striking instance is afforded

as a general canon of Psychology, that the unit of consciousness is a *judgment;* in other words, that every act of consciousness, intuitive or discursive, is comprised in a conviction of the presence of its object, either internally in the mind or externally in space. The result of every such act must thus be generally stated in the proposition, "This is here." Consequently, at least with reference to the primary and spontaneous, as distinguished from the secondary and reflex acts of consciousness, it is more correct to describe Apprehension as the analysis of Judgments, than Judgment as the synthesis of Apprehensions.[1]

In a psychological point of view, therefore, it is incorrect to describe Simple Apprehension as the first operation of the mind. In one sense, indeed, the relation of prior and posterior is altogether out of place: Chronologically, inasmuch as every Apprehension is simultaneous with a Judgment, and every Judgment with an Apprehension; and logically, inasmuch as Judgment cannot exist without Apprehension, nor Apprehension without Judgment. In another sense, however, we may properly say that Judgment is prior to Apprehension; meaning that the subject and the object are first given in their mutual relation to each other, before either of them can itself become a separate object of attention. But when a corresponding division is adopted of the operations of Thought, properly so called, the same order of priority cannot be observed. Every operation of thought is a judgment, in the psychological sense of the term; but the psychological judgment must not be confounded with the logical. The former is

by Wolf, in his account of Apprehension and Judgment. *Phil. Rat.*, §§ 33—39.

[1] See Reid, *Intellectual Powers*, Essay iv. ch. 3, with Sir W. Hamilton's Commentary.

the judgment of a relation between the conscious subject and the immediate object of consciousness; the latter is the judgment of a relation which two objects of thought bear to each other. The former cannot be distinguished as true or false, inasmuch as the object is thereby only judged to be present at the moment when we are conscious of it as affecting us in a certain manner; and this consciousness is necessarily true. The latter is true or false according as the relations thought as existing between certain concepts are actually found in the objects represented by those concepts or not. The logical judgment necessarily contains two concepts, and hence must be regarded as logically and chronologically posterior to the conception, which requires one only. The psychological judgment is coëval with the first act of consciousness, and is implied in every mental process, whether of intuition or of thought. It cannot, therefore, be called prior or posterior to any other mental operation, for there is no mental operation in which it does not take place; but the judgments of intuition are logically and chronologically prior to the judgments of thought.[1] Conception is a psychologi-

[1] Of the important distinction between *chronological* and *logical* priority (the *tempore* and *natura* of the scholastic post-predicaments), it will be sufficient to quote one ancient and one modern exposition. Aristotle (for name and thing), *Categ.* ch. 12: Πρότερον ἑτέρου ἕτερον λέγεται τετραχῶς, πρῶτον μὲν καὶ κυριώτατα κατὰ χρόνον, καθ' ὃ πρεσβύτερον ἕτερον ἑτέρου καὶ παλαιότερον λέγεται. . . . Δεύτερον δὲ τὸ μὴ ἀντιστρέφον κατὰ τὴν τοῦ εἶναι ἀκολούθησιν, οἷον τὸ ἓν τῶν δύο πρότερον· δυοῖν μὲν γὰρ ὄντων ἀκολουθεῖ εὐθὺς τὸ ἓν εἶναι, ἑνὸς δὲ ὄντος οὐκ ἀναγκαῖον δύο εἶναι. *Metaph.* viii. 8. 2. Πάσης δὴ τῆς τοιαύτης προτέρα ἐστὶν ἡ ἐνέργεια καὶ λόγῳ καὶ τῇ οὐσίᾳ· χρόνῳ δ' ἔστι μὲν ὥς, ἔστι δ' ὡς οὔ. Cousin, *Programme d'un cours de Philosophie:* "Une connaissance est antérieure à une autre dans l'ordre logique, en tant qu'elle l'autorise; elle est alors son antécedént logique. Une connaissance est antérieure à une autre dans l'ordre psychologique, en tant qu'elle se produit avant elle dans l'esprit humain; elle est alors son

cal judgment, but not a logical one, and is properly ranked as the first operation of Thought, inasmuch as it is the simplest.

As the design of the present essay is not to consider Psychology in itself, but Psychology in its relation to Logic, I shall content myself with accepting the three operations of Thought as they are commonly distinguished by Logicians, examining them with a view of ascertaining what light Psychology can throw on the province and laws of each. Other points of view, and other principles of classification, need not be further discussed in this place. In relation to their several logical products, the three operations may be distinguished as follows.

Conceiving has been already explained as the individualizing of certain attributes comprehended in a general notion and expressed in a general term; the representation, namely, of such attributes as coëxisting in a possible object of intuition. Language, as before observed, is, in its earliest operations, a sign, not of concepts, but of intuitions. Its earliest terms are employed as the proper names of individual objects. Conception does not take place till after we have learned to give the same name to various individuals presented to us with certain differences of attributes, and hence to associate it with a portion only, not with the whole, of what is presented in each. This may be distinguished as *Abstraction*, a spontaneous, though not always a voluntary act, the concentration of the mind on certain portions only of a given object in relation to its name. This must not be treated, as is frequently done by Logicians, as a conscious process of

antécédént psychologique." For some admirable applications of the above distinction, see the same author's criticism of Locke, *Cours de Philosophie*, leçon 17.

thought, being only a preliminary condition to thinking, taking place in the majority of cases unconsciously, during the gradual acquisition of speech.[1] Our names thus gradually acquire a signification, being transformed from proper names to appellatives. Finally, the act of conception consists in contemplating the attributes thus combined in the signification of a name as coëxisting, along with individual features, in a possible object of intuition, and hence, apart from the individual features, as indifferently representing all such objects. This representative collection of attributes, combined by means of a sign, is a *Concept.*

In the above remarks, the office of language is considered as it now exists and is taught, not as it might possibly have been originally created. We do not form our own language, but receive it ready formed; and its teaching, whether true or deceitful, whether promoting or distorting the right development of the mind, does, as matter of fact, impress us from our infancy upwards with certain associations, and casts our earliest thoughts in a certain mould, from which no future effort can wholly emancipate us. I am not now considering what might have been the course of our mental growth had we been the original inventors of our mother tongue, or if we had been born among a people with whom (as in a hypothesis

[1] Abstraction, as described by Stewart, *Elements,* vol. i. ch. 4, answers in essential points to what I have here described. It should be observed, however, that by language as it now operates, whatever may have been the case in its first formation, the question as to what attributes shall be abstracted and what retained, is in a great measure determined for us. The process must thus be distinguished from the voluntary abstraction implied in all operations of thought. On Abstraction, as distinguished from Attention, see Tissot, *Anthropologie,* vol. i. p. 142.

of Reid's[1]) every sound represented a complete sentence. Language is not here considered as it might have been invented by a conclave of imaginary philosophers, or as it may have influenced the thoughts of Adam in Paradise; but as it does influence the thoughts of children born into the world, the offspring of articulately-speaking parents.

As in Conception a single general notion is considered in its relation to a possible object of intuition, so in Judgment two such notions are considered as related to a common object. When I assert that A is B, I do not mean that the attributes constituting the concept A are identical with those constituting the concept B,—for this is only true in identical judgments,—but that the object in which the one set of attributes is found is the same as that in which the other set is found. To assert that all philosophers are liable to error, is not to assert that the signification of the term *philosopher* is identical with that of *liable to error;* but that the attributes comprehended in these two distinct terms are in some manner united in the same subject. To ask what constitutes unity or identity in a subject of attributes, is to enter on a deep metaphysical question, the discussion of which must be postponed to a later stage of our inquiry; it is sufficient for the present to observe, that the common language and common thought of mankind universally acknowledge something of the kind, assuming, whether they can explain it or not, that a certain smell and color and form, which are distinct attributes, are in some way related, as parts or qualities, to some one thing which we call a rose; and that, when I assert that the rose is fragrant, I imply that the thing

[1] *Correspondence,* Letter xi. to Dr. James Gregory. See p. 71 of Sir W. Hamilton's edition.

which affects in a certain way my power of sight is in some manner identical with that which affects in a certain way my power of smell. The metaphysical problem thus lies at the bottom both of Conception and of Judgment, and, whether it admits of satisfactory explanation or not, must be included as a fact in any description of the several operations of Thought.

Reasoning is the most complex of the three operations, as in it two concepts are determined to be in a certain manner related to each other, through the medium of their mutual relations to a third concept. This operation is therefore treated last in order.[1] The several relations asserted in the premises and deduced in the conclusion, are of the same nature as those implied in Judgment, and lead to the same metaphysical difficulties. These, together with the logical and psychological character of the Laws of Thought, will be considered in a future chapter. For the present it will be sufficient to attempt, in accordance with the above observations, a definition of the products of the several acts of Thought, the Concept, the Judgment, and the Syllogism, the legitimate objects of Formal Logic.

A Concept is a collection of attributes, united by a sign, and representing a possible object of intuition.

A Judgment is a combination of two concepts, related to one or more common objects of possible intuition.

[1] "Judicium notiones conjungit vel separat, adeoque eas supponit. Ratiocinando ex notionibus et judiciis præviis elicitur judicium ulterius, adeoque ratiocinatio notiones et judicia supponit. Ergo notio est operatio prima, judicium secunda, discursus tertia." — Wolf, *Phil. Rat.* § 53. But Wolf, as before observed, has not accurately distinguished between the perceptive and discursive faculties. His remark is true, though only in a much narrower sense than that in which he designed it.

A Syllogism is a combination of two judgments, necessitating a third judgment as the consequence of their mutual relation.

The definition above given of a Judgment renders necessary a few remarks on a class of propositions, whose true logical character has been considerably misapprehended by eminent authorities. According to the above definition, every judgment in Logic must be regarded as a combination of concepts; every term of such judgment, as the sign of a concept. This is no less true of singular than of common judgments, and the neglect of it has given rise to some errors in the logical treatment of propositions. "Proper names," says Mr. Mill, "denote the individuals who are called by them; but they do not indicate or imply any attributes as belonging to those individuals. When we name a child by the name Mary, or a dog by the name Cæsar, these names are simply marks used to enable those individuals to be made subjects of discourse. It may be said, indeed, that we must have had some reason for giving them those names rather than any others; and this is true: but the name, once given, becomes independent of the reason. A man may have been named John, because that was the name of his father; a town may have been named Dartmouth, because it is situated at the mouth of the Dart. But it is no part of the signification of the word John, that the father of the person so called bore the same name; nor even of the word Dartmouth, to be situated at the mouth of the Dart."[1]

These remarks are true so far as the name alone is concerned, or as regards the reason of its being imposed, at a certain time, on a certain man. But, then, the man, as an individual existing at some past time, cannot become im-

[1] Mill's Logic, vol. i. p. 40.

mediately an object of thought, and hence is not, properly speaking, the subject of any logical proposition. If I say, "Cæsar was the conqueror of Pompey," the immediate object of my thought is not Cæsar as an individual existing nearly two thousand years ago, but a concept now present in my mind, comprising certain attributes, which I believe to have coëxisted in a certain man. I may *historically* know that these attributes existed in one individual only; and hence my concept, virtually universal, is actually singular, from the accident of its being predicable of that individual only. But there is no *logical* objection to the theory that the whole history of mankind may be repeated at recurring intervals, and that the name and actions of Cæsar may be successively found in various individuals at corresponding periods of every cycle.

> "Alter erit tum Tiphys, et altera quæ vehat Argo
> Delectos heroas: erunt etiam altera bella;
> Atque iterum ad Trojam magnus mittetur Achilles."

These remarks will suggest a correction of the ordinary logical account of the quantity of propositions, which should have been made long ago. The subjects of all logical judgments are concepts: the true singular proposition in Logic is not one in which the concept is *materially* limited to an individual by extralogical considerations, but one in which it is *formally* so limited by a sign of individuality. In scholastic language, only *individua demonstrativa*, and not, as is vulgarly taught, *individua signata*, are properly the subjects of singular propositions.[1] Indefinite, or, as they should rather be called, indesignate[2]

[1] Cf. Fries, *System der Logik*, § 22. His principle is sound, though some of his instances are inaccurate.

[2] Properly speaking, particular propositions are indefinite, singulars and

propositions, are an anomaly in Logic, no less when the subject is a singular than when it is a common term. In both, the quantity can only be known by the matter, and, in both, an appeal to the matter is extralogical.

The same considerations will also show the propriety of Aristotle's limitation of the logical verb to the present tense only. All thought is a consciousness of present mental acts, and its object is not the past event, but the present concept of it. Hence the office of the verb in Logic is not to declare the past or future connection of an attribute with its subject in the represented fact, but to declare the present coëxistence of two concepts in the representative act of thought.[1]

Before quitting this portion of the subject it will be desirable to compare the conclusions arrived at with those of two eminent philosophers, from both of whom they appear, verbally at least, to differ in a slight degree.

Locke's well-known definition of knowledge, "The perception of the agreement or disagreement of two ideas," has been somewhat severely commented on by his illustrious critic, M. Cousin.[2] The French philosopher shows clearly that, in many of our judgments, we cannot be said

universals definite. For when I say *Some A is B*, I leave it altogether undetermined how many, and whether any given A is included or not. For this reason it is better to adopt the term *indesignate*, suggested by Sir W. Hamilton.

[1] "Copula non est nisi verbum substantivum præsentis temporis. Denotat enim nexum inter subjectum et prædicatum intercedentem, qualis nempe repræsentatur in ideis nostris. Cum igitur in omni judicio nexus ille semper sit aliquid præsens, copula non esse potest nisi verbum substantivum præsentis temporis." — Wolf, *Phil. Rat.* § 202.

[2] *Cours de Philosophie*, leçon 23. Compare Jouffroy's Reid, Preface, pp. 130, 133, sqq. For other criticisms, see Reid, *Intellectual Powers*, Essay I. ch. 7; Essay VI. ch. 3; Leibnitz, *Nouveaux Essais*, IV. 1.

to have distinct notions of terms united, prior to pronouncing on the fact of their agreement. The distinctions drawn in the preceding remarks will, I think, furnish a ground for a more exact decision of the point at issue than has been given either by the English philosopher or his French censor. Locke's definition abounds in verbal inaccuracy, for which, however, the author is not entirely responsible, as it is partly owing to the unsettled signification, in his day, of philosophical terms, which have since been more accurately determined. Taking *Perception* in the strict sense to which it has been determined by Reid and his successors, it is not correct to say, in general terms, that the agreement of ideas is in all cases *perceived.* Extending *Knowledge*, as Locke himself does, to include the evidence of the senses,[1] it is incorrect to say that, in all knowledge, we have a distinct consciousness of two ideas and their agreement. And the term *Idea* itself, used loosely by Locke, as by Descartes, for any object of consciousness, admits of a variety of subordinate senses, in some of which the definition is assuredly inaccurate. But, as limited to the logical judgment proper, as it has been above distinguished from the psychological, the definition is substantially correct, though susceptible of some verbal improvement. In every logical judgment there is a union of concepts; and every concept is represented by a sign. The concepts themselves must be regarded as existing in the mind before their union; and, the signs being practically furnished by the existing terms of a language, the logical judgment may be properly described as formed by the combination of concepts; as its representative, the proposition, is formed by the combination of terms. But to the judgments distinguished as psychological the defi-

[1] *Essay*, B. IV. ch. 2. § 14.

nition of Locke is inapplicable; and here the objections of M. Cousin may be urged with full effect. Such are all the spontaneous judgments of the perceptive and imaginative faculties. Such, too, is the Cartesian *cogito, ergo sum*, a primitive judgment, not of the senses, but of the internal consciousness, which the opponents of Descartes, from Gassendi to Kant, have misrepresented as a logical reasoning from concepts.[1] The definition of Locke is therefore correct, as far as regards judgments of thought, properly so called; judgments formed by means of concepts, and, consequently, of language, and whose constituent parts are given piecemeal in words, and put together by the mind in the act of judging. It is incorrect, as regards all judgments, whether concerning the *ego* or the *non-ego*, which the mind forms for itself, by an immediate act of consciousness, without the aid of verbal or other signs of voluntary intuition.

From the definition of Locke we proceed to consider that of Kant. In the Critical Philosophy, Thought and Judgment are synonymous, and the act of the understanding. The understanding may be defined indifferently, the faculty of *thinking*, or the faculty of *judging;* for all thought is cognition by means of concepts; and all concepts are the predicates of possible judgments, and are, by such judgments, referred to objects of sensible intuition, either immediately, or through the interposition of lower

[1] See an article in Cousin's *Fragments Philosophiques*, "Sur le vrai sens du *cogito, ergo sum.*" To this I am indebted for the following quotation from Descartes himself: "Cum itaque quis advertit se cogitare, atque inde sequi se existere, quamvis forte nunquam antea quæsiverit quid sit cogitatio nec quid existentia, non potest tamen non utramque satis nosse, ut sibi in hac parte satisfaciat." — *Responsio ad sextas objectiones.* See also Clauberg, *Logica*, Qu. clx.

concepts.[1] The intuitions of sense being, according to Kant's theory of perception, immediate representations of objects, the judgment is thus the mediate cognition of an object, or the representation of a representation.[2]

In a psychological point of view, the Kantian definition of Judgment is too narrow; as it virtually denies that any act of Judgment whatever is performed in the exercise of the intuitive faculties; a denial which the author repeats still more explicitly in other passages.[3] In a logical point of view, it is too wide; the province of Judgment being made coëxtensive with the whole of Thought, including, therefore, under it, Conception or Simple Apprehension. Every concept, according to Kant, is the predicate of a possible judgment, in which it may be affirmed of any of the objects of intuition included within its sphere. He might have gone further, and said that, in all positive thinking, the possible judgment becomes an actual one. But it is a psychological, not a logical judgment. It

[1] "Wir können alle Handlungen des Verstandes auf Urtheile zurückführen, so dass der Verstand überhaupt als ein Vermögen zu urtheilen vorgestellt werden kann. Denn er ist nach dem Obigen ein Vermögen zu denken. Denken ist das Erkenntniss durch Begriffe. Begriffe aber beziehen sich, als Prädicate möglicher Urtheile, auf irgend eine Vorstellung von einem noch unbestimmten Gegenstande."—*Kritik der r. V.* p. 70, ed. Rosenkranz.

[2] "Da keine Vorstellung unmittelbar auf den Gegenstand geht, als blos die Anschauung, so wird ein Begriff niemals auf einen Gegenstand unmittelbar, sondern auf irgend eine andre Vorstellung von demselben (sie sey Anschauung oder selbst schon Begriff) bezogen. Das Urtheil ist also die mittelbare Erkenntniss eines Gegenstandes, mithin die Vorstellung einer Vorstellung desselben."—*Kritik der r. V.* p. 69.

[3] "Wahrheit oder Schein sind nicht im Gegenstande, so ferne er angeschaut wird, sondern im Urtheile über denselben, so ferne er gedacht wird. Man kann also zwar richtig sagen: dass die Sinne nicht irren, aber nicht darum, weil sie jederzeit richtig urtheilen, sondern weil sie gar nicht urtheilen."—*Kritik der r. V.* p. 238.

affirms only the mental existence of the object, as now present in thought; and the affirmation is necessarily true, whatever be the nature of the object. To make the doctrine of Kant consistent, the province assigned to Judgment must be either extended or contracted. It must either be extended, to denote every consciousness of a relation between subject and object, *i. e.*, to every operation of mind, or it must be contracted, to denote the consciousness of a relation between two objects of thought; in which case it does not extend beyond the logical judgment by means of, at least, two concepts.

Having thus pointed out the distinction of Thought from other mental acts, and its various subdivisions relatively to Logic, I shall proceed to offer a few observations on the nature of Law, in so far as that term is applicable to a conscious subject.

CHAPTER III.

ON LAW, AS RELATED TO THOUGHT AND OTHER OBJECTS.

THE following passage from Archbishop Whately's Logic may serve as an appropriate introduction to this part of our subject. "What may be called a *mathematical* impossibility, is that which involves an absurdity and self-contradiction; *e. g.*, that two straight lines should inclose a space, is not only impossible, but inconceivable, as it would be at variance with the definition of a straight line. And it should be observed, that inability to accomplish anything which is, in this sense, impossible, implies no limitation of *power*, and is compatible even with omnipotence, in the fullest sense of the word. If it be proposed, *e. g.*, to construct a triangle having one of its sides equal to the other two, or to find two numbers having the same ratio to each other as the side of a square and its diameter, it is not from a defect of power that we are precluded from solving such a problem as these; since, in fact, the problem is in itself unmeaning and absurd: it is, in reality, *nothing* that is required to be done."[1]

Substantially, perhaps, this is not far from the truth. But it may be stated in a more satisfactory form by divesting it of a hypothesis which, even if true (and this we have no

[1] Whately's Logic, p. 353. (Sixth edition.)

means of ascertaining), may for the present purpose be dispensed with.[1]

When anything is said to be *inconceivable*, it is thereby acknowledged that the human mind is not altogether unrestricted in its operations. It is bounded not only as regards the sphere of objects of which it is permitted to take cognizance, but also as regards the manner in which it is capable of thinking about objects within that sphere. In other words, there are *laws* under which the mind is compelled to think, and which it cannot transgress, otherwise than negatively, by ceasing to think at all.

The existence, then, of laws of thought is a fact of which our every-day consciousness assures us. Necessity, of whatsoever kind, implies a necessary agent; that is, an agent acting under a law. If, then, any question can be proposed to the mind of man which he feels himself compelled to decide in one way only, that compulsion is at once an evidence of the existence of laws which, as a thinker, he is compelled to obey.

And this admission is all that is required for the solution of such difficulties as that suggested above. If our whole thinking is subject to certain laws, it follows that we cannot think of any object, not even of omnipotence itself, except as those laws compel us. The limitation does not lie in the object of which we think, but in the thinking subject. "Whatsoever we imagine," says Hobbes, "is *finite*. Therefore there is no idea or conception of anything we call *infinite*. No man can have in his mind an

[1] In venturing to criticize this note, one of the most valuable portions of the Archbishop's work, I beg to state, that it is to the wording only of the first part that my remarks are intended to apply. With the just and philosophical distinction laid down in the same place between the three senses of the word *impossibility*, I have only to express full concurrence.

image of infinite magnitude; nor conceive infinite swiftness, infinite time, or infinite force, or infinite power. When we say anything is infinite, we signify only that we are not able to conceive the ends and bounds of the things named; having no conception of the thing, but of our own inability."[1]

It may be, indeed, that the conditions of possible thought correspond to conditions of possible being, that what is to us inconceivable is in itself non-existent.[2] But of this, from the nature of the case, it is impossible to have any evidence. If man, as a thinker, is subject to necessary laws, he cannot examine the absolute validity of the laws themselves, except by assuming the whole question at issue. For such examination must itself be conducted in subordination to the same conditions. Whatever weakness, therefore, there may be in the object of criticism, the same must necessarily affect the critical process itself.

We may indeed believe, and ought to believe, that the powers which our Creator has bestowed upon us are not given as the instruments of deception. We may believe, and ought to believe, that, intellectually no less than morally, the present life is a state of discipline and preparation

1 *Leviathan*, i. 3. (p. 17, ed. Molesworth.) This opinion of Hobbes has been severely censured by Cudworth, *Intellectual System*, B. I. ch. v. § 1, who, however, mistakes the meaning of the assertion, both in what it expresses and in what it implies. The error of Cudworth in this respect has been corrected by his learned translator, Mosheim, who, though no friend to Hobbes's views in general, admits that in this particular his doctrine is not liable to the objections urged against it. See Harrison's edition of Cudworth, vol. ii. p. 522.

2 *In itself*, distinguished from, *as an object of thought*. As the latter, it is of course impossible. The distinction between things *per se* and things as objects of thought, will be familiar to every reader of Kant. It is, in fact, the cardinal point of the whole Critical Philosophy.

for another; and that the portion of knowledge which our limited faculties are permitted to attain to here may indeed, in the eyes of a higher Intelligence, be but partial truth, but cannot be absolute falsehood. But, in believing thus, we desert the evidence of Reason to rest on that of Faith, and of the principles on which Reason itself depends it is obviously impossible to have any other guarantee.

But such a faith, however well founded, has but a regulative and practical, not a speculative application. It bids us rest content within the limits which have been assigned to us: it cannot enable us to overleap them, or to exalt to a more absolute character the conclusions obtained by finite thinkers concerning finite objects of thought.[1] For the same condition which disqualifies us from criticizing the laws of thought, must also deprive us of the power of ascertaining how much of the results of those laws is true in itself, and how much is relative and dependent upon the particular bodily or mental constitution of man during the present life. To determine this question, it would be necessary to examine the same conclusions with a new set of faculties,[2] and under new conditions of thought, so as to separate what is merely relative to the existing state of

[1] When Kant (*Kritik der r. V.* p. 49) declares that the objects of our intuition *are not* in themselves as they appear to us, he falls into the opposite extreme to that which he is combating: the Critic becomes a Dogmatist in negation. To warrant this conclusion, we must previously have compared things as they are with things as they seem; a comparison which is, *ex hypothesi*, impossible. We can only say that we have no means of determining whether they agree or not. And, in the absence of proof on either side, the presumption is in favor of what is at least subjectively true. The *onus probandi* lies with the assailant, not with the defender, of our faculties. Cf. Royer-Collard, Jouffroy's Reid, vol. iv. p. 412.

[2] See Reid, *Intell. Powers,* Essay vi. ch. 5. (p. 447, ed. Hamilton.)

human consciousness, from what is absolute and common to other intelligences.[1]

In accordance with these views, we are naturally led to regard all the hitherto unsolved problems of Metaphysics as requiring to be treated from a psychological, instead of an ontological point of view. Instead of asking what are the circumstances, in the constitution of things, by virtue of which they present such and such difficulties and contradictions to human understanding, we must ask what are the circumstances of the human understanding itself, by virtue of which a distinction exists between the conceivable and the inconceivable. Such, in fact, was the revolution introduced by Kant into metaphysical speculation; a revolution which he aptly compares to that effected in Astronomy by Copernicus, when he thought of investigating the apparent motion of the heavens from the side of the spectator, instead of from that of the objects. The advantages of such a treatment are obvious. From the objective view, we obtain only the fact that certain questions have up to the present time remained unsolved. From the subjective view, we learn why they are insoluble; and the answer to this question determines the laws and limits of thought. The abuse of the method appears in

[1] Truth relative to *no intelligence* is a contradiction in terms, as it implies a relation existing after one of the correlatives has been annihilated. Our only possible notion of absolute truth is a truth relative to all intelligences. If all truth is subjective which implies a cognitive power, Omniscience itself has but subjective truth. "Aux termes de la philosophie de Kant," says M. Cousin, "la raison divine serait donc aussi frappée de subjectivité, par cela même que cette raison réside dans un sujet déterminé qui est Dieu." (*Leçons sur Kant*, p. 350.) Within the limits of human knowledge the same principle is allowed by Kant himself: "so bedeutet die objective Gültigkeit des Erfahrungsurtheils nichts anders, als die nothwendige Allgemeingültigkeit desselben."— *Prolegomena*, § 18.

the attempts of the successors of Kant, especially of Schelling and Hegel, to construct a philosophy of the absolute from the subjective side, by denying in certain relations the validity of those laws of thought which they acknowledge in others, and endeavoring thereby to do away with relation in consciousness altogether. Such a system, with whatever ability it may be constructed, carries in its fundamental conception the germ of its own refutation. It commences by giving the lie to consciousness; it proceeds by dividing the human mind against itself, the understanding against the reason, and the reason against the understanding; it ends by leaving no test by which its own truth can be determined. But the philosophy of Kant is like the spear of Achilles, and possesses virtue to heal the wounds which it has itself inflicted. While it is impossible to deny the lineal descent of the philosophy of Schelling and of Hegel from a one-sided view of Kantian principles, it is equally clear that the only satisfactory refutation of the extravagances of that philosophy must be based on a sober acknowledgment of those laws and limits of the mental faculties which Kant has been mainly instrumental in pointing out.

We must admit, then, that our present faculties are trustworthy guides to that portion of knowledge which God designs us to attain to in our present state; that the laws to which these faculties are subjected, though perhaps not absolutely binding on things in themselves, are binding upon our mode of contemplating them; that, while we obey these laws, we seek after truth, according to our kind and in conformity with the end of our intellectual being; and that, when we neglect them, we abandon ourselves to every form of error; or, rather, we lose all power of discerning between error and truth; we commence by an act of intellectual suicide, and construct a system which, by virtue of its fundamental principle, must disclaim all superiority over, and decline to combat with, any rival theory; its sole claim to attention being, that it may, for aught we know, be true or false, or both, or neither.

To apply these principles to the question with which we commenced: Among the limitations to which even omnipotence is regarded as subject, none is of older birth, or has been more frequently alleged, than the impossibility of undoing an act already done,

μόνου γὰρ αὐτοῦ καὶ Θεὸς στερίσκεται,
ἀγένητα ποιεῖν ἅσσ' ἂν ᾖ πεπραγμένα.

Now, it may be that Time and Space are, as Kant maintains, merely subjective conditions of human sensibility. As such, they limit the whole exercise of human thought. But the limits of the thinking faculty are limits of things as objects of thought only; and beyond that sphere we know nothing. It may be that the whole distinction of past, present, and future, has no place relatively to other intelligences than ours. Still, that distinction continues to influence all human thought; and every act, as an object of thought, must be regarded as taking place according to the conditions of temporal succession. If we cease to regard it in this light, we do not extend our knowledge, but abandon the problem as (humanly speaking) *unthinkable*. The limitation, then, is not of omnipotence in itself, but of all power as the object of human thought.[1] The ulti-

[1] This distinction is drawn by Locke, in his Second Reply to the Bishop of Worcester. "But it is further urged, that we cannot conceive how matter can think. I grant it: but to argue from thence that God, therefore, cannot give to matter a faculty of thinking, is to say God's omnipotency is limited to a narrow compass, because man's understanding is so; and brings down God's infinite power to the size of our capacities."

mate consequence of this admission will be, that the unlimited is not an object of human *thought* at all.[1] It may be an object of human *belief*, but the two provinces are not coëxtensive.

So again with reference to the impossibility of reversing a necessary truth, such as those of Geometry. To whom is the problem to construct a triangle, one of whose sides shall be greater than the other two, "unmeaning?" Clearly to the geometer, whose science has already shown him the necessary truth of a contradictory proposition. By a law of thought, he is compelled to deny that two contradictory assertions can be true at the same time. Why they may not both be true at different times, — why a mathematical proposition once demonstrated is held always and everywhere true, and its contradictory always and everywhere false; while other truths, however certain at present, are allowed only to a limited extent under temporal or local restrictions, — requires some further consideration.

Necessity is the result of law, and law implies an agent whose working is regulated thereby.[2] But it is a law only to that which works under it: to an observer, who sees the results of the law without being subject to its influence, it is no more than a fact evidenced by or inferred from sensible observation, and can never obtain higher value than that of a generalization from a more or less extended experience. Hence arise two very different kinds

[1] See the admirable Article on M. Cousin's Philosophy by Sir Wm. Hamilton, *Discussions*, p. 1.

[2] "All things that are have some operation not violent or casual. . . . . That which doth assign unto each thing the kind, that which doth moderate the force and power, that which doth appoint the form and measure of working, the same we term a Law." — Hooker, *E. P.* i. 2.

of necessity, the results respectively of laws of the *ego* and of the *non-ego*;[1] of laws under which I feel myself compelled to think, and of laws under which I see other agents invariably working. These two it is essential to all sound thinking to distinguish from each other; and the more so, inasmuch as they have been perpetually confounded together. The distinctive features of each have been overlooked by the disciples of opposite schools. By one party, laws of thought have been degraded to generalizations from experience; by another, empirical laws have been invested with the character and authority of original principles of mind.[2] And yet, apart from the psychological tenets of any particular school, it would seem as if a distinctive criterion might *à priori* be determined, from a mere analysis of the notion of law and its operation.

Setting aside, for an instant, the question how the mind of man is actually constituted, let us suppose an intelligent being, subject to laws under which he is compelled to think, and placed in the midst of a world of material

[1] It is much to be wished that these expressions, or some equivalent, were more naturalized in English philosophy. In Germany and France they are fully established as technical terms, and the foundation of the most important distinctions in mental science. In adopting here the Latin expressions instead of English equivalents, I have been guided by the authority of Sir W. Hamilton, *Reid's Works*, p. 100, supported by that of Mr. Hallam, *Literature of Europe*, vol. ii. p. 436. (Second edition.) The latter observes, of the term Ego, "It seems reasonable not to scruple the use of a word so convenient, if not necessary, to express the unity of the conscious principle. If it had been employed earlier, I am apt to think that some great metaphysical extravagances would have been avoided, and some fundamental truths more clearly apprehended."

[2] The opposite theories of Dr. Whewell and of Mr. Mill, on the nature of axiomatic principles, exhibit the extreme views in a remarkable degree. See *Appendix*, note A.

agents, subject to laws under which they must act. What would be the distinctive character presented to his mind by these respective laws of himself and of the world without? The laws of the planetary motions are absolutely binding on the moving bodies themselves, independently of the existence of astronomical science. But it is optional with an intelligent being to study astronomy or not; and, when he does so, he observes, as matter of fact, how such laws influence their own subordinate agents; but he does not himself become an agent under their influence. As facts of his experience,[1] they are known solely in and through his observation; as laws within their own sphere, they are independent of his knowing aught about them. But the laws of his mind come into operation as laws when the act of thinking commences, and are binding, not on this or that class of physical phenomena, but upon the thinker himself, in the contemplation of all of them. Hence it is not optional with him whether he will think according to these or other conditions. Choose what object of study he will, he cannot think at all, he cannot conceive his liberty of choosing, without being *ipso facto* under their influence. Hence arises an obvious criterion. A law which is not binding on me as a thinker, may at any time be reversed, without affecting my mode of observing the same agents under their new conditions. And I have no difficulty in conceiving such a reversal as at any moment possible, because, antecedent to experience, I had no internal bias which required the recognition of the existing law rather than of any other. I have only to discard an ad-

[1] "Les vérités primitives sont de deux sortes, comme les dérivatives. Elles sont du nombre des vérités de raison, ou des vérités de fait. Les vérités de raison sont nécessaires, et celles de fait sont contingentes." — Leibnitz, *Nouv. Essais*, iv. 2.

ventitious knowledge. But the reversal of a necessary law of thought, supposing that there are such, is, from the nature of the case, inconceivable; for conception is itself the servant of the law, and, *ex hypothesi*, cannot rebel against it. I cannot by an act of thought annihilate the conditions by which all thought is governed. I can, indeed, admit the possibility that there may be other beings thinking under other laws; but I can form no positive conception of their nature. Such a supposition is not thought, but its negation. A mind cannot think by other laws than its own.

Now, how far is this hypothesis supported by facts? Is it a matter of fact, that men are acquainted with certain truths which they acknowledge to be necessary only while the present laws of nature remain in force, and which they can conceive as reversible at any moment, and others which they are compelled to regard as necessary under all circumstances of which they are capable of thinking? Is it a matter of fact, that men do not attribute the same necessity and universality to physical as to mathematical truths? Do they not acknowledge that, while the laws of the physical world continue as they are, seed-time and harvest, and cold and heat, and summer and winter, and day and night, shall never cease; and yet, have they any difficulty in conceiving the earth's motion stopped by some superior power, and one-half of the globe left from that time forth in perpetual daylight?[1] Or do they see the least

[1] "Tous les exemples qui confirment une vérité générale, de quelque nombre qu'ils soient, ne suffisent pas pour établir la nécessité universelle de cette même vérité: car il ne suit pas, que ce qui est arrivé arrivera toujours de même. Par exemple, les Grecs et les Romains et tous les autres peuples ont toujours remarqué, qu'avant le décours de vingt quatre heures le jour se change en nuit, et la nuit en jour. Mais on se seroit trompé si

improbability, not to say impossibility, in the supposition, that in some remote part of space there may exist worlds in which the alternations of the seasons have no place? On the other hand, can they conceive the same power forming a triangle with more or less than two right angles? Can they conceive an occurrence taking place in any portion of space without a cause? or an object possessing neither of two contradictory attributes? If such a distinction exists, and our daily consciousness assures us that it does, the fact at once affords at least a strong presumption that the necessity in the one case is a necessity of observation only, depending on the laws of the world without, in the other a necessity of thought, depending on the laws of our mental constitution.

But, granting that thought has its laws, how are these to be discovered? Only by reflection upon the phenomena of actual thinking, and the restriction to which, in all cases, we experience it to be subject. To learn how we think, we must in the first place actually think; and a multitude of successive acts of thought will be necessary, before we become aware that certain conditions are contingent, and limited to some of those acts only, while others are necessary, and cannot but be present in all.[1] If, therefore, *Experience* be taken in a wide sense, as coëxtensive with the whole of consciousness, to include all of which the mind is conscious as agent or patient, all that it does

l'on avoit crû, que la même règle s'observe partout, puisqu'on a vu le contraire dans le séjour de Nova Zembla. Et celui-là se tromperoit encore, qui croiroit, que c'est au moins dans nos climats une vérité nécessaire et éternelle, puisqu'on doit juger, que la Terre et le Soleil même n'existent pas nécessairement, et qu'il y aura peut-être un temps, où ce bel astre ne sera plus avec tout son Système, au moins en sa présente forme."— Leibnitz, *Nouveaux Essais, Avant-Propos.*

[1] See Hamilton on Reid, p. 772, and Cousin, *Cours de Philosophie,* Leç. 22.

from within, as well as all that it suffers from without, — in this sense, the laws of thought as well as the phenomena of matter, in fact all knowledge whatever, may be said to be derived from *experience*.[1] But further, experience in its narrower and more common meaning, as limited to the results of sensation and perception only,[2] is, though not the *source*, the indispensable *condition* of discovering the laws of mind as well as of matter. For, to think actually, we must think about something; this something, the object-matter of thought, whatever it may be, must in the first instance be supplied through the medium of the senses; for thought itself does not become an object of thought till after it has been called into exercise by objects presented from without.[3] But while the material or external element varies with every successive act of thought, the formal or internal remains the same in all; and thus the necessary law, binding on the thinker in every instance, is distinguished from the contingent objects, about which he thinks on this or that occasion.

The last consideration necessitates a further division of those truths which have already been distinguished as necessary, and therefore not derived from experience. While we maintain that all necessary truths must have

[1] In this extended sense, Wolf derives the principle of contradiction from experience: "*Experiri* dicimur, quicquid ad perceptiones nostras attenti cognoscimus. *Solem lucere* cognoscimus ad ea attenti, quæ visu percipimus. Similiter ad nosmet ipsos attenti cognoscimus, nos non posse assensum præbere contradictoriis, v. gr. non posse sumere tanquam verum, quod simul pluat vel non pluat."—*Ph. Rat.* § 664. Here it should be observed that *perception* is used in a wider sense than that to which Reid and the Scottish Philosophers after him restrict it.

[2] Ἐκ μὲν οὖν αἰσθήσεως γίνεται μνήμη, ἐκ δὲ μνήμης πολλάκις τοῦ αὐτοῦ γινομένης ἐμπειρία. — Arist. *Anal. Post.* ii. 19.

[3] Cf. Arist. *De Anima*, iii. 4, 7.

their origin in the constitution of the mind itself, and are virtually prior to all experience, they cannot all of them be referred to Laws of Thought, properly so called. For thought, as thought, cannot be limited to any special class of objects: its laws must operate in all cases alike, whatever be the matter on which it is engaged. That every triangle has its angles equal to two right angles, is indeed a necessary truth; but it is true of triangles only, and cannot be applied to any other object. But that the same subject cannot possess contradictory attributes, is a principle equally applicable to the objects of geometrical demonstration and to the most contingent facts of sensible experience. It is equally certain, that no man can at once be standing and not standing, as that the angles of a triangle cannot be both equal and unequal to two right angles. Hence the criterion of absolute necessity, though valid as far as it goes, is not adequate to determine the whole question. It serves to distinguish judgments *à priori* from judgments of experience: it does not distinguish between different classes of the former, nor explain their several relations to the mind, which is the common source of all. Of the various judgments which have been enumerated by philosophers as necessary truths, it will be sufficient for our present purpose to select three classes, which may be severally distinguished as Mathematical, Metaphysical, and Logical Necessity. All these, being in different ways regarded as absolutely and universally necessary, must be considered as in different ways dependent on laws of our mental constitution. From all must be distinguished what is commonly called Physical Necessity, or belief in the permanence of Laws of Nature. The several distinctions may be represented by the following questions:

I. Why do I judge that a triangle can, under no circumstances whatever, have its angles greater or less than two right angles?

II. Why do I judge that every sensible quality must belong to some subject, and that every change is and must be brought about by some cause?

III. Why do I judge that two contradictory attributes can, under no circumstances whatever, coëxist in the same subject?

IV. Why do I judge that the alternations of day and night will not, under the existing circumstances of our globe, cease to take place?

The last of these obviously stands on a different ground from the other three. I am immediately cognizant of law only as I am conscious of its obligation upon *myself*. The law itself may be physical, intellectual, or moral; but to know it *as a law*, I must know it as a condition which I cannot or ought not to transgress. Law, in this sense, as a discerned obligation, can obviously exist only in relation to a conscious agent; and even with regard to conscious agents, other than myself, I only infer the existence of the law from a supposed similarity between their constitutions and my own. But, as regards unconscious agents, *Law* means no more than a constantly observed fact in its highest generalization. When I speak of the alternations of day and night as consequent on a *law* of nature, I mean no more than that the alternation has invariably been observed to take place; and, when I resolve such alternations into the law of the earth's rotation, I mean only that the earth does constantly revolve on her axis once in twenty-four hours. Or, if I could resolve all the phenomena of the material world into a universal law of gravitation, I should obtain no more than the universal fact, that all particles of matter in the universe do gravitate towards each other, and that certain subordinate combinations of those particles present certain phenomena in so doing. But I have not, by this resolution, got any nearer to *necessity*; for the gravitation of bodies in the inverse ratio of the square of the distance is, like the ebb and flow of the tides, or the elliptical orbits of the planets, an observed fact in the order of nature, and it is no more.[1] *My belief* in the continuance of this observed order may perhaps be explained by some law of my mental constitution; but, as thus explained, it is a law of mind, and not of matter. Under what circumstances certain facts of nature may be resolved into others, and what kinds of experiment and observation will contribute to this end, are questions which, with all their importance, are totally distinct from those which form the object of the present inquiry.

I shall only observe here, that to call such questions a portion of Logic — that is, to regard the New Organon as a supplement to the Old, and both as forming parts of the same Science — is to confound two essentially distinct branches of knowledge, distinct in their end, in their means, and in their evidence.[2] "We do not enlarge the sciences," says Kant, "but disfigure them, when we suffer their boundaries to run into one another." The confusion produced in the present instance is perhaps the most injurious of all to sound thinking — a confusion between the mental self and its sensible objects, the *ego* and the *non-ego*, the positive and negative poles of speculative philosophy.

[1] See Stewart, *Elements*, vol. ii. ch. 2, § 4.

[2] On this distinction some excellent remarks will be found in M. Jouffroy's Preface to his translation of Reid, p. 43.

CHAPTER IV.

ON THE PSYCHOLOGICAL CHARACTER OF MATHEMATICAL NECESSITY.

It has been already observed, that whatever truths we are compelled to admit as everywhere and at all times necessary, must have their origin, not without, in the laws of the sensible world, but within, in the constitution of the mind itself.[1] Sundry attempts have, indeed, been made to derive them from sensible experience and constant association of ideas;[2] but this explanation is refuted by a criterion decisive of the fate of all hypotheses: it does not account for the phenomena. It does not account for the fact, that other associations, as frequent and as uniform, are incapable of producing a higher conviction than that of a relative and physical necessity only. And, indeed, this might have been expected beforehand; for the utmost rigor in a law of the sensible world may furnish a sufficient reason why phenomena must take place in a certain manner, but furnishes no reason at all why I must think so.

But it is one thing to recognize the operation of a men-

1 "La preuve originaire des vérités nécessaires vient du seul entendement, et les autres vérités viennent des expériences ou des observations des sens. Notre esprit est capable de connoitre les unes et les autres, mais il est la source des premières, et quelque nombre d'expériences particulières qu'on puisse avoir d'une vérité universelle, on ne sauroit s'en assurer pour toujours par l'induction, sans en connoitre la nécessité par la raison."— Leibnitz, *Nouv. Essais*, l. i. ch. 1.

2 See, for example, Mill's Logic, vol. i. p. 305.

tal law, and another to discover the law itself. The distinction above noticed between Mathematical, Metaphysical, and Logical Necessity, implies, that, although the origin of all is to be sought for in the mind itself, they are in some way differently related to one or other of the special faculties of their common source. We must further inquire, what is the peculiar relation of the mind to mathematical ideas,[1] by virtue of which not merely the general laws of all thinking, but the special applications of those laws in Arithmetic and Geometry, possess a necessity which is not found when they are applied to concepts generalized from experience. How is it that in some reasonings both matter and form can be furnished by the mind itself, while in others the form alone is from the mind, the matter being derived from experience?

Before entering upon this question, it will be necessary to give some account of Kant's celebrated distinction between Analytical and Synthetical Judgments. An Analytical or Explicative Judgment contains nothing in the predicate but what has been already implied in the conception of the subject. For example: since the conception of body implies extension, the proposition, "All bodies are extended," is an Analytical Judgment. Of this character are all propositions in which, in scholastic language, the predicate is said to be of the essence of the subject; whether a part of the essence, as in the predication of genus or differentia, or the sum of the parts, as in a definition.[2] In a Synthetical or Ampliative Judgment, on the

[1] The word *idea* is here used intentionally, as, in modern philosophy, the most vague and indeterminate that could be selected. It would be an anticipation of what has yet to be determined to give any more definite expression.

[2] The substitution of *definition* for *species* is intentional.

other hand, the predicate adds an attribute to the subject which has not been already thought therein. Thus the proposition, "All bodies are heavy," is a Synthetical Judgment; the attribute *heavy* not being thought in the mere conception of body. Of this kind are all propositions in which the predicate is said to be joined to the essence of the subject as a property or accident.[1]

All Analytical Judgments are formed by the mind *à priori*, whether the notion analyzed be empirical or not. For the mind, having once gained this notion as a subject, has no occasion for any additional experience to determine the predicate which is already given therein.[2] Any Science whatever may therefore have abundance of necessary truths of this kind; but such do not contribute in any way to the extension of our knowledge, but only to a more distinct consciousness of what we already possess. A Synthetical Judgment, on the other hand, is a positive extension of our knowledge, but requires for its formation something more than the concept which stands as its subject. All empirical judgments are synthetical;[3] but mathematical necessity requires that the mind should be able to form for itself synthetical judgments not dependent on experience.

The axioms of Geometry contain specimens of both kinds of judgment. Those which relate exclusively to geometrical objects, — such as, "A straight line is the shortest distance between two points,"[4] "Two straight lines cannot enclose a space," "Two straight lines which, being met by a third, make the interior angles less than two right

[1] See Kant, *Kritik der r. V.* p. 21; *Prolegomena*, p. 16, ed. Rosenkranz.

[2] Kant, *Proleg.*, p. 17.

[3] Kant, *Kritik der r. V.* p. 700; *Proleg.*, p. 18.

[4] This is sometimes given as a definition, but it is properly synthetical.

angles, will meet if produced"—have been shown by Kant to be synthetical;[1] and it is with reference to these that he discusses the well-known question, How are synthetical judgments *à priori* possible? But those axioms which are not peculiar to Geometry, the *common principles* of Aristotle,[2] — such as, "The whole is greater than its part," "Things that are equal to the same are equal to each other," "If equals be added to equals, the sums are equal,"—are analytical.[3] The two last, indeed, may be easily shown to be merely various statements of the Principle of Identity, "Every thing is equal to itself," or, "A = A." Thus, if the common magnitude of the first pair of equals be represented by A, and that of the second by B, the axiom, "If equals be added to equals, the sums are equal," is expressed in the identical judgment, "A + B = A + B."[4]

The former class of axioms determine the peculiar

[1] "Dies sind die Axiome, welche eigentlich nur Grössen als solche betreffen."—Kant, *Kritik der r. V.* p. 143; cf. p. 703, etc.; *Proleg.* p. 20. Hence the error of Leibnitz, in maintaining that all axioms (excepting, of course, identical judgments themselves) may be demonstrated from definitions and the judgments of identity. (*Opera,* Erdm. p. 81.) He selects as a specimen the analytical judgment, "The whole is greater than its part," and of such his theory is correct; but no synthetical judgment can be proved solely from analytical premises; and without synthetical axioms Geometry is impossible.

[2] Synthetical axioms are not included, as they should have been, under the *peculiar principles* (ἴδιαι ἀρχαί) of Aristotle, which are divided into definitions and hypotheses. With the exception of this omission, Aristotle's account of geometrical demonstration is far more accurate than any that can be found in modern philosophy before Kant.

[3] Cf. Kant, *Kritik der r. V.* p. 143.

[4] Dr. Whewell (*Phil. Ind. Sc.* vol. i. p. 134) speaks of this axiom as a condition of the intuition of magnitudes. This is a confusion of the common axioms of Logic with the peculiar axioms of Geometry. Stewart (*Elements,* vol. ii. ch. 1) falls into the opposite error, regarding all the truths of Geometry as deduced from *definitions.*

character of all the conclusions of Geometry; the latter have no peculiar relation to Mathematics, but depend on the general conditions of all thinking whatever, and have therefore a logical, not a mathematical necessity. The whole question of the superior necessity of Geometry to Physical Science depends upon the manner in which we account for the origin of the synthetical axioms relating to magnitudes as such. As an instance, we may take the proposition, "Two straight lines cannot enclose a space."

An eminent writer of the present day has labored hard to prove that this principle is nothing but a generalization from experience, and, consequently, that our belief in the superior necessity of mathematical as compared with physical truths is a mere self-deception. He lays much stress on one of the characteristic properties of geometrical forms, their capacity of being painted in the imagination with a distinctness equal to reality; in other words, the exact resemblance of our ideas of form to the sensations which suggest them.[1] But while it is impossible to deny the ability with which Mr. Mill combats the notion of an *à priori* necessity in Mathematics, it is impossible to assent to an argument which contradicts the direct evidence of consciousness. Nor does this reasoning against Doctor Whewell, however powerful as an *argumentum ad hominem*, meet the real question at issue. What is required is to account, not for the necessity of geometrical axioms as *truths* relating to objects without the mind, but as *thoughts* relating to objects within. Mathematical judgments are true of real objects only hypothetically. If there exist anywhere in the world a pair of perfect straight lines, those lines cannot enclose a space. But if such lines exist nowhere but in my imagination, it is

[1] Mill's Logic, vol. i. p. 309.

equally the case that I cannot think of them as invested with the contrary attribute. That which is to be accounted for is, not the physical fact that certain visible objects possess certain properties, but the psychological fact that, in the case of geometrical magnitudes, I am compelled to invest imagined objects with attributes not gained by mere analysis of the notion under which they are thought; — a compulsion of which I am not conscious with regard to the most uniform associations of phenomena within the field of sensible experience. A sensible object may have been familiar to me from childhood; but, suppose the external reality destroyed, I can assert nothing with certainty of its imaginary representative, except what is contained in the concept itself. So long as I have to conform my judgments, not to the actual laws of the existing course of nature, but to the possible conditions of an imaginary state of things, I have no difficulty in attributing contradictory attributes successively to the same object. I may imagine the sun rising and setting as now for a hundred years, and afterwards remaining continually fixed in the meridian. Yet my experience of the alternations of day and night has been at least as invariable as of the geometrical properties of bodies. I can imagine the same stone sinking ninety-nine times in the water, and floating the one-hundredth; but my experience invariably repeats the former phenomenon only. Whereas, in the case of two straight lines, which, so far as they are objects of experience, stand only on a level with the above and similar instances, the mind finds itself compelled to assert as necessary one attribute, not contained in the concept, and to reject its contradictory as impossible.

The possibility of forming synthetical judgments *à priori*

in Geometry admits of only one adequate explanation, viz., that the presentative intuition, as well as the representative notion, is derived from within, not from without; in other words, that both the matter and form of the judgment are determined subjectively. If it can be shown that the object of which pure Geometry treats is not dependent on sensibility, but sensibility on it; that it is a condition under which alone sensible experience is possible, it is obvious that its characteristics must accompany all our thoughts concerning any possible object of such experience; that its laws must be equally binding upon the imaginary representation as upon the sensible percept: for, abstract as we may from this or that particular phenomenon of experience, we are clearly incompetent to deprive it of those conditions under which alone experience itself is possible.

Such a condition is furnished to us by the intuition of *Space*. That this is a subjective condition of all sensible perception, and not a mere empirical generalization from a special class of phenomena, is evident from the fact that it is impossible, by any effort of thought, to contemplate sensible objects, save under this condition. We may shift our attention at will from this object to that; but we can think of none save as existing in space. We may conceive the whole world of sensible phenomena to be annihilated by the fiat of Omnipotence; but the annihilation of space itself is beyond the power of thought to contemplate. That things *in themselves* must exist in space, and, as such, must be so presented to every possible intelligence, is more than we may venture to affirm; but this much is certain, that man, by a law of his nature, is compelled to perceive and to think of them as so existing.

Upon this law of the mind depends the certainty of geometrical axioms as *thoughts*, though not as *truths*. The peculiar figures of space must, indeed, be originally suggested empirically, from observation of the actual figures of body; but this experience is still subject to the same condition. Bodies cannot be perceived or imagined, but in space: bodies of this or that figure cannot be perceived or imagined, but as occupying a similarly figured space. The modifications originally suggested by the former become an object of thought as existing in the latter; and the features exhibited now and here in the one, we are compelled to think as existing always and everywhere in the other.

The sensationalist is therefore, in a certain sense, right in deriving geometrical axioms from experience. It must be conceded to him that, had we never seen two straight lines, had we never observed that as a matter of fact they did not in that particular instance enclose a space, we should never have arrived at the conviction that they cannot do so in any instance. But this is equally true of any product of the imagination. If I had never seen separately the upper parts of a man and the lower parts of a horse, I could not unite them together in the fantastic image of a centaur. If I had never seen a black object, I could not combine that color with a known form, so as to produce the imagination of a black swan. But why is it that in the one case I find no difficulty whatever in going beyond or against the whole testimony of my past experience, while in the other such transgression is altogether out of my power? Experience has uniformly presented to me a horse's body in conjunction with a horse's head, and a man's head with a man's body; just as experience has uniformly presented to me space enclosed within a pair of curved lines, and not within a pair of straight ones. Why do I, in the former case, consider the results of my experience as contingent only and transgressible, confined to the actual phenomena of a limited field, and possessing no value beyond it; while, in the latter, I am compelled to regard them as necessary and universal? Why can I give in imagination to a quadruped body what experience assures me is possessed by bipeds only? And why can I not, in like manner, invest straight lines with an attribute which experience has uniformly presented in curves?

Can it be said that the ideas in the latter case are contradictory, and that their union is therefore forbidden by the laws of formal thinking? By no means. *Straight* and *curved*, viewed merely as objects of sense, are opposed only as *black* and *white*, or as *biped* and *quadruped;* they cannot, that is, be thought as existing at the same time in the same subject: but that property which experience testifies to have universally accompanied curved lines is not, merely by virtue of that experience, more incompatible with straight ones than the head which has uniformly accompanied a biped body is incompatible with a quadruped one; or than the form which experience has uniformly connected with a white surface is incompatible with a black one. Nor does the impossibility arise from any defect in the simple ideas, such as exists in the case of a man who can form no idea of a color which he has never seen. We have all the simple ideas, or combinations of simple ideas, which experience can give: man's head and horse's body, in the one case; straight lines and space enclosed, in the other. Why is not the latter conjunction as easy to the imagination as the former?

That it is not so, is a matter not of this or that theory, but of psychological fact; and, as such, requires explanation, under any theory whatever. In fact we may demand, as a *sine qua non*, of every hypothesis concerning the character of human knowledge, that it shall accept and account for this fact, instead of neglecting or denying it. Only two theories can be mentioned as having fairly attempted to fulfil this condition. The one is that of Leibnitz, who treats mathematical principles as mere analytical judgments, dependent on the laws of formal thought. On this supposition, the distinction between Logical and Mathematical necessity vanishes altogether.[1] But the solution, though applicable to the general axioms which Geometry, in common with all other Sciences, tacitly or openly presupposes in so far as it contains reasoning at all, fails when applied to those on which all that is especially geometrical depends. By no mere analytical process, as Kant has shown,[2] can the conception of not enclosing a space be elicited from that of two straight lines. In this, and all similar principles, the predicate of the proposition is not developed out of, but added to, the subject.

The other, and far more satisfactory, solution, is that of Kant himself. Whatever we are compelled to regard as necessary, must be so in consequence of laws, not of the object, but of the subject. But there are subjective laws of the presentations of sense, as well as of the representations of thought. We can perceive only as permitted by the laws of our perceptive faculties, as we can think only in accordance with the laws of the understanding. If, then, by a law of my sensibility, I am compelled to regard all external objects as existing in space, any attributes which are once presented to me as properties of a given portion of space, the same must necessarily be thought as existing

[1] *Opera*, ed. Erdmann, p. 81. [2] *Prolegomena*, § 2.

in all space, and at all times. For to imagine a space in which such properties are not found, would not be to imagine merely a different combination of sensible phenomena, such as continually takes place without any change in the laws of sensibility; it would be to imagine myself as perceiving under conditions other than those to which, by a law of my being, I am subjected. The attempt to realize such imagination is not a new train of thinking; it is the refusal to think at all. It does not inquire what new objects may possibly be presented to my present faculties; it requires me to determine how objects may appear to a being whose faculties are differently constituted from mine. Thought, as has already been observed, is representative, and can only be exercised on objects presented to it. It is therefore restricted by the conditions under which alone such presentation is possible. If I am to exercise my thought on sensible objects at all, I must think of such objects under such determinations as the conditions of my sensibility require.

Geometrical principles cannot, therefore, properly be called laws of thought, inasmuch as they do not govern every operation of the thinking faculty, but only regulate the application of thought to a special class of objects. But they are laws relative to the subjective condition of one portion of our intuitions — those, namely, which are presented to the senses — the condition of their presentation being *Space*. But a condition is discernible only in conjunction with that of which it is the condition. Space, therefore, and its laws can be made known to consciousness only on the occasion of an actual experience of sense. Hence the twofold character of geometrical principles: empirical, as suggested in and through an act of experience; necessary, as relating to the conditions under which alone such experience is possible to human faculties.[1]

The same considerations will explain another important feature of geometrical judgments, in which they represent a striking contrast to truths properly called empirical. Imagination plays its part in both; but in the former case it determines, in the latter it is determined by, the phenomena given in experience. The mental image which I can form of this or that individual possesses more or less of truth and reality, as it represents with more or less accuracy the features of the sensible object; just as the value of a portrait depends on the accuracy with which it represents the features of the original. The imagination, again, may of itself form new combinations of attributes; but these also are hypothetically regarded as real or fictitious, according as we may or may not hereafter discover such combinations to exist in sensible objects. But in Geometry the case is reversed. Its propositions are primarily and necessarily true of objects existing in the imagination; they are only secondary and hypothetically true of sensible objects, in so far as they conform to the imaginary model. If there is such a thing in the visible world as a perfect triangle, its angles are equal to two right angles. But if there is not, the proposition is still true of the triangle as it exists in my imagination. And

[1] This character of the special axioms of Geometry is remarkably expressed in the language of Aristotle. For example: *αἴσθησις, οὐχ ἡ τῶν ἰδίων, ἀλλ' οἵᾳ αἰσθανόμεθα ὅτι τὸ ἐν τοῖς μαθηματικοῖς ἔσχατον τρίγωνον.*—*Eth. Nic.* vi. 9. And again: *Ταῦτα δ' ἐστὶν οἷον ὁρᾶν τῇ νοήσει.*—*Anal. Post.* i. 12. With which may be compared the language of Kant, *Logik*, § 35: "Die ersten können in der Anschauung dargestellt werden." Had Aristotle been aware of the distinction between the analytical and the synthetical axioms, he might almost have anticipated Kant's view of the whole question.

the whole of Geometry, as a speculative science, would be unaffected by the annihilation of every material square or triangle in existence, whatever might become of its merely approximate applications to purposes of practical utility. Whereas, the truths of Zoölogy, or Botany, or Mineralogy, are dependent entirely on the existence of animals, or plants, or minerals, not as images within the mind, but as entities without. The cause of this distinction is manifest from what has been said above. The truths of Geometry, though subsequent to, are not consequent on, experience: they relate not to the empirical figures of body, but to the figures of that space upon which sensible experience is dependent. They are therefore unaffected by the destruction of the visible bodies, and could only become fictitious by the annihilation of space itself. But the truths of Physical Science depend upon experience alone: they are true of the objects only as actually presented to the senses; and their reality depends entirely on the real existence of the sensible type.

As Geometry is a science of necessary truths relating to continuous quantities or magnitudes, so Arithmetic is a science of necessary truths relating to discrete quantities or numbers. The two sciences, however, present some important features of distinction. Almost all the truths of Geometry are deductive. It contains very few axioms, properly so called, *i. e.*, synthetical judgments, derived immediately from the intuition of space; and its processes consist in the demonstration of a multitude of dependent propositions, from the combination of these axioms with analytical principles. On the other hand, the fundamental operations of Arithmetic, Addition, and Subtraction,[1] pre-

[1] "Though in some things, as in numbers, besides adding and subtract-

sent to us a vast number of synthetical judgments; each of which, however, is derived immediately from intuition, and cannot, by any reasoning process, be deduced from any of the preceding ones.[1] Pure Geometry cannot advance a step without demonstration; and its processes are therefore all reducible to the syllogistic form. Pure Arithmetic contains no demonstration; and it is only when its calculus is applied to the solution of particular problems that reasoning takes place, and the laws of syllogism become applicable. It is not reasoning which tells us that two and two make four;[2] nor, when we have gained this proposition, can we in any way deduce from it that two and four make six. We must have recourse, in each separate case, to the senses or the imagination, and, by presenting to the one or the other a number of individual objects corre-

ing, men name other operations, as *multiplying* and *dividing*, yet they are the same: for multiplication is but adding together of things equal; and division, but subtracting of one thing, as often as we can."— *Hobbes, Leviathan*, part i. ch. 5.

[1] Subtraction may be demonstrated from Addition, if all the truths of the latter be supposed given, or *vice versa;* though it is simpler to regard Subtraction as an independent process of *denumeration*, as is done by Condillac, *Langue des Calculs*, ch. i. But no result of either can be derived from a preceding result of the same operation.

[2] Nothing, at first sight, can appear more satisfactory than Leibnitz's proof of this proposition. *Nouv. Essais*, 1. iv. ch. 7. But that demonstration assumes the definitions of the higher numbers (2 is 1 + 1; 3 is 1 + 1 + 1, etc.), and this, as will hereafter appear, is in fact begging the whole question. The real point at issue is not whether 4 and 2 + 2 are at bottom identical, so that, *both being given*, an analysis of each will ultimately show their correspondence; but whether the former — notion, definition and all — is contained in the latter. In other words, whether a man who has never learned to count beyond two, could obtain three, four, five, and all higher numbers, by mere dissection of the notions which he possesses already. This remark applies also to Stewart (*Elements*, vol. ii. ch. 1), and to Hegel's attempted critique of Kant (*Werke*, vol. v. p. 275).

sponding to each term separately, *envisage* the resulting sum.[1] The intuition thus serves nearly the same purpose as the figure in a geometrical demonstration; with the exception, that in the latter case the construction is adopted to furnish premises to a proposed conclusion, while in the former it gives us a judgment which we have no immediate purpose of applying to any further use.

An apparent objection, which meets us at the outset, must not be left unnoticed. If the results of Arithmetic are altogether intuitive, how is it that they extend to cases of which sense has never furnished us with the occasion of judging? I may have never seen a thousand objects of any kind together, yet I am as fully convinced that $976 + 24 = 1000$, as I am that $2 + 2 = 4$, of which I see instances every day of my life. And, even if I have seen examples of the former as well as of the latter, how far does the observed fact help in the formation of the judgment? Is my sight so acute that I can distinguish at a glance a group of 1000 objects from one of 999? Can I then, in any case, be said to have seen the fact verified? And if not, how is it that I do not merely know that what I have seen in a single case must be true universally, but even can be assured of the necessity of truths which I have never accurately observed in any actual instance?

This objection is based on a confusion of intuition in general with the special presentations of sight.[2] When the

[1] See Kant, *Kritik der r. V.* p. 703. I have availed myself of the term *envisage*, as the best English equivalent that has yet been proposed to the German *anschauen*, a word which is applied generally to any presentation of individual objects in sense or imagination. Etymologically, both the German and the English word are drawn from the sense of sight only. If uniformity alone were to be consulted, the substantive *Anschauung*, usually translated *intuition*, should be rendered by *envisaging*.

[2] A confusion to which Kant himself has perhaps, in some degree, con-

propositions of Arithmetic are said to be intuitive, it does not follow that their truth must have been observed in visible instances; that we must have seen, for example, that two and three make five, in lines, or pebbles, or the fingers of the hand. It implies only that we must have perceived the truth of the proposition in some *individual series*, it may be of visible objects, it may be of audible sounds, it may be of states of our own minds present to internal observation. In none of these cases do we deal with representative concepts, but with individual objects presented to the external or internal sense.

Now, how, as a matter of fact, are arithmetical judgments usually formed? We see inexperienced calculators arrive at their results by running through, orally or mentally, the several units of the numbers to be added together. If we do not remember that 18 and 7 make 25, as readily as that 2 and 2 make 4, we supply the defect by summing up severally 19, 20, 21, etc. The artificial aids to which we have recourse in larger sums, by adding up, for instance, the corresponding digits in separate columns, are but abbreviated steps of the same process.

Setting aside, as belonging to art rather than science, all those methods whose aim is merely to extend or facilitate already existing processes, the psychological foundation of Arithmetic is to be found in the consciousness of successive mental states; and its earliest actual process consists in giving names to the several members of the series. Such a process, which may be denominated *natural*, as distinguished from *artificial* numeration, would proceed steadily forward, from one member arbitrarily selected as

tributed, by representing (*Proleg.* § 2) five visible points as the intuition of the number; thus by implication connecting Arithmetic with space rather than with time.

the starting-point, acknowledging no relation between the several steps beyond that of succession to its predecessor, until the computation ceases from the inability of the memory to carry on the series. Such a system, however limited in its practical results, would rest on precisely the same foundation as the more perfect methods which art has supplied us, and will, consequently, contain all the data required for determining the nature of the necessary truths of Arithmetical Science.

As Arithmetic, as well as Geometry, contains such truths, it must be equally regarded as founded on an internal law or condition of our mental constitution. This condition is that of *Time*, a condition which governs not merely our external perceptions, but our universal consciousness of all that takes place within or without ourselves. Every successive modification of the conscious mind can be made known to us only as a change of state; a change which is only possible under the condition of succession in time,—a transition from an earlier to a later phase of consciousness. Of Time, as an absolute existence, we cannot form any idea whatever: it is made known to us only as the condition or form of successive states of consciousness. To ask, therefore, whether Time has any existence out of our own minds, is, in the only intelligible mode of putting the question, to ask whether other orders of intelligent beings are subject to the same conditions of intelligence as ourselves; whether they, like us, are conscious of various mental states, one succeeding another. Put in this form, the question is sufficiently intelligible, but obviously one which we have no data for determining; put in any other form, it is absolutely void of meaning; it contains not the material for thought, but only a negation of all thinking whatever.

It might indeed be argued, with some show of probability, that the condition of successive consciousness is essentially the condition of a finite and imperfect intelligence, consequent only upon its very limited power of simultaneous consciousness.[1] The scholastic doctrine of an eternal *Now*, or *nunc stans*, so contemptuously treated by Hobbes, in this respect contains assuredly no *prima facie* absurdity.[2] The error of such speculations is of another kind. It consists in mistaking the negation of all thought for an act of positive thinking. As our whole personal consciousness is subject to the condition of successiveness, we can form no positive notion of a different state: we only know that it is something which we have never experienced. The nature and attributes of an Infinite Intelligence must be revealed to us in a manner accommodated to finite capacities. How far the accommodation extends, we have no means of determining, as we cannot examine the same data with a different set of faculties. The importance of this distinction between positive

[1] Vide Boeth. *De Consol. Phil.*, lib. v. pros. vi.

[2] It is surprising to see how near some of the earlier views on this point approached to, without actually arriving at, the doctrine of Kant. Had the question been considered subjectively as well as objectively, on the psychological as well as on the metaphysical side, the most important conclusion of the Critical Philosophy would have been anticipated. When Hobbes, in his controversy with Bramhall, said, "I never could conceive an *ever-abiding now*," he was right; but he was wrong in supposing that this was decisive of the point at issue. We can only conceive in thought what we have experienced in presentation; and all our past presentations have been given under the law of succession. But this does not enable us to decide what may be the condition of other than human intelligences. In this respect, the remark of Bramhall is exactly to the purpose: "Though we are not able to comprehend perfectly what God is, yet we are able to comprehend what God is not; that is, he is not imperfect, and therefore he is not finite." Reid (*Intell. Powers*, Essay iii. ch. 3) treats the *nunc stans* as a contradiction, which it is not.

and negative thinking will be more closely examined hereafter.

But, to return to the question of mathematical necessity: To construct the whole science of Arithmetic, it is only requisite that we should be conscious of a succession in time, and should be able to give names to the several members of the series. And since in every act of consciousness we are subject to the law of succession, it is impossible in any form of consciousness to represent to ourselves the facts of Arithmetic as other than they are. To the art, not to the science, of Arithmetic belong all the methods for facilitating calculation which imply anything more than the mere idea of succession. Such a method, and a powerful one, is afforded by the invention of Scales of Notation, in which, to the idea of *succession*, is added that of *recurrence;* the series being regarded as commencing again from a second unit, after proceeding continuously through a certain number of members, ten for example, as in the common system. Hence we are enabled to repeat over again, in the second and subsequent decades, the operations originally performed in the first, and thus indefinitely to extend our calculus in the form of a continually recurring series; but the calculus, though thus rendered infinitely more efficacious as an instrument, remains in its psychological basis unaltered.

From these considerations it follows that the several members of an arithmetical series are incapable of definition. Succession in time, and the consciousness of *one*, *two*, *three*, etc., are not complex notions abstracted from and after a multitude of intuitions, but simple immediate intuitions, differing, as far as numeration is concerned, only in the order of their presentation. They are not by any act of thought compounded, the latter from the earlier:

they cannot be resolved into any simpler elements of consciousness, presentative or representative, being themselves the *à priori* conditions of consciousness in general. Hence the failure of all attempts to analyze numerical calculation as a deductive process. Leibnitz, and subsequently Hegel, have endeavored to represent the arithmetical processes as operations of pure analysis. Assuming, for example, 12 and 7 and 5, as *given concepts*, they show that the first may be ultimately analyzed into the same constituent units as the two last; and this is regarded as an explanation of the whole process of Addition. They overlook the fact that, in that process, 12 is not given, but has to be determined by the addition of the two other numbers. Arithmetic is not, like Geometry, a science whose definitions are *genetic* and preliminary to its processes. The analysis of any number into its constituent units presupposes the whole operation which it professes to give rise to. We may call, if we please, such an analysis *definition;* but we must not suppose that it in any degree corresponds to the definitions of Geometry, or answers the same purpose in the operations of the science.[1]

The above considerations are sufficient for our present purpose, which is to determine the psychological basis of mathematical judgments, and their consequent special character as necessary truths, in a distinct sense from that in

[1] Writers of a very different school from that of Leibnitz or Hegel have fallen into a similar error with regard to the nature of arithmetical processes. Mr. Mill, for example, regards the whole science of numbers as derived from the common axioms concerning equality, and the definitions of the several numbers. Stewart appears to have been of the same opinion. On the contrary, the whole essentials of the science must be in existence before the so-called definitions can be formed. The applications of the calculus as an instrument must not be confounded with its essential constituents as a science.

which the term is applied to logical or physical principles. Mathematical judgments are synthetical, based on the universal conditions of our intuitive faculties, and are necessary, not, properly speaking, as laws of thought, but because thought can only operate in conjunction with matter given by intuition, and intuition cannot be emancipated from its own subjective conditions. Hence we are compelled to think of our intuitions under the same laws according to which they are invariably realized in consciousness. Judgments of logical necessity, on the other hand, are analytical, and rest on the laws of thought, properly so called. Their analytical character is a necessary consequence of the constitution of the thinking faculty, and is so far from being a proof of the unsoundness or frivolity of logical speculations, that it is the strongest evidence of their truth and scientific value, and leads to most important consequences, both in Logic and in Psychology.

The nature of these judgments, as well as of those distinguished as metaphysically necessary, will be examined in the following chapters.

CHAPTER V.

ON THE PSYCHOLOGICAL CHARACTER OF METAPHYSICAL NECESSITY.

A DISTINCTION between necessary and contingent matter is found, somewhat out of place it is true, but still it is found, in most of the older, and, among English writers, in most also of the recent treatises on Logic.[1] The boundaries of each, however, are not in the majority of instances determined with any approach to accuracy. Among the schoolmen, the favorite example of a proposition of the highest degree of necessity was *omne animal rationale est risibile;* an example consistent enough with the mediæval state of physical science, but which in the present day will scarcely be allowed a higher degree of certainty than belongs to any other observed fact in the constitution of things. An eminent modern Logician gives as an example of a proposition in necessary matter, "All islands are surrounded by water;" an example which is only valid in

[1] Matter in this sense must not be confounded with the modality recognized by Aristotle, and by most of the modern German Logicians. The former is an *understood* relation between the terms of a proposition, — the form of the proposition being in all cases "A is B,"— and is supposed to be of use in determining the quantity of indefinites. The latter is an *expressed* relation, the form of the necessary proposition being "A must be B;" and this is applicable to universal and particular propositions indifferently. The admission of the latter is still a point of dispute among eminent authorities; the admission of the former will be tolerated by no Logician who understands the nature of his own science.

so far as the predicate forms part of the notion of the subject, and which, therefore, has no other necessity than belongs to all analytical judgments, — a necessity derived from the form, not from the matter.[1] The distinction itself, though altogether out of place when Thought is considered merely in its relation to Logic, is, in a psychological point of view, of considerable importance. The following remarks will, it is hoped, throw some light on its true character.

All analytical judgments are necessary; but they cannot properly be said to be in necessary *matter*. They are all ultimately dependent on the Principles of Identity and Contradiction, "Every A is A," and "No A is not A:"[2] principles, the necessity of which arises solely from their form, without any relation to this or that matter. That every triangle has three sides, arises from a mere analysis of the notion of a triangle; as that every island is surrounded by water, arises from a mere analysis of the notion of an island. This necessity is derived solely from the laws of formal thinking.

Of synthetical judgments, every statement of a physical fact is in contingent matter; at least if the opposite term be used in its highest sense. However rigidly certain phenomena may be deduced from the assumption of a

[1] Examples of this kind were indeed indiscriminately admitted by the scholastic Logicians, who held any proposition to be in necessary matter in which the predicate was part of the essence, or necessarily joined to the essence, of the subject. But this classification, though tenable perhaps in connection with realist metaphysics, is inconsistent with an accurate discrimination between the matter and the form of thought.

[2] Kant, *Kritik der r. V.* p. 133; *Proleg.*, § 2. He derives all analytical judgments from the Principle of Contradiction. It would be more accurate to distinguish this principle from that of Identity, and to derive the negative judgments from the former, the affirmative from the latter.

general law of nature, the law itself remains nothing more than an observed fact, of which we can give no other explanation than that it was the will of the Creator to constitute things in a certain manner. For example: that a body in motion, under certain conditions of projection, and attracted by a force varying inversely as the square of the distance, will describe an ellipse having the centre of attraction in one of the foci, — this is matter of demonstration; but that the earth is such a body, acted upon by forces of this description, is matter of fact, of which we can only say that it is so, and that it might have been otherwise. The original premise being thus contingent, all deductions from it are materially contingent likewise.

The same is the case with all psychological judgments, so far as they merely state the fact that our minds are constituted in this or that manner. But there is one remarkable difference between this contingency and that which is presented by physical phenomena. The laws of the latter impose no restraint on my powers of thought: relatively to me, they are simply universally observed facts. There is, therefore, no impediment to my uniting in a judgment any two notions once formed; though the corresponding objects cannot, consistently with existing laws of nature, be united in fact. I may thus conceive a mountain moving, or a stone floating on the water; though my experience has always presented to me the mountain as standing, and the stone as sinking. But as regards Psychology, the powers of my mind cannot be presented to consciousness, but under one determinate manifestation. The only variety is found in the objects on which they operate. I am thus limited in my power of forming notions at all, in all cases where I am, by mental restrictions, prevented from experiencing the corresponding intuition. I have thus a negative idea only of the nature of an intelligent being constituted in a different manner from myself; though I have no difficulty in supposing that many such exist. I can *suppose*, for instance, that there may exist beings whose knowledge of material objects is not gained through the medium of bodily senses, or whose understanding has a direct power of intuition; but to *conceive* such a being is beyond my power; conception being limited to the field of positive intuitions. In another point of view, both physical and psychological judgments may be called necessary; as the consequence of certain established laws, which laws, however, might have been otherwise. In this sense, both might be classified as *hypothetically necessary;*[1] in opposition to another class of judgments, those relating to human actions, which, as will hereafter appear, are, in the fullest sense of the term, *contingent.* For logical purposes, however, the former classification is preferable.

On the other hand, mathematical judgments have been almost universally regarded as belonging to the province of necessary matter.[2] We can suppose the possibility of beings existing whose consciousness has no relation to space or time at all. We can suppose it possible that some change in our mental constitution might present us with the intuition of space in more than three dimensions. This is no more than to admit the possible existence of intelli-

[1] For this expression see Leibnitz, *Théodicée*, § 37; Duval-Jouve, *Logique*, p. 78.

[2] Universally among those who have accurately distinguished *intelligible* from *sensible* magnitude. The objections of Sextus Empiricus in ancient, and of Hume in modern times, among skeptics, so far as they have any special relation to Geometry, as well as those of M. Comte and Mr. Mill, among sensationalists, are mainly based on a confusion of these two.

gent creatures otherwise constituted than ourselves, and, consequently, incomprehensible by us. But to suppose the existence of geometrical figures, or arithmetical numbers, such as those with which we are now acquainted, is to suppose the existence of space and time as we are now conscious of them; and, therefore, relatively to beings whose mental constitution is so far similar to our own. Such a supposition, therefore, necessarily carries with it all the mathematical relations in which time and space, as given to us, are necessarily thought. For mathematical judgments strictly relate only to objects of thought, as existing in my mind; not to distinct entities, as existing in a certain relation to my mind. They therefore imply no other existence but that of a thinking subject, modified in a certain manner. Destroy this subject, or change its modification, and we cannot say, as in other cases, that the object may possibly exist still without the subject, or may exist in a new relation to a new subject; for the object exists only in and through that particular modification of the subject, and on any other supposition is annihilated altogether. It is thus impossible to suppose that a triangle can, in relation to any intelligence whatever, have its angles greater or less than two right angles, or that two and two should not be equal to four; though it is possible to suppose the existence of beings destitute of the idea of a triangle or of the number two. This is *necessary matter*, in the strict sense of the term; a relation which our minds are incapable of reversing, not merely positively, in our own acts of thought, but also negatively, by supposing others who can do so.

There is one other science which has frequently been supposed to share this necessity with Mathematics. Metaphysics, though, so far as it deals in merely analytical judgments, it has been sufficiently shown by Kant to be incapable of leading to any scientific results, is frequently regarded as possessing a certain number of synthetical axioms, which, under the various names of Principles of Necessary Truth, Fundamental Laws of Human Belief, and sometimes even (however incorrectly) of Laws of Thought,[1] have held a prominent place in various systems of philosophy down to the present time. Two of these principles may be especially selected for examination, partly on account of the importance attached to them by eminent writers, and partly on account of their relation to the Forms of Thought recognized by Logic.

1. The Principle of Substance. All objects of perception are Qualities which exist in some Subject to which they belong.

2. The Principle of Causality.[2] Whatever begins to exist must take place in consequence of some Cause.

"I perceive," says Reid, "in a billiard-ball, figure, color,

[1] This nomenclature is sanctioned by the authority of M. Royer-Collard. "Trois lois de la pensée concourent dans la perception.

1°. L'étendue et l'impénétrabilité ont un *sujet* auquel elles sont inhérentes, et dans lequel elles coëxistent.

2°. Toutes les choses sont placées dans une durée absolue, à laquelle elles participent comme si elles étaient une seule et même chose.

3°. Tout ce qui commence à exister a été produit par une cause." — Jouffroy's *Reid*, vol. iv. p. 447.

[2] Called also the Principle of *Sufficient Reason*, or of *Determining Reason*; though these expressions, as Sir William Hamilton has observed, are used ambiguously to denote, conjunctly and severally, the two metaphysical or real principles: 1°, Why a thing *is*; 2°, Why a thing *becomes* or *is produced*; and, 3°, The logical or ideal principle, Why a thing is *known* or *conceived*. — Hamilton on Reid, p. 624. Cf. Leibnitz's Fifth Letter to Clarke, § 125, where he states the principle in three forms: "Ce principe est celui du besoin d'une raison suffisante, pour qu'une chose existe, qu'un événement arrive, qu'une vérité ait lieu." For a criticism on the principle as thus given, see Herbart, *Lehrbuch zur Einleitung in die Philosophie*, § 39.

and motion; but the ball is not figure, nor is it color, nor motion, nor all these taken together; it is something that has figure, and color, and motion. This is a dictate of nature, and the belief of all mankind."[1]

On the other hand, Bishop Berkeley had labored hard to prove that it was much more consonant to nature, and to the common sense of mankind, to deny altogether the existence of this imperceptible substance, the supposed support of perceptible attributes. "I do not argue," he says, "against the existence of any one thing that we can apprehend, either by sense or reflection. That the things I see with mine eyes and touch with my hands do exist, really exist, I make not the least question. The only thing whose existence we deny, *is that which philosophers call matter*, or corporeal substance. And in doing of this there is no damage done to the rest of mankind, who, I dare say, will never miss it. The atheist, indeed, will want the color of an empty name to support his impiety; and the philosophers may possibly find they have lost a great handle for trifling and disputation."

"It will be urged," he continues, "that thus much at least is true, to wit, that we take away all corporeal substances. To this my answer is, that if the word *substance* be taken in the vulgar sense, for a combination of sensible qualities, such as extension, solidity, weight, and the like — this we cannot be accused of taking away. But if it be taken in a philosophic sense, for the *support of* accidents or *qualities without the mind* — then indeed I acknowledge that we take it away, if one may be said to take away that

[1] *Intellectual Powers*, Essay ii. ch. 19. Compare Descartes, *Meditatio Secunda*, who adduces the changes in a piece of wax as an argument to show that the thing itself is conceived as something distinct from its sensible qualities.

which never had any existence, not even in the imagination."[1]

But after Berkeley came Hume, who applied to the phenomena of internal perception the same process of reasoning which Berkeley had applied to the external. Within myself, he argued, I am conscious only of impressions and ideas. The substance called Mind is a mere fiction, imagined for the support of these, as the substance called Matter is imagined for the support of sensible qualities.[2] In opposition to these skeptical conclusions, Reid and his disciples appealed to the authority of certain universally acknowledged axioms, distinguished as Principles of Common Sense, or Fundamental Laws of Human Belief, of which we can give no other account than that such is our constitution, and we must think accordingly. One of these is the Principle of Substance, mentioned above.

It is necessary to speak with diffidence on a point disputed by philosophers of such eminence; but if there be any truth in the psychological distinction between Thought and Intuition, noticed in my first chapter, it will appear that the Scottish philosophers, in endeavoring to overthrow Hume and Berkeley at once, abandoned the only position from which an attack might have been successfully made on either of them separately. Hume's philosophy is not a legitimate development of Berkeley's, unless we allow that our consciousness of mind, as well as of matter, is *representative* only. If it be true that neither mental nor material substance, as distinguished from the various states and attributes of either, is in any manner *presented intuitively*, the two theories must stand or fall together. And

[1] *Principles of Human Knowledge*, xxxv., xxxvii.

[2] *Treatise of Human Nature*, part iv. §§ 5, 6.

this point is over and over again conceded by Reid and Stewart.[1]

Under this concession, the appeal to a fundamental law of belief is insufficient. Such a law can only state the fact, that we are by our constitution compelled to believe in a certain relation between two given notions: it does not explain how either of such notions could have entered into the mind in the first instance. But the appeal becomes self-contradictory in the hands of any one who admits the views of Locke, or of Kant, concerning the limits of the understanding.[2] Either a presentative origin must be found for the notions of substance and cause, or we must admit that, in these instances, the act of thought has created its own objects.

We are therefore compelled to ask, Is this asserted analogy between our modes of consciousness in relation

[1] For example: "The attributes of individuals is all that we distinctly conceive about them. It is true, we conceive a subject to which the attributes belong; but of this subject, when its attributes are set aside, we have but an obscure and relative conception, whether it be body or mind." — Reid, *Int. Powers*, Essay v. chap. 2. "It is not matter, or body, which I perceive by my senses; but only extension, figure, color, and certain other qualities, which the constitution of my nature leads me to refer to something which is extended, figured, and colored. The case is precisely similar with respect to mind. We are not immediately conscious of its existence, but we are conscious of sensation, thought, and volition; operations which imply the existence of something which feels, thinks, and wills." — Stewart, *Elements*, Introd. part i.

[2] Yet Kant, no less than Reid, allows that we are not immediately conscious of mind, but only of its phenomena. In his hands, however, the concession is perfectly suicidal, and forms the weak part of the Critical Philosophy. The reader who bears this inconsistency in mind, may perhaps find an easier solution to some of Kant's Paralogisms and Antinomies of Pure Reason than could have been given by the author himself. On this subject, the admirable remarks of M. Cousin, in his Sixth Lecture on Kant, should be consulted.

11

to matter and mind really tenable? Does it not rather appear a flat self-contradiction to maintain that I am not immediately conscious of myself, but only of my sensations or volitions? Who, then, is this *I* that is conscious; and how can I be conscious of such states as *mine?* In this case it would surely be far more accurate to say, not that I am conscious of my sensations, but that the sensation is conscious of itself; but, thus worded, the glaring absurdity of the theory would carry with it its own refutation.[1]

The one *presented substance*, the source from which our data for thinking on the subject are originally drawn, is *myself*.[2] Whatever may be the variety of the phenomena

[1] Since the publication of the first edition of this work, the author has met with the following passage in Jouffroy's *Nouveaux Mélanges Philosophiques*, p. 275, in which the above argument has been anticipated in substance, and almost in language: "Thèse singulière à soutenir que je ne saisis pas la cause qui est *moi*, que je sens ma pensée, ma volonté, ma sensation, mais que je ne me sens pas pensant, voulant, sentant! Mais d'où saurais-je alors que la pensée, la volonté, la sensation que je sens, sont miennes, qu'elles émanent de moi, et non pas d'une autre cause? Si ma conscience ne saisissait que la pensée, je pourrais bien concevoir que la pensée a une cause; mais rien ne m'apprendrait quelle est cette cause, ni si elle est *moi* ou toute autre. La pensée ne m'apparaîtrait donc pas comme *mienne*. Ce qui fait qu'elle m'apparaît comme mienne, c'est que je la sens émaner de moi; et ce qui fait que je la sens émaner de moi, c'est que je sens la cause qui la produit et que je me reconnais dans cette cause."

[2] Thus Descartes observes (*Meditatio Tertia*): "Ex iis vero quæ in ideis rerum corporalium clara et distincta sunt, quædam ab idea mei ipsius videor mutuari potuisse, nempe substantiam, durationem, numerum, et si quæ alia sunt ejusmodi." This passage perhaps suggested the observation of an illustrious French disciple of the Scottish philosophy, who has thus supplied a marked deficiency in the system of his masters: "Le moi," says M. Royer-Collard, "est la seule *unité* qui nous soit donnée immédiatement par la nature; nous ne la rencontrons dans aucune des choses que nos facultés observent. Mais l'entendement qui la trouve en lui, la met hors de lui par induction, et d'un certain nombre de choses coëxistantes il crée des unités artificielles." — Jouffroy's *Reid*, vol. iv. p.

of consciousness, sensations by this or that organ, volitions, thoughts, imaginations, of all we are immediately conscious as affections of one and the same self. It is not by any after-effort of reflection that I combine together sight and hearing, thought and volition, into a factitious unity or compounded whole: in each case I am immediately conscious of myself seeing and hearing, willing and thinking. This self-personality, like all other simple and immediate presentations, is indefinable; but it is so because it is superior to definition. It can be analyzed into no simpler elements, for it is itself the simplest of all; it can be made no clearer by description or comparison, for it is revealed to us in all the clearness of an original intuition, of which description and comparison can furnish only faint and partial resemblances.

The extravagant speculations in which Metaphysicians attempted to explain the nature and properties of the soul as it is not given in consciousness, furnish no valid ground for renouncing all inquiry into its character as it is given, as *a power, conscious of itself*.[1] That there are many metaphysical, or, rather, psychological difficulties, still unsolved, connected with this view of the subject, must be allowed;[2] but, so long as we remain within the legitimate field of consciousness, we are not justified in abandoning them as insoluble. To this class belongs the question of Personal Identity, or the reference of earlier and later states of consciousness to the same subject; an immediate consciousness being of present objects only.

350. But the French writer to whom this portion of philosophy is most indebted is Maine de Biran.

[1] See Cousin, *Leçons sur Kant*, p. 197; Damiron, *Psychologie*, l. i. ch. iv.

[2] See Herbart, *Lehrbuch zur Einleitung in die Philosophie*, § 124; *Hauptpuncte der Metaphysik*, §§ 11, 12.

The following question may perhaps furnish a hint of the data from which the solution of this problem may be attempted. Time and Space are given as forms or conditions of the several phenomena of internal or external consciousness; but are the same conditions strictly applicable to the conscious subject itself? I may speak, accurately enough, of my earlier or later thoughts or feelings; but, apart from metaphor, can I, with any philosophical accuracy, speak of an earlier or later *self*, even as a mere logical distinction for the purpose of afterwards identifying the two? To identify is to connect together in thought objects given under different relations of space or time, as when I pronounce the sovereign now lying on my table to be numerically one with that which I received yesterday at the bank. But is the conscious self ever given under these different relations at all? Is it not rather that from which our original notion of numerical identity was drawn, and which cannot be subjected to later and analogical applications of the same idea?

This one presented substance, *myself*, is the basis of the other notions of substance which are thought representatively in relation to other phenomena. When I look at another man, I do not perceive his consciousness. I see only a compound body, of a certain form and color, moving in this or that manner. I do not immediately know that he perceives, feels, and thinks, as I do myself. He may be an exquisitely formed puppet, requiring perhaps more mechanical skill in the construction than has ever been attained by man, but still a mere machine, a possible piece of clockwork. When I attribute to him personality and consciousness, I mediately and reflectively transfer to another that of which I am directly cognizant only in myself. In this case, the phenomena are given in a sensible intuition; the substance is added to them by a representative act of thought.

Beyond the range of conscious beings, we can have only a negative idea of substance. The name is applied in relation to certain collections of sensible phenomena, natural or artificial, connected with each other in various ways: by locomotion, by vegetation, by contributing to a common end, by certain positions in space. But here we have no positive notion of substance distinct from phenomena. I do not attribute to the billiard-ball a consciousness of its own figure, color, and motion; but, in denying consciousness, I deny the only form in which unity and substance have been presented to me. I have therefore no data for thinking one way or the other on the question. Some kind of unity between the several phenomena may exist, or it may not; but if it does exist, it exists in a manner of which I can form no conception; and if it does not exist, my faculties do not enable me to detect its absence.

Such an acknowledgment of the negative character of certain supposed thoughts, *i. e.*, of their not being really thoughts at all, is very different from skepticism. It does not teach a distrust of our faculties within their proper limits, but only tells us that they have limits, and that they cannot transgress them. In this there is no more of paradox than in asserting that we cannot see a man or a tower at a thousand miles' distance. The fault of Berkeley did not consist in doubting the existence of matter, but in asserting its non-existence. If I cannot see a spot a thousand miles off, I am, as far as sight is concerned, equally incompetent to assert that there is or is not a tower standing upon it. In like manner, it is characteristic of all mere negative notions, that we have no direct evidence whether their supposed objects exist or not. To maintain that matter is a fiction, invented for the support of attributes, is to dogmatize in negation, and, after all, to give a partial solution only of the question; for fictions as well as facts have their psychological conditions, under which alone their invention is possible.[1] Had Berkeley's theory been accompanied by an inquiry into the origin of negative notions and their influence on thought and language, it could scarcely have given rise either to the extreme skepticism of his successor, or to the strange misunderstandings of some of his adversaries.

The conclusion to be drawn from the above remarks is sufficiently obvious. The general assertion, that all sensible qualities belong to a subject, cannot with any propriety be called a principle of necessary truth; inasmuch as it is a principle which may be either true or false, and we have no means of determining which. Nor is it correct to call it a fundamental law of human belief; if by that expression is meant anything more than an assertion of the universal tendency of men to liken other things to themselves, and to speak of them under forms of expression adapted to such likeness, far beyond the point where the parallel fails. The true law or principle which connects attributes with a substance extends no further than to the phenomena of the personal consciousness, which are neces-

[1] "It seems to be a judgment of nature," says Reid (*I. P.* ii. 19), "that the things immediately perceived are qualities which must belong to a subject; and all the information that our senses give us about this subject is, that it is that to which such qualities belong." In point of fact, our senses tell us nothing of the kind; and, were these our only intuitive faculties, we should never have supposed such a subject to exist. To refer any belief to a principle of our nature, is insufficient, unless we can at the same time psychologically account for the origin of the notions which that belief implies.

sarily apprehended as attributes of *myself;* and this principle does not warrant us in asserting that the whiteness and roundness and hardness of the billiard-ball are attributes of the ball, in the same manner as my thoughts and feelings and sensations are attributes of me. Nevertheless, there is a real, though an incomplete analogy between the two cases; which may serve in some degree to account for the association which has led to the apparent recognition, in the universal language of mankind, of a relation which has no warrant in our immediate consciousness. Though bodily attributes are not perceived as related to a substance, they are in all cases perceived as related to each other. The perception by sense of any phenomenon of matter is necessarily accompanied by an intellectual apprehension of its relations to space, as occupying it, and contained in it. Color cannot be perceived without extension, nor extension without solidity; and solidity is not a single attribute, but includes in its comprehension the three dimensions of length, breadth, and thickness. But we can analyze in language what we cannot analyze in consciousness; and by the appropriation of distinct names to the related attributes we are enabled to speak of them apart, though we cannot perceive them except in conjunction. This is the real distinction indicated by the use of concrete or abstract terms: the round, hard, white body denotes the attribute as perceived in space; the roundness and hardness and whiteness severally denote the same attributes as separated in language. This real distinction is coupled with an association transferred from the personal consciousness; and men speak of the roundness and hardness and whiteness *of the ball*, as they speak of *my* thoughts and *my* feelings and *my* desires, without being aware that the relation which in the latter case is a fact of consciousness, is in the other an imaginary parallel, which cannot be positively verified by consciousness, though for the same reason it cannot be positively denied.

But, though there is thus no speculative reason for accepting or rejecting Berkeley's theory as true or false, or for attempting to adapt to it common forms of speech, there may, in certain philosophical inquiries, be a practical reason for accepting or rejecting it as convenient or inconvenient. If the method of metaphysical research can in any degree be simplified by divesting it of the hypothesis of a substratum of sensible attributes, this will be a sufficient reason for accepting the theory as *pro tanto* valid. Such simplification will not, however, be effected by taking the Berkeleian theory in its whole extent. The admission of *ideas* as the immediate objects of perception, whether in Berkeley's form, as entities distinct from the mind, or in Fichte's, as modifications of the mind itself, and the necessary consequence that nothing exists except when it is perceived, is too repugnant to the common sense of mankind to have any ultimate value in philosophy. There is still room, however, for an attempt to construct a similar theory, viewed from the objective side, which, banishing the hypothesis of a substratum, shall regard the sensible attributes as the things themselves. Whether such a theory would offer any ground for constructing Metaphysical Science on a surer basis, or whether it would share the fate of preceding systems, remains to be seen.[1]

Much of the above reasoning is applicable to the Prin-

[1] Something of this sort may perhaps be attempted in connection with Sir William Hamilton's doctrine of Natural Realism. But that doctrine, admirable as it is in many of the fragments that have been published, is unfortunately least complete in its ontological relations. On the really weak side of Berkeley's Philosophy, see *Appendix*, note B.

ciple of Causality likewise. I hold a piece of wax to the fire, and it begins to melt.[1] Here my senses inform me only of two successive phenomena: the proximity of the fire, and the melting of the wax. That the one is the *productive cause* of the other, is an addition to the sensible data, which, so far as this particular instance is concerned, is not *given*, but *inferred*. Here, again, it becomes necessary to inquire whether we shall abandon the belief in Causes altogether; whether we shall concede that Thought alone is competent to create the notion; or whether we can discover any intuition in which Causality, as distinct from mere Succession, is immediately presented.

Hume, and subsequently Brown, denied altogether the existence of Cause in this sense of the term. With these philosophers, a cause is nothing more than something prior to the change, and constantly conjoined with it. "We give the name of *cause*," says Brown, "to the object which we believe to be the invariable antecedent of a particular change; we give the name of *effect* reciprocally to that invariable consequent; and the relation itself, when considered abstractly, we denominate *power* in the object that is the invariable antecedent, — *susceptibility* in the object that exhibits, in its change, the invariable consequent. We say of fire, that it has the *power* of melting metals, and of metals, that they are *susceptible* of fusion by fire, — that fire is the *cause* of the fusion, and the fusion the *effect* of the application of fire; but in all this variety of words we mean nothing more than our belief, that when a solid metal is subjected for a certain time to the application of

[1] See Locke, *Essay*, b. ii. ch. 26, who erroneously regards the *production* of change as perceptible by the senses. The other and very different origin suggested by the same philosopher (*Essay*, b. ii. ch. 21) is the germ of the theory of Maine de Biran.

a strong heat, it will begin afterwards to exist in that different state which is termed liquidity, — that in all past time, in the same circumstances, it would have exhibited the same change, — and that it will continue to do so in the same circumstances in all future time."[1]

Thus far Hume and Brown are at one. Into the subordinate question at issue between them, as to the origin of our belief in the uniformity of nature, it is foreign to my present purpose to enter. I have at present to do only with that portion of the theory in which both philosophers are agreed, — the resolution of *cause* into *invariable antecedent;* concerning which Reid remarks, that we may learn from it that night is the cause of day, and day the cause of night; for no two things have more constantly followed each other since the beginning of the world.

In the theory of causation, as above stated, two very distinct principles are fused into one; and the fusion is indicated by the two words *invariable antecedent.* Admitting for the moment that causation means no more than immediate antecedence in time, it is obviously one thing to say that every event must have *some antecedent or other*, and another to say that this particular event must always have *this particular antecedent.* The latter assertion, which implies the assumption of the uniformity of nature in her operations, is, even granting its universal truth, obviously a law of things, and not of thought, the contradictory of which is at any time perfectly conceivable. There is no absurdity in the supposition, whether it be true or not as a fact, that the phenomenon C may at one time be preceded by A, and at another by B; the other circumstances being in both cases exactly alike. Whether such a variation actually takes place under the existing constitution

[1] *Inquiry into the Relation of Cause and Effect,* p. 12.

of the world which we inhabit, is another question; but there is certainly no difficulty in conceiving that in an imaginary world it may take place. This portion of the principle being thus excluded from the class of necessary truths, the remaining portion will not be difficult to explain. The assertion that every event must have some antecedent or other, implies no more than that we cannot conceive it as standing at the absolute beginning of all time, apart from any relation to a preceding series of phenomena. This is an obvious result of the subjection of our consciousness to the law of time. For our consciousness of time is not of time in the abstract, but of phenomena as taking place in time; and the law which compels us to conceive every event as occurring in time, obviously compels us also to conceive it as related to some temporal antecedent.[1]

But, as thus limited, the principle, however necessary, is obviously inadequate as a theory of *causation*. We cannot help feeling that there is a deficiency even in the original theory as stated by Hume; we feel that cause implies something more than invariable antecedent, and that Reid's instance of day and night, if it does not amount to a philosophical refutation of the theory, is at least a practical proof of its insufficiency. The feeling becomes still stronger when the element of invariability itself is shown to be an adventitious accretion, and the original principle is reduced to the mere acknowledgment of a temporal antecedent of some kind or other. Rightly or wrongly, all men do in fact unite with the idea of temporal antecedence that of *productive power*, and regard this

[1] In thus acknowledging one element of the principle of Causality to depend on the mental law of existence in time, I have partially adopted the theory of Sir W. Hamilton. For some observations on the remainder of that theory, see *Appendix*, note C.

addition as essential to the conception of a *Cause.* A belief so universal, even if it be delusive in a portion of its extent, can only be explained, even as a delusion, by the supposition that it has an origin in truth; that there is such a notion as *power* given in the actual facts of consciousness, however it may be extended in imagination beyond the data which suggested it.

The philosophers of the school of Reid could not fairly meet Hume's theory of causation, for the same reason that they could not fairly meet his theory of substance; because they denied the existence of an immediate consciousness of *mind*, as distinguished from its several states. It was easy for Hume to show that volition is but one phenomenon, and motion is but another; and that the former is so far from being the necessary cause of the other, that a stroke of paralysis may put an end even to the uniformity of the sequence. It was also easy for him to show that, as the motion of the arm is not the immediate consequent of the volition, but is separated from it by an intervening nervous and muscular action, of which we are unconscious, the one cannot be directly given as produced by the other. The intuition of Power is not immediately given in the action of matter upon matter; nor yet can it be given in the action of matter upon mind, nor in that of mind upon matter; for to this day we are utterly ignorant how matter and mind operate upon each other. We know not how the material refractions of the eye are connected with the mental sensation of seeing, nor how the determination of the will operates in bringing about the motion of the muscles. We can investigate severally the phenomena of matter and of mind, as we can examine severally the constitution of the earth and the architecture of the heavens: we seek the boundary-line of their junction, as the child chases the horizon, only to discover that it flies as we pursue it.

There is thus no alternative, but either to abandon the inquiry after an immediate intuition of power, or to seek for it in *mind as determining its own modifications;*[1] a course open to those who admit an immediate consciousness of self, and to them only. My first and only presentation of power or causality is thus to be found in my consciousness of *myself as willing.* In every act of volition I am fully conscious that it is in my power to form the resolution or to abstain; and this constitutes the presentative consciousness of free will and of power. Like any other simple idea, it cannot be defined; and hence the difficulty of verbally distinguishing causation from mere succession. But every man who has been conscious of an act of will, has been conscious of power therein; and

[1] This is clearly and accurately stated by M. Cousin: "Cherche-t-on la notion de cause dans l'action de la bille sur la bille, comme on le faisait avant Hume, ou de la main sur la bille, et des premiers muscles locomoteurs sur leurs extrémités, ou même dans l'action de la volonté sur le muscle, comme l'a fait M. de Biran, on ne la trouvera dans aucun de ces cas, pas même dans le dernier, car il est possible qu'il y ait une paralysie des muscles qui rende la volonté impuissante sur eux, improductive, incapable d'être cause et par consequent d'en suggérer la notion. Mais ce qu'aucune paralysie ne peut empêcher, c'est l'action de la volonté sur ellemême, la production d'une résolution, c'est-à-dire une causation toute spirituelle, type primitif de la causalité, dont toutes les actions extérieures, à commencer par l'effort musculaire, et à finir par le mouvement de la bille sur la bille, ne sont que des symboles plus ou moins infidèles." — *Fragments Philosophiques,* Préface de la première édition. James Mill (*Analysis of the Human Mind,* vol. ii. p. 256) speaks of the idea of power in the relation of cause and effect as "an item altogether imaginary." Such a thorough-going imagination is a psychological impossibility: the item must be given in one relation before it can be imagined in another. No effort of imagination can create its object out of nothing.

to one who has not been so conscious, no verbal description can supply the deficiency.

Here again, as in the case of substance, as soon as we advance beyond the region of consciousness we find ourselves in the midst of negative notions, which we can neither conceive, nor affirm, nor deny. Our clearest notion of efficiency is that of a relation between two objects, similar to that which exists between ourselves and our volitions.[1] But what relation can exist between the heat of fire and the melting of wax, similar to that between a conscious mind and its self-determinations? Or, if there is nothing precisely similar, can there be anything in any degree analogous? We cannot say that there is, or, if there is, how far the analogy extends, and how and where it fails. We can form no positive conception of a power of this kind: we can only say that it is something different from the only power of which we are intuitively conscious. But, on the other hand, we are not warranted in denying the existence of anything of the kind; for denial is as much an act of positive thought as affirmation, and a negative idea furnishes no data for one or the other.

The principle of Causality is thus precisely analogous to that of Substance, in its origin and legitimate application, as well as in its perversion. The idea of power cannot legitimately be extended beyond the phenomena of personal consciousness in which it is directly manifested. But the phenomena of matter are thus far similar to those of mind, that both alike are subject to the law of time; the phenomena of nature being in all cases preceded by other phenomena, as the phenomena of volition are preceded by a productive energy of the person willing. The relation which is given in the latter alone is transferred by

[1] See Reid, *Active Powers,* Essay i. ch. v.

association to the former; and men speak of the *power* of fire to melt wax, as they speak of their own power of self-determination, without being aware that, in departing from the field of consciousness, they have departed from the only province in which the term *power* has any positive significance.[1] What is meant by *power* in a fire to melt wax? How and when is it exerted, and in what manner does it come under our cognizance? Supposing such power to be suspended by an act of omnipotence, the Supreme Being at the same time producing the succession of phenomena by the immediate interposition of his own will,—could we in any way detect the change? Or suppose the course of nature to be governed by a preëstablished harmony, which ordained that at a certain moment fire and wax should be in the neighborhood of each other; that, at the same moment, fire by itself should burn, and wax by its own laws should melt, neither affecting the other,—would not all the perceptible phenomena be precisely the same as at present? These suppositions may be extravagant, though they are supported by some of the most eminent names in philosophy; but the mere possibility of making them shows that the rival hypothesis is not a necessary truth; the various principles being opposed, only like the vortices of Descartes and the gravi-

[1] Thus M. Engel observes: "Dans ce que nous appelons force d'attraction, d'affinité, ou même d'impulsion, la seule chose connue (c'est à-dire représentée à l'imagination et aux sens), c'est l'effet opéré, savoir, le rapprochement des deux corps attires et attirant. Aucune langue n'a de mot pour exprimer ce *je ne sais quoi* (*effort, tendance, nisus*), qui reste absolument caché, mais que tous les esprits conçoivent nécessairement comme ajouté à la représentation phénoménale." (See De Biran, *Nouvelles Considérations*, p. 23.) The *ce je ne sais quoi* expresses exactly the negative character of the notion in question.

tation of Newton, as more or less plausible methods of accounting for the same physical phenomena.

Before we can positively assert, as a principle of necessary truth, that all physical phenomena must have a cause, we must ascertain clearly what meaning we attach to the word *cause.* If we eliminate the notion of power, which has no positive significance in this relation, and confine ourselves to that of chronological succession, we may assign three different meanings to the term *cause,* and three different degrees of certainty to the corresponding principle. If we mean no more than that every event must have some chronological antecedent, the principle is a necessary truth, dependent upon an original law of the human consciousness, by which we are compelled to contemplate all phenomena as taking place in time. If we advance a step beyond this, and add to the notion of *succession* that of *invariability,* or repetition of similar phenomena under similar circumstances, the principle may be stated in two different ways. We may interpret Cause to mean simply *invariable antecedent,* in which case the principle may be expressed as follows: Every phenomenon which takes place in nature is preceded by some other phenomenon, or aggregate of phenomena,[1] with which it is invariably conjoined. Or, secondly, regarding the invariability as one of consequence and not of antecedence, we may enunciate the principle in a some-

[1] This last limitation is necessary: the cause, to speak accurately, is the sum total of the conditions, whose united presence is followed invariably by the effect. It is not any single phenomenon, unless we can, by successive experiments, eliminate all the concomitants save one, and thus show that, as far as the given effect is concerned, they are indifferent. This, however, in practice, is seldom the case. On this subject some valuable remarks will be found in Mill's *Logic,* book iii. ch. 5.

what more complex form: Every phenomenon which takes place has, among its immediate antecedents, some one phenomenon or aggregate of phenomena, which being repeated, the same consequent phenomenon will invariably recur.

As stated in the first of the above forms, the Principle of Causality is no more than an induction from experience, and can never at highest amount to more than the assertion of a general fact in nature. We are not warranted in stating, prior to observation, that the two phenomena A and B are so invariably connected together that nature never presents, and man can never produce, a single instance of the latter without the precedence of the former. Such a conclusion may be established, as a matter of fact, by a long course of observation: it may be regarded as extremely probable beforehand, from what observation teaches us of the uniformity of nature in other instances: but in these cases it is not a principle of necessary truth; it is an inductive law or general fact in the constitution of nature as now established by the will of God. It is thus, and it might be otherwise.

In point of fact, the principle, as thus explained, is so far from being necessary, that it has not yet been ascertained to be true. As far as observation has hitherto gone, the same phenomenon occurs at different times with totally different antecedents. Thus, as Mr. Mill has observed, one set of observations or experiments shows that the sun is a cause of heat; another, that friction is a cause of it; others, that percussion, electricity, and chemical action, are also causes. It is very possible, indeed highly probable, that further observation may hereafter discover some one uniform feature running through these several sources; but this is only a probability supported by the analogy of nature in other instances; it is not a necessary law of our own minds compelling us, prior to experience, to pronounce that a plurality of physical causes is impossible.

The second form of the principle is less open to exception. For, though it may be a matter of question whether the same phenomenon may not proceed from a variety of physical causes, it appears to be beyond all doubt that any one of those causes, whenever it takes place, will be adequate to the production of the effect. Thus expressed, the law in question is identical with that belief in the universal connection of similar events, which Hume reduces to the result of association, which his antagonists of the Scottish school refer to an original principle of our nature; while Mr. Mill holds it to be itself an instance of induction, and induction by no means of the most obvious kind.

None of these solutions is entirely satisfactory. That of Hume has been sufficiently refuted even by the disciple of his general theory, Brown; and the refutation holds good, whether we suppose, with Brown, that the theory in question is a dogmatic position maintained by Hume himself, or whether, with Sir W. Hamilton, we regard it merely as the *reductio ad absurdum* of the dogmatism then in vogue. That of an original principle of our nature, though true as far as it goes, is too vague, and confounds under one general term things which it should be the principal object of any mental classification to distinguish. There are some original principles of our nature of immutable obligation; and there are others which are perpetually leading us astray. There are some which lead us to truths which we cannot reverse even in thought; and there are others which point out only contingent and variable phenomena. Sight and hearing, appetite and desire, the law of conscience, and the intuitions of space and time, are all equally original principles of our nature; that is, we can ultimately give no account of them, but that it has pleased our Maker so to constitute us. Mr. Mill's explanation overlooks the fact, that when the principle in question is found in apparent conflict with experience, it is invariably assumed to be in the right, and experience in the wrong; which is not the case with merely inductive laws: to say nothing of the paralogism of making the ground and principle of all induction itself dependent upon induction, and upon induction only. Our earliest and unphilosophical inductions appear as often to indicate variety in the operations of nature as uniformity. The sun rises and sets, the tide ebbs and flows, with regularity; but storm and calm, rain and sunshine, appear to observe no fixed order of succession. But, in any instance whatever of physical causation, let an apparent repetition of the cause not be followed by that of the effect, and all men alike, philosophical or unphilosophical, will at once assert that there was some latent variety in the circumstances, and not a change in the uniformity of their succession.

The Principle of Causality, as thus exhibited, seems to combine in one formula two separate elements, the one necessary, the other empirical. That matter in every relation is subject to some law, by virtue of which a given antecedent admits at any one time of only one possible consequent, seems to be a necessary and unavoidable conviction. That this law will be manifested by the production of similar phenomena on similar occasions, is the result of a combination of this necessary conviction with the experience of the actual evidence of law in our own world, in those cases which are most open to observation. I can suppose it possible that in another world the law may be manifested in another way, according to which the phenomena of matter may have no settled relations to each other, but phenomena at one time and in one place connected, as cause and effect, may at another time or in another place have no connection at all. But even in this case, I can only conceive the material agents as passively obeying the law of their organization, not as enabled, by their own caprice, to obey or disobey on different occasions. Whether the perceptible results be more or less regular, I am still compelled to believe that, in any single instance, the antecedent circumstances being given, the consequent cannot but be determined by them in one way and in one way only; whether a similar antecedent will on a future occasion be followed by a similar consequent or not.

At the same time I am not entitled to pronounce, *à priori*, that matter cannot possibly disobey its own law; though assuredly I am unable to conceive how it can do so. And we have thus a remarkable parallel between the general law of causation, as applicable to physical phenomena, and the psychological facts of our own constitution, the reverse of which, as was observed at the beginning of the present chapter, may be *supposed*, but cannot be *conceived*. And this parallel, I am inclined to think, furnishes a key to the true character of the law. If we were told of an instance on our own globe in which the repetition of exactly similar phenomena had apparently not been followed by the same effect, we should without hesitation account for it on one of two grounds: either the phenomena were not really exactly similar, or the interposition of some intelligent being had prevented the natural result. And if we were asked why these two alternatives alone are admissible, we should probably reply, "Because matter cannot change of itself." And probably, if we were informed that in some other world, where the laws of matter are manifested otherwise than by regular succession, the natural relation had in any given instance not taken place, we should ascribe it in like manner to some external intervention, not to any power of obedience or disobedience residing in the matter itself. Whatever relation of cause and effect is conceived as existing between two material phenomena, whether limited to a single occasion or repeated in orderly recurrence, we find it impossible to attribute to the phenomena at that particular time anything like self-action, or a choice of alternatives to determine or be determined in this way or that. Now, why cannot we think of matter as acting by itself? Because *power* and *self-determination* have never been given to us, save in one form, that of the actions of the conscious self. What I am to conceive as taking place, I must conceive as taking place in the only manner of taking place in which it has ever been presented to me. This reduces the law of Causality, in one sense indeed, to an empirical principle, but to an empirical principle of a very peculiar character; one, namely, in which it is psychologically impossible that experience should testify in more than one way. Such principles, however empirical in their origin, are coëxtensive in their application with the whole domain of thought. They cannot, properly speaking, be called inductive truths; for they require no accumulation of physical experience. The course of Nature is thought as uniform, because, so long as Nature alone is spoken of, that element is absent which alone we can think of as originating a change — Intelligence. And for the same reason, so long as the several phenomena of Nature are believed to be each under the control of a separate intelligence, the axiom of her uniformity will admit of perpetual modification. The winds may blow north or south, as suits the caprices of Æolus; Xanthus may neglect the laws of his periodical rise and fall, to arrest the progress of Achilles; and even the steady-going coachman, Phœbus, may alter upon occasion the pace of his chariot, to gratify the wishes of his roving parent.

To call the Principle of Causality, as thus explained, a Law of Thought, would be incorrect. We cannot think the contrary, not because the laws of thought forbid us, but because the material for thought is wanting. Thought is subject to two different modes of restriction: firstly, from its own laws, by which it is restricted as to its form; and, secondly, from the laws of intuition, by which it is restricted as to its matter. The restriction, in the present instance, is of the latter kind. We cannot conceive a course of nature without causation, as we cannot conceive a being who sees without eyes or hears without ears; because we cannot, under existing circumstances, experience the necessary intuition. But such things may, notwithstanding, exist; and, under other circumstances, they might become objects of possible conception, the laws of the process of conception remaining unaltered. This will be more clearly seen hereafter, when we come to treat of Logical Necessity and the Laws of Thought.

The Principle of Causality may thus, as far as its necessity is concerned, be referred to an intermediate place between the axioms of mathematics and the generalizations of physical science, being contingent in some degree as compared with the former, and necessary in some degree as compared with the latter. It is contingent, inasmuch as it relates to circumstances to which our experience is subjected in the present state of things, and those circumstances might possibly have been different. It is necessary, inasmuch as, while those circumstances remain as they are, the conviction produced by them is unavoidable, in thought no less than in fact. The necessity has thus a negative, not a positive origin; and this origin suggests a practical caution as regards the employment of the principle. Our immediate intuition of power, as has been before observed, is to be found in the consciousness of mind as modifying itself, the *ego* determining its own volitions. That mind *operates upon* matter, we are not immediately conscious. It is not given in any intuition that the determination of the will *acts upon* the muscles of the arm; though the motion of the latter follows the generation of the former. Hence, though we are compelled to ascribe all change to the only power of which we are conscious, we are unable to ascribe it in the only manner of operation of which we are conscious. For purposes of scientific investigation, the principle is thus purely negative, though it serves to regulate our belief. We know not to this day, and we never can know in this life, how mind operates upon matter; though we must believe that, in some way or other, it does so operate. It is impossible, therefore, to construct deductively any system of Natural Philosophy from the Principle of Causality, or from any other axiom expressing the agency of mind upon matter. The value of such principles is purely psychological.

From the view above given of the Principle of Causality, some important consequences might be drawn relatively to other sciences; which, however, my present limits do not permit me to attempt. One such remark, however, will, I trust, be tolerated, both from the intrinsic importance of the question to which it relates, and from its connection with the doctrines of an eminent author,[1] to whom I have

[1] For the argument of Mr. Mill, here alluded to, see *Appendix*, note D.

been considerably indebted in the preceding pages. If the view above taken be sound, we are enabled to detect a fundamental fallacy in the argument in favor of necessity from the determination of the will by motives. If every thing in nature, it is argued, must have a cause or sufficient reason, the determinations of the will cannot be exempted from this general law. If I am determined by motives in the formation of every act of volition, then there is something previous to such act which made it to be necessarily produced. If I am not so determined, there is an effect in nature without a cause. In this argument, there is a latent ambiguity of language. As applied to Physics, the *cause* of a phenomenon is a certain antecedent fact, which being repeated, the phenomenon will recur. This notion of cause is gathered from material phenomena, and can only by an imperfect analogy be applied to mental. In this sense, motives addressed to the will are not causes; for, in every act of volition, I am fully conscious that I can at this moment act in either of two ways, and that, all the antecedent phenomena being precisely the same, I may determine one way to-day, and another way to-morrow. To speak of the determinations of the will as *caused* by phenomena, in the same sense in which the fusion of metal is *caused* by fire, is to give the lie to consciousness for the sake of theory. On the other hand, if *cause* be interpreted to mean an agent with power, my only positive notion of cause in this sense is derived from the consciousness of myself as determining, not as determined. Of the *power* of motives upon my will, consciousness tells me nothing; but only that the one is presented and the other follows; not, however, as in Physics, uniformly. My notion of causes with power, other than myself, is derived from the primary intuition of myself as a cause, and cannot be made to reäct upon that intuition, without the fallacy of deducing the known from the unknown. Of myself, as necessitated by motives, my immediate consciousness tells me nothing. It is a mere inference from a supposed general law of causality, which law is itself derived from the consciousness of the very reverse. You are conscious, says the necessitarian, of yourself as a determining cause; therefore you must be a determined effect. By what logic does this follow? If these considerations suggest a limit to the universality of the principle of sufficient reason, so be it. No principle can consistently be allowed so much universality as to overthrow the intuition from which it had its rise.[1]

Another observation will not be deemed unimportant by those who are aware how many philosophical theories have been constructed on the sole basis of philosophical phraseology.[2] Locke has laid some stress on the fact, that the names which stand for insensible actions and notions are derived from those of sensible objects. "To imagine, apprehend, comprehend, adhere, conceive, instil, disgust, disturbance, tranquillity, etc., are all words taken from the operations of sensible things, and applied to certain modes of thinking. By which we may give some kind of guess what kind of notions they were, and whence derived, which filled their minds who were the first beginners of lan-

[1] The above cursory remarks are of course not designed as a full examination of the problem of necessity, but only as a hint for examining one of the arguments advanced in its support. More would be out of place here. A few additional observations will be found in the *Appendix*, note E.

[2] It will scarcely be credited that a philosopher of Hegel's eminence should have connected a logical theory of judgment with the fact that the German word *Urtheil* etymologically means *original part*. Such a method of philosophizing could hardly have been surpassed by Conradus Crambe, or his facetious relative Mr. Swan, Gamester and Punster of the City of London.

guages; and how nature, even in the naming of things, unawares suggested to men the originals and principles of all their knowledge."[1] The fallacy of the theory attached to this fact by Locke himself, and by Horne Tooke, has been fully exposed by Dugald Stewart; but it should also have been observed that, in point of fact, the obligation is not entirely on one side. While, as regards attributes and phenomena, the language of mental science has mostly been borrowed from that of sensation; in all that relates to the notions of cause or force, as has been well remarked by Maine de Biran, the language properly belonging to the mental fact has been transferred by analogy to the physical. As the basis of a theory, the fact is of no great value; but its weight, such as it is, should at least be acknowledged to bear on both sides of the question.

Before closing the present remarks it is necessary to say a few words in reference to an objection which will probably have frequently suggested itself to those conversant with the literature of the subject. The origin here assigned to the principle of causality (and the same may in some degree be said of that of substance also) may perhaps appear to be of too empirical a character to consist with the amount of universality assigned to the principle itself; besides being in some respects at variance with the opinions of those philosophers to whom the preceding pages are mostly indebted.[2] Sir William Hamilton has remarked, that, if the conception of active power is derived, as Reid asserts, from our voluntary exertions, our notion of causality would be of an empirical derivation,

[1] *Essay*, b. iii. ch. i. § 5.

[2] A point at issue between two eminent French philosophers, to whose writings I am under considerable obligations, will be considered in the *Appendix*, note F.

and without the quality of universality and necessity.[1] Reid himself, in another passage, admits the same thing. "The proposition to be proved," he says, "is not a contingent, but a necessary proposition. It is not that things which begin to exist commonly have a cause, or even that they always in fact have a cause; but that they must have a cause, and cannot begin to exist without a cause. Propositions of this kind, from their nature, are incapable of proof by induction. Experience informs us only of what *is* or *has been*, not of what *must* be; and the conclusion must be of the same nature with the premises."[2]

That experience is the chronological antecedent of all our knowledge, even of the most necessary truths, is now generally admitted. But a distinction is frequently drawn, and has been more than once adverted to in the preceding pages, between truths or notions of which experience is the *source*, and those of which it is only the *occasion*. The mind, instead of being compared to a *tabula rasa*, on which experience impresses the whole writing, is likened to a seed, which must indeed be planted before it will grow; but contact with the soil is only the occasion which calls forth the hidden germ of the plant. Both analogies are imperfect; and both, as regards the present question, tend rather to darken than to illustrate. The point may be better explained by laying aside, as far as is possible, physical imagery altogether, and by examining separately the relation to experience of notions or concepts, and of judgments; instead of confounding both under the vague expression, *origin of ideas.*

Every general concept is in one sense empirical; for every concept must be formed from an intuition, and every

[1] *Reid's Works*, p. 604.

[2] *Intell. Powers*, Essay vi. ch. 6 (p. 455 of Sir W. Hamilton's edition).

intuition is experienced. But there are some intuitions which, from our constitution and position in the world, we cannot help experiencing; and there are others which, according to circumstances, we may experience or not. The former will give rise to concepts which, without any great impropriety of language, may be called *native*, or *à priori;* being such as, though not coëval with the mind itself, will certainly be formed in every man as he grows up, and such as it was preördained that every man should have. The latter will give rise to concepts which, for a like reason, may be called *adventitious*, or *à posteriori;* being such as may or may not be formed, according to the special experience of this or that individual. To the former class belong the notions of time and space, as implied in all our intuitions, internal or external: to this class belong also the notions of seeing, hearing, and such other mental operations as, in some manner or other, are performed by every man not physically deficient in the requisite organs. Of the same kind are the notions of right and wrong, which must necessarily arise in the mind of every man who has ever performed an action of which his conscience approves or disapproves, — and all men must at times do both. The numerous controversies concerning the existence of a moral sense may be considerably simplified by this consideration.[1] On the other hand, to the class of adventitious notions belong those of this or that color, sound, etc.; in short, of all simple or complex objects of perception which it is possible may have been presented to the experience of one man and not to that of another.

But a necessity of which I am conscious, can, like truth and falsehood, exist only in judgments. It may be ordained by the laws of my constitution that I must neces-

[1] See *Appendix*, note G.

sarily form certain notions; but those notions are not therefore thought by me as necessary. The simplest form in which necessity can be presented to my consciousness is that of a judgment, A must be B. This character belongs to all such judgments as by the laws of his constitution a man must form, *supposing him to be possessed of the constituent concepts.*

There are certain concepts which, whether native or adventitious in their own origin, must, when once gained, necessarily be thought in conjunction; there are others which we are at liberty to connect or not, according to circumstances. This necessity or contingency of judgments is generally confounded with necessity or contingency in the corresponding concepts; but the fact is, that they are not even coëxtensive in their provinces. There may be thousands of men who never heard of a circle or its radius: there is not one who, those notions being once acquired, can fail to see that all the radii of a circle must be equal to each other.

Necessity in judgments is dependent sometimes on the laws of thought, sometimes on the laws of other parts of our constitution; and the term may, in another sense, be applied to that character in certain judgments which arises from the limitation of our faculties, and from the circumstances in which all men alike are placed. Thus, by the laws of thought, every part of any given concept, be its origin what it may, must be thought as identical with itself; and hence arises the logical necessity of all analytical judgments. By the laws of our intuitive faculties, all objects of external perception have a certain relation to Space, and all objects of internal perception to Time; and hence arises the mathematical necessity of geometrical and arithmetical judgments. Again, the limitations imposed on our intuitive faculties restrict us, in the case of certain intuitions, to one relation only between them; and hence arises the psychological necessity of certain judgments, of which we can *suppose*, but cannot *conceive*, the contrary. The restriction in this case is not properly a law regulating acts which we can perform, but a bar separating us from acts which we cannot perform. None of these classes of judgments can properly be termed empirical; being dependent, not on experience alone, but on experience in conjunction with certain laws and limitations of our mental constitution. They are thus, to adopt Shaftesbury's correction of Locke, if not *innate*, at least *connatural;* the constitution of man being such that, being adult or grown up, at such or such a time, sooner or later (no matter when), they will infallibly, inevitably, necessarily spring up in him. These laws and limitations of our constitution render necessary the adoption of Leibnitz's addition to the sensationalist axiom,[1] "Nihil est in intellectu, quod non fuerit in sensu, *nisi ipse intellectus*." And even with this addition, *sense* must be understood with extreme latitude, for every possible kind of external or internal presentation. There is another class of judgments in regard to which our experience is restricted by the circumstances in which

[1] *Nouveaux Essais*, l. ii. ch. 1. This axiom has been attributed to Aristotle, who, in *De Anima*, iii. 4, compares the intellect before its actual exercise to a tablet with nothing actually written upon it (γραμματεῖον ᾧ μηθὲν ὑπάρχει ἐντελεχείᾳ γεγραμμένον). But Aristotle does not regard the blank as filled up by the senses, but by the activity of the intellect itself. A nearer approach to the sensational *tabula rasa* may be found in the doctrine attributed to the Stoics by (Pseudo) Plutarch, *De Plac. Phil.* iv. 11: Οἱ Στωϊκοί φασιν· ὅταν γεννηθῇ ὁ ἄνθρωπος, ἔχει τὸ ἡγεμονικὸν μέρος τῆς ψυχῆς, ὥσπερ χάρτης ἐνεργῶν εἰς ἀπογραφήν· εἰς τοῦτο μίαν ἑκάστην τῶν ἐννοιῶν ἐναπογράφεται· πρῶτος δὲ ὁ τῆς ἀναγραφῆς τρόπος ὁ διὰ τῶν αἰσθήσεων. Compare Zeller, *Philosophie der Griechen*, iii. p. 31.

we are universally placed. This is the case with the results of existing physical laws of the universe, which we can perfectly conceive reversed, though within our actual experience they never are so. I am fully convinced, for example, that, under the existing state of things, a stone thrown into the water will sink to the bottom; but it is perfectly conceivable that it might float. Lastly, there is a class of judgments which are, in the strictest sense, contingent; such as relate to the conduct of a voluntary agent, who is subject to no necessary restraint, whatever may be his moral obligations.

The above remarks are not designed as an exact statement of the theory of any previous philosopher,[1] nor as an explanation of language which has been hitherto employed in describing a supposed origin of our ideas. They are offered only as expressing what I believe to be a more exact and accurate account than is conveyed by the physical analogies already mentioned, by the vague phraseology of *source* and *occasion*, or by the obscure notions of *potential* and *actual* consciousness. They likewise help to distinguish, what it is important to keep separate from each other, necessity in the acquisition of concepts, and necessity in their combination in judgments. It is hardly correct, for example, to call mathematical notions *native*, or *à priori;* since it is by no means necessary or universal among mankind to form the concept of a circle or a triangle, still less of an ellipse or a parabola. But the judgments affirming the properties of these figures are necessary in the highest possible degree. On the other hand, the

[1] They approach closely to the view given by Maine de Biran in his 6th and 7th Answer to the objections of Stapfer; but that philosopher has hardly marked with sufficient distinctness the positive and negative elements.

conception of a cause is necessary in its origin; all men being, in some degree, conscious of the exertion of power in their voluntary acts. But the necessity of the principle of causality, as a proposition, is of an inferior degree to that of mathematical judgments.

The general results may be summed up as follows:

1. Judgments necessary in the first degree, or logical and mathematical necessity. These are dependent on the laws of our mental operations; and their contradictions are neither conceivable nor supposable.

2. Judgments necessary in the second degree, or psychological necessity. These are dependent on the restrictions of our mental constitution; and their contradictories are supposable, but not conceivable. To this class belong the principles of causality and of substance.

3. Judgments necessary in the third degree, or physical necessity. These are dependent on the laws of the material world; and their contradictories are both supposable and conceivable, but never actually true.

4. Judgments purely contingent, where either contradictory may be the true or the false alternative. Such are all judgments reducible to no law of causation.

To this class belong at the present moment many judgments on physical phenomena; but here the contingency solely arises from our ignorance of the law, and may hereafter be removed. Thus I am certain that the sun will rise to-morrow; but I am uncertain whether the wind will blow from the north or south. But this only means that we are acquainted with the laws of the one phenomenon, and ignorant of those of the other. The progress of science may raise all these judgments to cases of physical necessity. But my whole consciousness assures me that my own voluntary acts are subject to no invariable law, and that to dream of any amount of future science enabling a man to predict these, as he can now predict an eclipse, and may hereafter predict a change of weather, is perfectly chimerical. These last judgments are, therefore, in the strictest sense of the term, contingent; while those of the second and third class, as before observed, may be called contingent or necessary, according to the different points of view in which they are regarded.

It only remains to point out the relation of the present chapter to Logical Science. Accidentally, it may be applied to the correction of a few perversions of the Scholastic Logic, such as the theory of demonstrative syllogisms; but its essential connection with the Science will be found in the different *forms* of conceptions and judgments. Though the notions of substance and of cause are obscure and negative only, the processes of conception and judgment, in their primitive form, proceed upon the tacit acknowledgment of the existence of something of the kind. In the act of conception, for example, different attributes are regarded as forming one whole by relation to a common substance. My conception of gold, for example, is that of a yellow, hard, heavy body; but the color is perceived by the eye, the hardness is discerned by touch, the weight is made known by its pressure as it lies in my hand. When I conceive these various attributes as forming one thing, *the gold* is neither the color, nor the hardness, nor the weight, but the *something* to which all these qualities belong. Again, having conceived gold as yellow, and hard, and heavy, I afterwards discover it to be soluble. Here, in forming the judgment, *gold is soluble*, I regard the attributes forming the subject and the predicate as coëxisting in a common substance; and this identity of substance is expressed by the copula. Our ordinary modifications of thought and speech thus contain certain negative elements, the notions attached to which no amount of reflection or analysis can render perfectly clear and distinct; though they have been instinctively adopted by all mankind, and underlie forms of speech and thought which are found among all nations. No language can in these respects be constructed upon principles of philosophical analysis; for analysis cannot take place till language has arrived at a certain stage of maturity; and, till that period, it must be suffered to grow up with all the imperfections consequent on a hasty generalization from the data of personal intuition. The logical character of these negative notions will be more fully explained when we come to examine the distinction between the matter and the form of thought.

A preliminary examination of the principles of substance and causality is also necessary, before we can inquire into the character of the logical laws of thought. If it were strictly accurate to regard the principle of causality, with M. Cousin,[1] as a Principle of the Reason; — if it were true that one term of the judgment, that of change, being given, the mind is competent by its own act to add the other, and assert "change supposes a cause;" and that this term thus added contains a positive element of thought, and not a mere negation of the existence of data for thinking; — if this were the case, the whole Science of Logic would have to be remodelled accordingly. The Reason, as distinguished in Kant's sense from the Understanding, would become a source of speculative truth; its principles would assume the character of Laws of Thought; and Logic would become, according to M. Cousin's conception, the passage from Psychology to Ontology: the process of

[1] *Cours de Philosophie,* Leçon 19.

pure Thinking would conduct us to the science of pure Being. A Logic of the Reason would thus become a necessary complement of the Logic of the Understanding; and a considerable portion, if not the whole, of the Hegelian Dialectic must be incorporated with the Formal Science of Kant. To show that such a treatment, instead of being a completion, would be a corruption of the Science, — instead of making Logic fruitful of truths, would make it prolific of chimeras, — instead of attaining knowledge, would aim at impossibilities, — has been one of the main objects of the preceding inquiry.

CHAPTER VI.

ON LOGICAL NECESSITY AND THE LAWS OF THOUGHT.

THE result of the two preceding chapters has been to mark off two classes of Necessary Truths, which, though dependent, as all such truths must be, upon mental laws and limitations, do not, properly speaking, exhibit the operation of Laws of Thought, nor come within the province of Logic. We have now to examine the psychological character of the laws of pure thinking, and the kind of necessity exhibited in consequence by strictly logical processes. The following passage from Mr. Mill's Logic may serve to introduce the subject:

"This maxim (the *dictum de omni et nullo*), when considered as a principle of reasoning, appears united to a system of metaphysics once indeed generally received, but which for the last two centuries has been considered as finally abandoned, though there have not been wanting, in our own day, attempts at its revival. So long as what were termed Universals were regarded as a peculiar kind of substances, having an objective existence distinct from the individual objects classed under them, the *dictum de omni* conveyed an important meaning; because it expressed the intercommunity of nature, which it was necessary upon that theory that we should suppose to exist between those general substances and the particular substances which were subordinated to them. That everything predicable of the universal was predicable of the various individuals contained under it, was then no identical proposition, but a statement of what was conceived as a fundamental law of the universe. The assertion that the entire nature and properties of the *substantia secunda* formed part of the properties of each of the individual substances called by the same name, — that the properties of Man, for example, were properties of all men, — was a proposition of real significance when man did not *mean* all men, but something inherent in men, and vastly superior to them in dignity. Now, however, when it is known that a class, a universal, a genus or species, is not an entity *per se*, but neither more nor less than the individual substances themselves which are placed in the class, and that there is nothing real in the matter except those objects, a common name given to them, and common attributes indicated by the name; what, I should be glad to know, do we learn by being told that whatever can be affirmed of a class may be affirmed of every object contained in the class? The class *is* nothing but the objects contained in it; and the *dictum de omni* merely amounts to the identical proposition, that whatever is true of certain objects, is true of each of those objects. If all ratiocination were no more than the application of this maxim to particular cases, the syllogism would indeed be, what it has so often been declared to be, solemn trifling. The *dictum de omni* is on a par with another truth, which in its time was also reckoned of great importance, 'Whatever is, is;' and not to be compared in point of significance to the cognate aphorism, 'It is impossible for the same thing to be and not to be;' since this is, at the lowest, equivalent to the logical axiom that contradictory propositions cannot both be true. To give any real meaning to the *dictum de omni*, we must consider it not as an axiom, but as a definition; we must look upon it as intended to explain, in a circuitous and paraphrastic manner, the meaning of the word *class*."[1]

I quote the above passage from a work of high and in many respects of deserved reputation, as a remarkable instance of the total misconception of the nature and purpose of Logic, arising from that erroneous view to which I have before alluded, which regards the Aristotelian and the Baconian Organon as forming portions of the same system, and as subservient to the same end, that of physical investigation or the discovery of "fundamental laws of the universe." That the deductive method may be advantageously *applied* to purposes of physical inquiry is unquestionable; and in this respect Mr. Mill has certainly not underrated its value. Any *single proposition* of any syllogism or chain of syllogisms may thus materially contain a fact or a law of nature; but that the fundamental principle on which all reasoning is supposed to depend can by any possibility exhibit a law of external nature and not a law of mind, is a supposition which, if tenable, would make a science of Logic impossible. If the *dictum de omni* were, as Mr. Mill supposes, formed on the hypothesis that universals had a distinct existence in nature apart from the mind that contemplates them, Logic might be entitled to rank with Optics or Astronomy, as a science of the laws of this or that order of natural phenomena; or it might, perhaps, aspire to the character of a general Cosmology, including these and other physical sciences as subordinate branches; but it could not pretend to the slightest knowledge of the laws which the mind obeys in thinking; and its principles, as mere generalizations from experience, could never attain to more than a

[1] Mill's *Logic*, vol. i. p. 234.

physical necessity, as the statement of certain facts in the existing constitution of the world.

A science is never ultimately benefited by dissembling any conclusion to which its principles appear fairly to lead; still less can it gain by adulterating those principles themselves with foreign matter, borrowed from other departments, in the hope of obviating the apprehended results. In the case of Logic especially, it may be confidently asserted that nine-tenths of the confusion and misunderstanding which still prevail concerning its nature and capabilities, have arisen from ill-judged attempts to invest it with an appearance of utility in matters alien to its province.[1] Let us therefore look the supposed charge fairly in the face, and ask what will be the consequences if we admit that the fundamental principles of pure thinking are, as they seem to be, analytical or identical judgments. Is Logic thereby determined to be false or futile? By no means. A system is futile only when it aims at the solution of questions beyond the reach of human faculties: and even then, the prosecution of such inquiries is attended with an indirect benefit; inasmuch as it is only after repeated failures that men learn to know the true limits of their mental powers, and can profit by the precept ultimately enjoined by a critical psychology:

"Tecum habita, et noris, quam sit tibi curta supellex."

It may indeed be humiliating to learn, what such an admission necessarily implies, that the understanding of man is not furnished with a power of intuition as well as

1 Rosenkranz, in his preface to Kant's Logic, speaks severely but truly on this point: "So ist denn auch die Logik hundertfach von philosophischen Stümpern *utiliter* gemisshandelt worden."

of thought; but only in the same way as it is humiliating to know that he cannot fly like a bird, nor swim like a fish. The restriction is one which the Maker of mankind has thought fit to impose upon his creatures; and, regret it as they may, they cannot escape from it. If Logic, indeed, supplied us with nothing but identical principles, it would by no means follow that the study of it is altogether useless; but, in point of fact, it does very much more. Viewed in connection with Psychology, it points to the important fact, that these principles are laws of mind; and this fact alone, applied to the past history and future prospects of Philosophy, will give rise to a series of practical rules of inestimable value in the direction of the mental powers.

To prove, then, that Logic is either futile or false, it must be shown either that it is impossible for a thinking being to attain to a knowledge of the laws by which he thinks, and to test thereby the legitimacy of the products of thought, or that the laws by which the human mind is actually governed are different from those universally assumed and insisted upon by Logicians. But if, on these two points, Logic and Psychology are found to be at one, each becomes the strongest possible guarantee of the truth and scientific value of the other. The laws which the logician has all along assumed as the basis of his system are now shown to be the very ones by which, from the actual constitution of the human mind, the operations of thought are regulated; the conclusions arrived at by a critical examination of the mental powers are shown to be the same laws of thinking which had before been accepted as principles from a critical examination of the mental products. Thus, by the united forces of Logic and Psychology, we advance a step in the most important of all speculative knowledge, the knowledge of ourselves and of our capacities; and so far is either science from being thereby proved futile, that they become the strongest possible safeguard against all futile speculations, by pointing out clearly the nature of the laws of the pure understanding, and the exact limits within which they are operative.

Enough has, I trust, been said to vindicate Logic from the charge of frivolity, whatever may be the conclusion concerning its principles to which our inquiries finally lead us. But, in the eyes of a philosopher, such a vindication is wholly unnecessary. The only question worthy of a liberal mind, as regards the result of any investigation, is not, Is it useful? but, Is it true? However fully persuaded we may be that every speculative truth has its practical advantages, to require a foresight of such advantages before entering on the inquiry, is to interpose the most effectual bar that can be devised to the progress of any knowledge, and the attainment of any benefit.[1] The only tenable po-

[1] This is indeed admitted, and ably maintained, by some of that class of writers whose researches are most to the taste of the Utilitarian. I am happy to be able to quote the following admirable vindication of the pursuit of truth for its own sake, from a philosopher with whose general principles I am by no means inclined to sympathize:

"Si la puissance prépondérante de notre organisation ne corrigeait, même involontairement, dans l'esprit des savans, ce qu'il y a sous ce rapport d'incomplet et d'étroit dans la tendance générale de notre époque, l'intelligence humaine, réduite à ne s'occuper que de recherches susceptibles d'une utilité pratique immédiate, se trouverait par cela seul, comme l'a très-justement remarqué Condorcet, tout-à-fait arrêtée dans ses progrès, même à l'égard de ces applications auxquelles on aurait imprudemment sacrifié les travaux purement spéculatifs; car, les applications les plus importantes dérivent constamment de théories formées dans une simple intention scientifique, et qui souvent ont été cultivées pendant plusieurs siècles sans produire aucun résultat pratique. On en peut citer un exemple bien remarquable dans les belles spéculations des géomètres grecs sur les sections coniques, qui, après une longue suite de générations, ont servi, en déterminant la rénovation de l'astronomie, à conduire finalement l'art de

sition that can be occupied by the assailants of Logic must be acquired by showing that men do not, as a matter of fact, reason consciously or unconsciously according to its rules; that the thinking process is not governed by laws at all; or that its laws are totally different from those which the logician lays down.

But it is time to examine the question itself which has given rise to these observations. Are the Laws of Thought in reality identical judgments or not? It may, perhaps, appear that the so-called frivolity of such judgments is the result of unsuspected causes, having their root in the nature of the mind itself; that the very feature which is selected as the especial object of contempt and ridicule is the strongest evidence of the truth and value of the principles which it characterizes. Supposing, then, that the act of thinking is governed by certain laws, what might we naturally expect to find as the prominent feature by which such laws will be distinguished? A new truth is in its very nature partial: it is new only because it is partial; — the discovery of the particular attributes of some particular thing or class of things. In a psychological point of view, the determination of the laws of thought (be their

la navigation au degré de perfectionnement qu'il a atteint dans ces derniers temps, et auquel il ne serait jamais parvenu sans les travaux si purement théoriques d'Archimède et d'Apollonius; tellement que Condorcet a pu dire avec raison à cet égard: 'le matelot, qu'une exacte observation de la longitude préserve du naufrage, doit la vie à une théorie conçue, deux mille ans auparavant, par des hommes de génie qui avaient en vue de simples spéculations géométriques.' "— Comte, *Cours de Philosophie Positive*, vol. i. p. 64.

An English philosopher, who has treated of the same subjects in a very different spirit, has expressed the same sentiment briefly and well: "It may be universally true, that Knowledge is Power; but we have to do with it not as Power, but as Knowledge."

character as judgments what it may) is as much a new truth as any other; being the discovery of a particular fact in the constitution of the human mind. But when we consider the same laws logically, in their application to the products of thought, how is it possible for any new truth to be determined by them? As general laws, they can have no special relation to this object of thought rather than that; and it is upon such special relations that the discovery of every new property must depend. Material knowledge arises from the observation of differences: the essential feature of laws of thought must be the abstraction from all differences.[1] A necessary law of all thinking, which shall at the same time ascertain the definite properties of a definite class of things, is a contradiction in terms; for it is optional, and therefore contingent, whether we shall apply our thoughts to that particular class of things or not. But if all men have been thinking, some on this thing, some on that, but all under one code of laws, what marvel if, when their attention is called to those laws, they should recognize them as what they have all along virtually acknowledged? Herein at once lies the explanation and the justification of the so-called frivolity of principles of this kind. They can determine only the general attributes common to all objects of thought as such; and these attributes must constitute the very analytical judgments which Logic is so much decried for offering. Surely, in the name of common sense and common honesty, never was outcry more absurd than that which finds fault with a science for accomplishing the very purpose which it professes to attempt, and for exhibiting the very features which, if its pretensions are well founded, and its method sound, it necessarily must exhibit.

[1] Kant, *Logik*, Einleitung vii. p. 219. Ed. Rozenkranz.

It is a remarkable fact in the modern history of philosophy, as regards identical judgments, that, while English philosophers, taking their departure from the principles of Locke, have been unsparing in their expressions of scorn and censure of them as mere verbal trifling, German philosophers, taking their departure from the principles of Kant, have placed them at the head of all philosophy, as the only absolute principles of truth and certainty. Yet Kant, as well as Locke, and with far more accuracy of discrimination, perceived and pointed out the impossibility of constructing a system of philosophy upon these judgments only. That both extremes are equally in error, — that both arise from a crude and one-sided view of a philosophy not perhaps in all respects consistent with itself, — and that the truth lies between the two, is a natural and obvious conclusion. To enter into the extravagances of Fichte and Schelling would be foreign to the purposes of the present work; but as regards the disciple of Locke, it may be observed, that he has no choice but of two alternatives: either to repudiate the attack of his master on frivolous propositions, or to retract his refutation of the doctrine of innate ideas. If the principles of thought are competent to supply any positive addition to what is given in intuition, it follows that the act of thought can in so far create its own materials. This brings us back, of necessity, to the theory of innate ideas. If, on the other hand, the understanding can only modify what is given out of the act of thought, it follows that analytical judgments are not mere verbal frivolities, but fundamental laws of the thinking faculty.

The Laws of Thought, properly so called, may thus be psychologically distinguished from the other elements of the process by the answers to the following questions:

1. What is the material which must be given prior to any act of pure thinking? 2. How is that material modified by the act of thought itself? 3. What are the conditions by which the understanding is bound in such modification? The third question will determine the fundamental laws of the several operations of Conception, Judgment, and Reasoning.

The act of conception consists in regarding certain attributes as coëxisting in a possible object of intuition. It has before been remarked, that when the object of intuition is actual, *i. e.*, now and here present, an act of thought is necessary to distinguish it as such from other objects simultaneously presented. This, however, is not pure conception, but conception in conjunction with intuition. In pure conception, the attributes are not presented in themselves, but represented by their signs. Hence the necessity, in some form or other, of language; and hence the object of intuition, in an act of pure conception, is not presented as actual, but represented as possible.[1]

Two preliminary conditions are thus requisite, prior to any act of pure conception. Firstly, attributes must be given which, in some combination or other, have been presented in a former intuition. For, as thought cannot create intuition, attributes which have never been experienced are not conceivable. They need not indeed have been experienced in their present relation, but in some relation or other. Thus, though I have never seen that combination of a man's head with a horse's body, which is supposed to constitute a centaur, yet the notion of such a conjunction is perfectly conceivable, because both the horse's body and the man's head have been presented in other combinations. Secondly, as the attributes are now

[1] Cf. Krug, *Logik*, § 15.

given in and through their signs, the import of those signs is presupposed to be known. A word which I cannot connect with some known attribute is, for all purposes of thought, like the terms of an unknown tongue. Pure thought can neither supply defects in the experience of things, nor ignorance of the meaning of words. Information on both these points is therefore presupposed.

These materials being given, how are they dealt with by the act of thought, and what are the laws and limits which govern or confine the operation? By the act of conception, the given attributes are combined in a unity of representation. Are there, then, any cases in which, certain attributes being given, I am compelled to think them as representing an object? are there any cases in which I am forbidden to do so? and are there any in which, as far as thought is concerned, I am left at liberty to do as I please? Pure conception being concerned with possible objects of intuition only, the first and third cases merge into one. The actual existence of any object can be determined only by its actual presence in this or that intuition; and even then the evidence extends only to its present existence now and here, not to its necessary existence at any future time when it may become an object of thought. As an object of a past intuition, it has then a possible and representative existence only.[1] The first law of pure thinking applicable to conception is thus indicated

[1] "As not *now present in time*, an immediate knowledge of the *past* is impossible. The past is only mediately cognizable in and through a present modification relative to and representative of it, as having been. To speak of an immediate knowledge of the past involves a contradiction *in adjecto*. For, to know the past immediately, it must be known *in itself;* and to be known in itself, it must be known as *now existing*. But the past is just a negation of the now existent; its very notion, therefore, excludes the possibility of its being immediately known." — Sir W. Hamilton, *Reid's Works*, p. 810.

by the negative criterion, that there are certain attributes which we cannot think as coëxisting in any possible object of intuition. This leads us to the well-known Principle of Contradiction,[1] the most general form of which is, "Nothing can be A and not-A;" or, "No object can be thought under contradictory attributes." But, though everything which is contradictory is thus inconceivable, it cannot be maintained, on the other hand, that everything which is not contradictory is conceivable.[2]

But the Principle of Contradiction, as above enunciated, can only be applied in thought cöordinately with another and a positive principle. If an object cannot be thought under contradictory attributes, the impossibility arises from its having a definite character of its own, including one of the contradictories and excluding the other. The universe of conceivable objects embraces both *A* and *not-A*: it is only when definitely conceived as the one that an object cannot be conceived as the other. Every object of thought, as such, is thus conceived by limitation and difference; as having definite characteristics by which it is marked off and distinguished from all others; as being, in short, *itself*, and nothing else. The indefinite ideas, therefore, corresponding to the general terms Thing, Object, Being in general, are not concepts, as containing no distinctive attributes; and the general object denoted by such terms is inconceivable. This second Law of Thought is expressed by the Principle of Identity, "Every A is A;" or, "Every object of thought is conceived as itself."[3]

[1] This law, as Krug has remarked (*Logik*, § 18), ought rather to be called the Principle of Non-Contradiction.

[2] On conceivability as a test of logical possibility, see Sir W. Hamilton, *Reid's Works*, p. 377.

[3] Cf. Krug, *Logik*, § 17, who contemplates the principle from the oppo-

But these two Laws of Thought necessarily involve a third. The object which I conceive is, by the Law of Identity, discerned as being that which it is, and by the Law of Contradiction is distinguished from that which it is not. But these two correlatives must also be regarded as constituting between them the universe of all that is conceivable; for the distinction above made is not between two definite objects of thought, but between the object of which I think and all those of which I do not think. *Not-A* implies the exclusion of *A* only, and of nothing else, and thus denotes the universe of all conceivable objects with that one exception. This relation, in its more general expression, constitutes a third Law of Thought, the Principle of Excluded Middle,[1] "Every possible object is either A or not-A." These three Principles, of Contradiction, Identity, and Excluded Middle, constitute the Laws of Pure Thinking, or of Thought as Thought.

Another limitation must be noticed, which, though perhaps not properly an *à priori* law arising out of the nature of thought itself, is at least a universally valid *à posteriori* restriction arising from the practical limits of our intuitive powers. Thought can only deal with such attributes as have been in some manner presented in intuition. Hence, in all cases where intuition is impossible, thought is im-

site side. He is wrong, however, in deducing from it the principle of Contradiction, which is an independent axiom. The two have been confounded or identified by many eminent philosophers; as Leibnitz (*Reflex. sur Locke*), Wolf (*Ph. Rat.* § 271), Kant (*Logik*, Einl. vii.), Herbart (*Einl. in die Philosophie*, § 39). Hoffbauer (*Logik*, § 23) shows that the two principles are independent, and that neither can be deduced from the other without a *petitio principii.*

[1] *Principium exclusi medii inter duo contradictoria.* For the history of this expression, and of the Law denoted by it, see Sir W. Hamilton's *Lectures on Logic*, p. 65.

possible likewise. Hence arises a class of practical limitations of thought based on the limitations of possible experience. Some of these are partial and accidental only; as in the case of a blind man, who can have no intuitive experience of colors. But one at least is common to all men, and, so far, psychologically, if not logically, necessary. Though, as far as the laws of thought are concerned, it is permitted to unite in an act of conception all attributes which are not contradictory of each other, it is impossible in practice to go beyond a very limited number. The number of attributes in the universe not logically repugnant to each other is infinite; and the mind can therefore find no absolute limits to its downward progress in the formation of subordinate notions. To arrive at a notion which shall comprehend within itself all conceivable compatible attributes, and which shall therefore admit of no further possible limitation but that of the individual conditions of presence in space and time, is an act which, if not *à priori* self-destructive, will at least in practice require an infinite grasp of mind and an infinite length of time for its accomplishment.[1]

Hence it follows at once that a logical Highest Genus, and a logical Lowest Species — *i. e.*, a notion so simple as to admit of no further subtraction, and a notion so complex as to admit of no further addition — are both *inconceivable.* The meaning of these two terms in Logic must not be

[1] This and the preceding condition are sometimes given as the *Laws of Homogeneity and Specification.* See Kant, *Kritik der r.* V. p. 510, ed. Rosenkranz; Krug, *Logik,* § 45, b; Fries, *Syst. der Logik,* § 21. I prefer to regard them as deductions from a higher law. It may be observed, that those logicians who insist on the Law of Homogeneity are not consistent in calling *thing* or *object* a *concept* (Begriff). The third law joined with these two, that of *Logical Affinity,* or *Continuity,* is questionable, both as regards truth and value.

confounded with that which is applicable to this or that branch of material science. The Highest Genus in any special science is the general class, comprehending all the objects whose properties that science investigates; the different Lowest Species are the classes at which that special investigation terminates. In Geometry, for example, under the *summum genus* of magnitudes in space, we find three coördinate *infimæ species* of triangles, the equilateral, the isosceles, and the scalene. The geometrical properties of the figures are not affected by any further subdivision. These three classes are therefore lowest species in Geometry, but not in Logic. For of geometrical limitations, the logician, as such, knows nothing. In a mere relation of concepts, the notion of an equilateral triangle whose sides are three feet long, is a further subdivision of the notion of an equilateral triangle; and out of this again we may form the subordinate notion, "an equilateral triangle whose sides are three feet long and divided into inches." This process may, as far as Logic is concerned, be continued *ad infinitum.*

The extreme limits of generalization and specification being thus inconceivable, we obtain from these conditions two characteristics of all logical concepts, namely, that they must have both *comprehension* and *extension.* Every notion, that is to say, as a condition of its conceivability, must contain a plurality of attributes, in consequence of which it is capable of subordination to a higher notion; and it must contain a limited number only of attributes, in consequence of which lower notions may be subordinated to it. This canon of conceivability, as we have seen, is not invalidated by the supposed highest and lowest classes of the logicians, which are limits never arrived at in any process of actual thought. Neither is it invalidated by the so-called *simple ideas*, which, according to the doctrine of Descartes and Locke, are the limits beyond which analysis is impossible. For a simple idea, like a *summum genus*, is by itself inconceivable. In every intuition it is presented as part of a complex object; and it can in no act of positive thought be contemplated out of that connection. Whiteness and redness, for example, are given to us in combination with extension; motion, with a moving body; pleasure and pain, with a conscious subject. We cannot represent to ourselves, as a possible object of intuition, a color unextended,[1] a motion without a moving body, a feeling without a mind. Simple ideas are thus never conceived as such, but only forming parts of a complex object. That they are indefinable (in Locke's view of definition), has been remarked in a former chapter; but this arises, not from their forming absolutely simple concepts, but from their being simple portions of a complex intuition.

From these two characteristics of all concepts follows their capability of *Definition* and *Division* — the former being an enumeration of the higher notions contained in the comprehension of a given concept; the latter, an enumeration of the lower notions contained in its extension. The manner, however, in which these two operations are commonly treated in logical writings manifests an utter confusion between the general laws of thinking as applicable to any matter, such as they are laid down in pure Logic, and the performance of a special act of thought about this or that matter, which forms a portion of this or that branch of applied Logic. The so-called Logical Laws

[1] The error of those philosophers who suppose that color can be conceived apart from extension, has been noticed by Sir W. Hamilton, *Reid's Works*, p. 860.

of Definition and Division are merely derived from an analysis of the notions of the operations themselves;—notions such as might be borrowed concerning any object from the art or science to which it materially belongs. In the *given notion* of Definition, as the enumeration of the parts comprehended in a concept, it is of course implied that it must be adequate, otherwise the parts are not enumerated; and that it is clear, otherwise they are not parts. And so of Division, substituting parts of extension for those of comprehension. Such an analysis furnishes no test even of the formal validity of any *single act* of division or definition; it only takes to pieces the general notion of the process. But it is obvious that any given notion, borrowed from any source whatever, may be analyzed in like manner by an application of thought. From the notion of weighing a pound of cheese, it follows of course, firstly, that the whole quantity weighed must be exactly a pound; secondly, that any part of the same must be less than a pound; thirdly, that the same ounce must not be weighed twice over. If this criterion be adopted, a chapter on cheese-weighing has as good a right to be placed in Logic, as a chapter on Division or Definition.

The question necessary to determine the true logical character of these processes is not, "Given the general notions of the two operations, to determine by analysis what those notions imply;" but, "Given any particular concept, how much can be ascertained by pure thinking concerning its relation to higher or lower concepts?" Viewed in this light, Definition, as a logical operation, is a portion of the act of Conception, governed by the same laws, and subject to the same limitations. We can determine thereby nothing concerning the actual possession of certain attributes by certain objects: we cannot even ascertain that objects of any kind really exist in nature. Conception being limited to possible objects of intuition only, Definition is confined to the analysis and separate exposition of the attributes contained in a given concept, and determines not their reality but their conceivability. Its only logical laws are the Principles of Identity and Contradiction: the one compelling us to regard any given concept as identical with the sum of its constituent parts, and the other pronouncing that a definition which enumerates attributes directly or by implication incompatible with each other is logically self-destructive. If the attributes are compatible, the definition is allowed as valid, as far as Logic is qualified to pronounce judgment: for further examination it must be referred to the tribunal of experience. The purpose of logical definition is thus not material accuracy, but formal distinctness as regards the *intension* or *comprehension*[1] of the concept.

It is obvious that the rules of definition commonly given in logical treatises have no value or significance except in extralogical applications. To say that a definition must be adequate *to the notion which I entertain*, is only to say that what I assign as the contents of a notion must be what I think to be the contents; which is, of course, implied in the fact of my assigning them. The rule acquires a material significance when interpreted to mean that the attributes assigned in the definition must exactly correspond to the characteristic features of *the object as it exists in nature.* But, then, to determine whether this rule is complied with or not is clearly beyond the province of the

[1] See Drobisch, *Neue Darstellung der Logik*, § 102. That analytical distinctness alone falls within the province of Logic is shown by Kant, *Logik*, Einl. viii.

logician. I may assign "rational animal," as an analysis of my notion of man; but to ascertain, as a matter of fact, that all men possess reason, and that all other animals are without it, is manifestly a question not of thought, but of experience. There is no alternative between exempting the logician as such from all material knowledge whatever, and requiring from him a minute acquaintance with every possible branch of human knowledge. If he is bound to know, as a matter of fact, that men are rational and horses hinnible, he is by the same rule bound to be conversant with the constitution and properties of every object which nature can present or art produce.

It is obvious also that Logic can admit one kind of definition, and one only. The so-called *nominal definition* by synonym or etymology would require of the logician a material knowledge of the vocabulary and construction of any given language, thus making Logic a compendium of all dictionaries and all grammars.[1] The so-called *accidental definition* is a logical absurdity. If the notion *homo*, for example, is composed of the notions *animal rationale*, it cannot at the same time contain the distinct attributes of *bipes implume*. To use the same word for both combinations is simply to employ language equivo-

[1] "In this place," says Archbishop Whately, "we are concerned with nominal definitions only, because all that is requisite for the purposes of *reasoning* (which is the proper province of Logic) is, that a term shall not be used in *different senses*: a *real* definition of anything belongs to the science or system which is employed about that thing." In the sense in which nominal and real definition were distinguished by the scholastic logicians, the exact reverse is the truth. Logic is concerned with real, *i. e.*, with notional definitions only: to explain the meaning of particular words belongs to the dictionaries or grammars of particular languages. But this is only one out of thousands of errors committed by various writers, through confounding the *thing* or notion in the mind with the *things* or individuals out of it. Even Kant (*Logik*, § 106) has not quite avoided this ambiguity.

cally. It *may so happen* that all the individuals possessed of reason are also provided with two legs and destitute of feathers; but this is not implied in the notion of rationality, and cannot be elicited by any act of pure thinking. For this reason those logicians are clearly right who consider the enumeration of properties or accidents, not as a *definition* of notions, but as a *description* of individuals. But such a description has clearly no connection with Logic, but solely with the natural history of the object described.

Division, on the other hand, corresponds in one sense to the remaining portion of the act of Conception, the union of the attributes in a possible object of intuition, and is thus regulated by the same laws as Definition. But Division, in this sense of the term, is not *Specification*, but *Individualization;* and moreover pays no attention to any coördinate members of the same class, but is solely occupied with the one object conceived. It thus belongs, not to symbolical, but to intuitive cognition; being not the mere enumeration of the constituent elements of a concept, but the verification of their conceivability by the aid of the imagination. Such an imagination is in one sense a Division; for it is impossible for me to imagine an individual triangle which shall be neither equilateral, isosceles, nor scalene: one of these attributes therefore enters into every actual intuition of a triangle, and thus far limits and divides the general notion. But, then, the attributes added are not in this case contemplated as the constituents of a lower class, but of a possible individual. In like manner, I cannot imagine a man of no color and no stature; but in adding these particulars to my conception, I do not think of them as related to any coördinate class, as constituting a division of men into tall and short, or white and not white. I think of them only as necessary to test the conceivability of the generic attributes with which they are combined. The office of Division in this respect is to make our conceptions *clear*, as that of Definition is to make them *distinct*.[1]

Beyond this, the process of Division, as contributing to distinctness in the *extension* of a Concept, cannot be regarded as an act of pure thinking,[2] or as solely determined by logical laws. Even in the case of dichotomy by contradiction, the principle of division must be given, as an addition to the attributes comprehended in the concept, before the logician can take a single step. For Division is not, like Definition, a mental analysis of *given* materials: the specific difference must be *added* to the given attributes of the genus; and to gain this additional material, it is necessary to go out of the act of thought, to seek for new empirical data. "Divide animal" is a command which no logician, as such, can obey; for the mere notion *animal* does not of itself suggest *rational* or *irrational*, any more than *mortal* or *immortal*, *virtuous* or *vicious*, or any other attributes not logically incompatible with the genus.[3] The principle of division must be given in addition to the concept to be divided; and when it is given, the process, thus raised from a material to a formal one,

[1] A conception is *clear* when its object, as a whole, can be distinguished from any other; it is *distinct* when its several constituent parts can be distinguished from each other. The merit of first pointing out these characteristics of the logical perfection of thought belongs to Leibnitz. See his *Meditationes de Cognitione Veritate et Ideis.*

[2] By *pure thinking* is not meant thinking which has no relation to any past experience; for without some experience, all thought is impossible. It means only that we can proceed to the act of thought without additional data being required prior to and out of the act itself. The relation of experience to thought is too often lost sight of in the Kantian philosophy.

[3] See Fries, *System der Logik*, § 92.

has, like definition, a potential only, not an actual value in relation to experience. If the differentia *rational* is given, I can divide animal into rational and not-rational; but if the differentia *mortal* is given, I can also, as far as Logic is concerned, divide into mortal and immortal. I must appeal to experience, and not to thought, to determine whether one or the other of these divisions is actually true; whether the Struldbrugs of Luggnagg or the Undying Fish of Bowscale Tarn are really existing animals or not. Every concept is potentially divisible by any two given differentiæ, contradictory of each other, and both compatible with the genus. And the laws by which the process is governed are, firstly, the Principle of Contradiction; and, secondly, that of Excluded Middle. By the first, we are forbidden to think that two contradictory attributes can both be present in the same object; by the second, we are forbidden to think that both can be absent. The first tells us that both differentiæ must be compatible with the genus: I cannot, for example, divide animal into animate and inanimate. The second tells us that one or the other must be found in every member of the genus; but in what manner this is actually carried out, whether by every existing member possessing one of the differentiæ and none the other, or by some possessing one and some the other, experience alone can determine.[1]

It thus appears that even dichotomy by contradiction is not, strictly speaking, a formal process, as Kant considers it;[2] but that it is partly material, and so far extralogical; and that the material element predominates still more, according as any other principle of division is adopted. Where the specific differences are not contradictory, so

[1] Trendelenburg, *Logische Untersuchungen*, i. 4.

[2] *Logik*, § 113. See, on the other side, Hoffbauer, *Logik*, §§ 134, 138.

that each naturally suggests the other, every one of them must be *given*, prior to any possible act of formal thinking. The only division of a concept which can be regarded as a purely logical process is that sometimes distinguished as *Determination*, which consists in the reünion of attributes previously separated by definition.[1] In a formal point of view, therefore, the arrangement of those logicians who treat of Definition before Division is preferable to the inverse order adopted by Aldrich, *Divisionem excipit Definitio.*

Throughout the preceding remarks, the presence of all the antecedent conditions requisite to the logical perfection of cognitions is presupposed. It is taken for granted that we are, prior to any act of conception, in possession of the materials necessary to complete *clearness* and *distinctness*, and that the act of thought consists merely in eliciting the concept with these qualities out of the sufficient data. And this supposition is the only one which can be admitted into a system of pure Logic, or into Psychology in its purely logical relation. The failure of materials for conception is precisely analogous to the failure of materials for reasoning. In the latter case, if a single premise only is given, or two premises so related that no necessary conclusion follows from them, the logician is not called upon to remedy the deficiency; he simply decides that the data are insufficient for reasoning at all. In like manner, if the empirical data for clear or distinct conception are wanting, the logician, as such, can only say that the materials for the thought are insufficient. The distinction between clear and obscure, distinct and indistinct conceptions, is as much out of the province of pure Logic, as a distinction between syllogisms whose premises

[1] See Drobisch, §§ 17, 29, 30.

necessitate their conclusion, and reasonings in which the consequence may with more or less probability be conjectured. In conception and in judgment, as well as in reasoning, there are processes necessitated by the laws of thought from certain data; there are others which are not necessitated, but which may be hazarded with more or less risk of error; the presumption in their favor amounting in some cases to a moral certainty, and binding upon our practice, but never reaching the height of logical necessity or speculative perfection.[1] The first class alone are recognized by Pure Logic, and that in relation not merely to reasoning, but to all three operations of thought. Applied Logic, in the Kantian sense of the term, may treat of the several practical imperfections of human thought, which lower in this or that special instance the logical standard of perfection. Here we may treat of notions more or less obscure or confused, of judgments more or less uncertain, of reasonings more or less inconsequent. The object of the present observations is rather to ascertain what light may be thrown by psychological considerations on the purely logical processes, and to call attention to the fact, that the distinction between material and formal thinking may and ought to be consistently carried out in reference to all the operations of the understanding.

Judgment is distinguished from Conception by the difference of its data. In Conception, attributes are given, to be united by thought in a possible object of intuition; in Judgment, concepts are given, to be united by thought in a common object. Like Conception, also, Judgment may be considered either as pure, or as combined with a present intuition. Pure judgments are those in which the given concepts are of such a character that their mutual relation

[1] Cf. Krug, *Logik*, § 35, Anm. 1.

of agreement or difference can be determined by an act of thought alone, without any appeal to experience. This is the case when the attributes comprehended in the one concept form either the whole or a part of those comprehended in the other; or where some attribute comprehended in the one is contradictory of one of those comprehended in the other. In the former case we are enabled at once, by the law of Identity, to unite the two concepts in an affirmative judgment, and in the latter, by the law of Contradiction, to separate them by a negative judgment. But this class of judgments (being those commonly known as analytical or explicative) may, with more propriety, be included under the head of Conception. The affirmative analytical judgment is in fact nothing more than the Definition, complete or partial, of the subject-notion; while the negative judgment expresses only the necessary condition of all conception, which, by discerning any notion as being that which it is, necessarily excludes it from all that it is not.

In synthetical or ampliative judgments, the act of thought is not sufficient to determine the relation of the concepts to each other, without the accompaniment of an intuition, pure or empirical. For example: in order to form the judgment, "Two straight lines cannot inclose a space," I must not only be able to conceive separately the two notions of a straight line and of an inclosing of space, but I must also, by the aid of imagination, construct a representation in my mind of two actual straight lines and their actual positions in space. I must perceive that these two straight lines are incapable of inclosing a space, before I pronounce the universal judgment concerning all pairs of straight lines. Here the relation between the two concepts is presented in a *pure* or *à priori intuition*, *i. e.*, in an intuition containing no adventitious element external to the mind itself. Again, in order to form the judgment, "Gold is heavy," supposing that my conception of gold does not in itself include the attribute of weight, I cannot, by merely thinking of gold as a hard, yellow, shining body, determine what effect it will produce when laid on the hand. I must actually place an individual piece of gold on my hand, and ascertain by experience the fact of its pressure. Here the relation between the two concepts is presented in a *mixed* or *empirical intuition*, *i. e.*, in an intuition caused by the presence of a body external to the mind itself.

Yet in this class of judgments, as well as in the former, when the necessary intuition has once been given, the act of thought itself is governed by the same laws of Identity and Contradiction. In pronouncing that two distinct notions are united in one and the same object, that it is *the gold* which is heavy, I unite the concepts "gold" and "heavy" in a complex notion comprehending both, and denoting the union of both in a common object. That which was before conceived as "gold," is now conceived as "heavy gold" (whether the new attribute becomes part of the meaning of the term gold or not is of no consequence), and this complex notion is now exhibited in the act of judgment, as analyzed into its constituent parts, and identified with them.[1] Synthetical judgments may thus, as far as the mere act of thought is concerned, be brought under the same law as analytical ones, namely, the Principle of Identity when the judgment is affirmative, and that of Contradiction when it is negative.

Another law of thought is sometimes given as the foundation of Judgment, under the name of the Logical Principle of Sufficient Reason. This law, which must be

[1] See Drobisch, *Neue Darstellung der Logik*, § 36.

carefully distinguished from the Metaphysical Principle of Causality, is enunciated, "Every judgment must have a sufficient ground for its assertion."[1] But, in truth, the relation of this principle to the act of judgment is merely negative: it forbids us in certain cases to judge at all, and it does no more. If the judgment is analytical, the law of Identity or of Contradiction is the sufficient reason for making it. If the judgment is synthetical, we have, previously to the given intuition, no reason at all; and, accordingly, we suspend our thought till we have referred the decision to the tribunal of experience. The only logical reason for a thought of any kind is its relation to some other thought; and this relation will in each case be determined by its own proper law. The Principle of Sufficient Reason is therefore no law of thought, but only the statement that every act of thought must be governed by some law or other.[2]

[1] See Kant, *Logik*, Einleitung vii.; Fries, *Syst. der Logik*, § 41; Krug, *Logik*, § 20; Thomson, *Laws of Thought*, p. 296.

[2] In excluding the Principle of Sufficient Reason from the laws of thought I am happy to find myself supported by the authority of Sir William Hamilton in the philosophical Appendix to his *Discussions*, published subsequently to the first edition of the present work. "The Principle of *Sufficient Reason*," he says, "should be excluded from Logic. For, inasmuch as this principle is not material (material = non-formal) it is only a derivation of the three formal laws; and inasmuch as it is material, it coincides with the principle of Causality, and is extralogical." Kant (*Logik*, Einleitung vii.) takes a different view. He regards the Principle of Contradiction as the criterion of the logical possibility of a judgment, that of Sufficient Reason as the criterion of its logical reality. But of judgments, as distinguished from the conclusions of syllogisms, the only logical reality is possibility. Directly I have ascertained two notions not to be contradictory to each other, I have made an actual judgment of the logical possibility of their coëxistence; and to take any step beyond this, experience is required, and not logic. The difference between problematical and assertorial judgments is extralogical, and depends on the

Hypothetical and Disjunctive Judgments must be reserved for a separate examination. At present, we must proceed to investigate the laws of Reasoning. This process differs from Judgment, as Judgment differs from Conception, in the nature of its preliminary data. In Judgment, concepts are given, thought being required to determine their possible coëxistence in an object. In Reasoning, one or more judgments are given, thought being required to determine what further judgments may be elicited from them. Under this head will thus be included not merely the ordinary Syllogism, but likewise (so far as they contain processes of thought at all) the immediate inferences of Opposition and Conversion. In all these, the material given prior to the act of thought is a judgment; and the process of judging from concepts is thus not included, but presupposed; the conclusion being always a different judgment, either in *form*, as regards Quantity, Quality, or Relation, which is the case in immediate consequences; or partially in *matter*, which is the case in mediate reasoning by syllogism.[1] The common arrangement, therefore, which places immediate inference in the second part of Logic, is objectionable.[2]

question whether a logical judgment is or is not determined by experience to be materially true.

[1] See Kant, *Logik*, § 44. His theory of contraposition affecting the *modality* of the judgment is untenable, and seems to result merely from that excessive love of system which must bring in *four forms* somehow. The supposed demonstrative character of the conclusion in contraposition is merely a necessity of consequence from the position of the premise; a character which is found in all logical reasoning whatever.

[2] This order, however, has by no means been uniformly adopted by Logicians. Aristotle treats of Opposition in the *De Interpretatione*, and of Conversion in the *Prior Analytics*. Wolf separates Opposition and Conversion, considered as relations between two given propositions, from the processes of inference derivable from each. The former is treated in con-

Opposition may be treated in two points of view. Firstly, as a relation between two *given* propositions; secondly, as a process of inference, in which, one proposition being given, another may be determined. In the former character, it is merely an explanation of the meaning of certain logical terms; in the latter, it is a process of reasoning, a deduction of one proposition as conclusion from another as premise, and governed, as we shall see, by the same laws as the mediate inference.[1] The primary processes, on which the rest may be made to depend, are those of Subaltern and Contradictory Opposition; the former being grounded on the Principle of Identity, and the latter on those of Contradiction and Excluded Middle. Thus in the proposition, "All A is some B," an identity is stated between the whole of the objects thought under the concept A, and a portion of those thought under B.[2]

nection with Judgment; the latter, under the name of Immediate Consequence, in connection with reasoning. Kant and his followers treat immediate consequences as reasonings, under the name of *Syllogisms of the Understanding;* an arrangement which is logically correct, whatever may be the psychological objections to the nomenclature.

[1] On account of this identity of law, various attempts have been made by ingenious writers to reduce immediate consequence to the mediate form. Thus Wolf exhibits subaltern opposition as a syllogism with the minor premise, "Some A is A;" thus perversely representing the law of thought, which governs the reasoning process in general, as a part of the special matter given preliminary to a particular act. Still more absurd is the elaborate system which Krug, after a hint from Wolf, has constructed, in which all immediate inferences appear as hypothetical syllogisms; a major premise being supplied in the form, "If all A is B, some A is B." The author appears to have forgotten that either this premise is an additional empirical truth, in which case the immediate reasoning is not a logical process at all, or it is a formal inference, presupposing the very reasoning to which it is prefixed, and thus begging the whole question.

[2] Throughout the following pages, in order to exhibit the law of thought more clearly in each case, I have, in conformity with the views of

The conclusion, "Therefore some A is some B," proceeds on the principle that every part of A must be identical with a part of that which has been given as identical with all A. This process resembles the inference in an affirmative syllogism, except that in the latter there is given a double identity; firstly, of the middle term with a part of the major; and secondly, of the minor with a part of the middle. The inferences of Contradictory Opposition are based on the Principles of Contradiction and Excluded Middle. By the former, when one of two contradictory judgments is given as true, we infer that the other is false; and by the latter, when one is given as false, we infer that the other is true. The remaining inferences of Opposition may be reduced to combinations of the above.

The several processes of Conversion, if the predicate is quantified as well as the subject, may be reduced to Simple Conversion only; and even under the old system, Conversion *per accidens* may be regarded as a combination of Simple Conversion with one of the inferences of Opposition.[1] Simple Conversion is thus the only one which it is necessary to examine. This cannot properly be regarded

Sir William Hamilton, stated the quantity of the predicate as well as of the subject in each proposition. Of the value of this addition to the ordinary logical forms, I have elsewhere expressed my opinion (*North British Review*, No. 29). I have not, therefore, thought it necessary to enter into an elaborate examination of it here; especially as it is sufficient for my purpose to bring forward only those forms of reasoning universally admitted by logicians. In quantifying the predicate in these instances, we only express what every treatise on Logic tells us to understand, viz., that the predicate of an affirmative proposition is not distributed; *i. e.*, is *thought as particular*.

[1] Thus Aldrich analyzes conversion *per accidens*. "Sit vera E: Ergo et ejus simpliciter conversa: Ergo et conversæ subalternata: quæ est expositæ conversa per accidens. Sit vera A: Ergo et ejus subalternata: Ergo et subalternatæ simpliciter conversa: quæ est expositæ per accidens."

as a process of judgment; for either the converted proposition is a new judgment distinct from the original one, or it is merely the same judgment expressed in different language. In the former case, it is an inference from a premise, and consequently a process of reasoning; in the latter, there is no process of thinking at all, but merely a change in the language by which a given thought is expressed. The former is the preferable view, so long as the subject and predicate of a proposition are viewed in the relation of whole and part, whether by the inclusion of the subject under the extension of the predicate, or of the predicate in the comprehension of the subject. For the inversion of the relations of whole and part is sufficient to constitute a new judgment. But in the system of Sir W. Hamilton, in which every proposition is reduced to an *equation*, or rather to an *identification* of object between the two terms, the latter view seems more accurate; it being manifestly the same thing to identify the object thought under A with that of B, and that thought under B with that of A.

To opposition and conversion must be added a third process, that of the immediate consequence of one equipollent proposition from another.[1] The equipollence in some cases can only be determined materially; and the consequence is then extralogical; as in the instance cited by Wolf, *Titius est pater Caii, ergo Caius est filius Titii;* but there are other instances in which the consequence is formal, and determined solely by the laws of thought. Thus, by the principle of contradiction, from the premise,

[1] See Wolf, *Philosophia Rationalis*, § 445; Fries, *System der Logik*, § 47. The former has not accurately distinguished the material from the formal cases of this consequence; and it was, probably, this confusion that led Kant to reject the inference altogether.

All A is B, follows the immediate inference, No A is not-B, in which is produced a change of quality from affirmative to negative. In this way, when one predicate is affirmed of a subject, its contradictory may always be denied. The process commonly called Conversion by Contraposition, is properly the simple conversion of this equipollent proposition.[1]

The whole of the preceding observations clearly point out the view in which Logic and Psychology must coincide concerning the nature and principles of the Syllogism. The former, as the science of the laws of pure thinking, has nothing to do with the inferences of more or less probability furnished by the analogies of this or that branch of physical science, nor even with the general constitution of the material world, so far as it is known to us only empirically as a fact. Its only province is with those inferences which are necessitated by the laws of thought; which, certain data being furnished, we cannot but draw as consequences. That the premises of a syllogism necessarily imply and contain the conclusion, is so far from being an imperfection in Logic, that it is a necessary consequence of the supposition that thought is governed by laws at all. And in accordance with this conclusion, Psychology teaches us that thought is representative and reflective, not presentative and intuitive; that, having no positive operation beyond the field of possible experience, its laws can only be analytical, and its processes must lead not to the acquisition of new knowledge, but to the modification of the old. It only remains to exemplify this result by applying it to the ordinary forms of the logical syllogism.

[1] This has been remarked by Fries (§ 49, c.), and recently by Mr. Karslake (*Aids to the Study of Logic*, p. 65).

Fig. 1.		Fig. 2.
All M is some P.	No M is any P.	No P is any M.
All S is some M.	All S is some M.	All S is some M.
∴ All S is some P.	∴ No S is any P.	∴ No S is any P.

Fig. 3.	
All M is some P.	No M is any P.
All M is some S.	All M is some S.
∴ Some S is some P.	∴ Some S is not any P.

The above examples will suffice as specimens of the different forms of affirmative and negative reasoning admitted by the three Aristotelian figures. The fourth figure might be easily subjected to the same treatment; but it is preferable to regard its moods as inverted forms of the first. On inspection of these specimens, it appears, that the Principle of Identity is immediately applicable to affirmative moods in any figure, and the Principle of Contradiction to negatives. In Barbara, for example, the minor term all S is identical with a part of M, and consequently with a part of that which is given as identical with all M, namely, some P. In Darapti, the minor term some S is identical with all M, and consequently with some P. The principle immediately applicable to both is the axiom, that what is given as identical with the whole or a part of any concept, must be identical with the whole or a part of that which is identical with the same concept. This may be briefly expressed by the Principle of Identity, Every A is A. In Celarent, Cesare, and Felapton, some or all S, being given as identical with all or some M, is distinct from every part of that which is distinct from all M.[1]

[1] Under the system of a quantified predicate, the second figure admits of affirmative syllogisms, which, like the rest, may be referred to the principle of Identity.

This is briefly expressed by the Principle of Contradiction, No A is not-A.

These two laws govern all the moods of Categorical Syllogism, including under them, as subordinate rules, the *dictum de omni et nullo*, or the nearly equivalent axiom, *nota notæ est nota rei ipsius;* as well as the distinct axioms which have been framed by different logicians as rules of the second and third figures.[1] The process of Reduction, which is properly and necessarily adopted by those logicians who, with Aristotle and Kant, acknowledge the principle of the first figure only, now becomes unnecessary and inconsistent; inasmuch as all the syllogistic figures are exhibited as equally direct exemplifications of the same general law. For the same reason, the distinction adopted by Kant between Syllogisms of the Understanding and Syllogisms of the Reason, in addition to the psychological impropriety of distinguishing two faculties of thought,[2] is now shown to be logically untenable also; the processes of immediate and mediate reasoning being exhibited as cognate acts of thought, governed by the same general laws, and differing only in their material data.

By bearing in mind what has been above said of the nature of thought and its laws, we shall also be enabled to take a juster view of a process more or less misrepresented in the majority of logical treatises, Induction. Scarcely any logician has accurately distinguished between *Formal Induction*, in which the given premises necessitate the

[1] As by Lambert, *Neues Organon*, part i. § 232; Kant, *Logik*, § 71; Sir W. Hamilton in Mr. Thomson's *Laws of Thought*, p. 248, where they are given correctly as special applications of a more general principle.

[2] On this question, see Sir W. Hamilton, *Discussions*, p. 17; Cousin, *Leçons sur la Philosophie de Kant*, p. 168; Krug, *Logik*, § 74.

conclusion in conformity with the laws of thought, and *Material Induction*, in which the conclusion may be inferred with more or less probability from additional data not furnished by the premises; between what we *must* know as thinkers, and what we *may* know as investigators of nature. By some logicians, Induction is treated as a Syllogism in Barbara, with the major or minor premise suppressed; the advocates of this view overlooking the fact, that the suppression of either premise leaves a deficiency to be supplied independently of the act of thought, and thus reduces the whole process from formal to material; to say nothing of the inversion of the reasoning as actually performed, and the destruction of all foundation for the syllogistic process from universals to particulars, by making every universal premise itself a deduction from a higher one. By others, Induction is represented, according to the Baconian view, as an *interrogation of nature*, by the selection, in any physical investigation, of such phenomena as may indicate the existence of a general law. Here it is forgotten that the fact that nature proceeds by uniform laws at all is a truth altogether distinct from the laws of thought, and, if not of wholly empirical origin, at least one which cannot be ascertained *à priori* by the pure understanding. Others again, struck by the physical difficulty of an exhaustive enumeration of individual cases, endeavor to effect a compromise between material probability and formal necessity, by describing the instances cited as *representatives* or *samples* of their class; as if the nature of samples and representatives could be made known by an innate principle of the mind, independently of experience. Even the wonderful acuteness of Kant in all questions between matter and form appears to have deserted him here; and by describing Induction as a *Syl-*

logism of the judgment, furnishing a *logical presumption* of a general conclusion, he not only encumbers the science with an extralogical process, but neglects altogether the really formal reasoning which it is the duty of the logician to take into account.[1]

The truth is that there are two totally distinct processes confounded under the general name of Induction. The Baconian or Material Induction proceeds on the assumption of general laws in the relations of physical phenomena, and endeavors, by select observations and experiments, to detect the law in any particular case. This, whatever be its value as a general method of physical investigation, has no place in Formal Logic. The Aristotelian or Formal Induction proceeds on the assumption of general laws of thought, and inquires into the instances in which, by such laws, we are necessitated to reason from an accumulation of particular instances to a general or partial rule. The process in this case may be affirmative or negative; and it is governed, like other formal reasonings, by the general laws of Identity and Contradiction. Specimens of its several forms may be exhibited as follows:

Affirmative Induction.

X, Y, Z, are some B.	X, Y, Z, are some B.
X, Y, Z, are all A.	X, Y, Z, are some A.
∴ All A is some B.	∴ Some A is some B.

Negative Induction.

X, Y, Z, are not any B.	X, Y, Z, are not any B.
X, Y, Z, are all A.	X, Y, Z, are some A.
∴ No A is any B.	∴ Some A is not any B.

Other moods may be added to these, by varying the quantity of the predicate in the major premise. By assign-

[1] Two distinguished exceptions to this general error must however be noticed. Aristotle's account of Induction, in *Anal. Pr.* ii. 23, incomplete as

ing, in conformity with the system of Sir W. Hamilton, a definite quantity to the predicate in all affirmative propositions, we are enabled to avoid that ambiguity of the copula which has hitherto been the main defect in the logical analysis of inductive reasoning.[1] The relation of whole and part between the terms of the proposition being thus dispensed with, the subject is no longer represented as at one time *contained under*, at another *constituting* its predicate; but each term, in every case, is *equated*, or *identified as to its object*, with the whole or a part of the other.

Under this system it is no longer necessary to distinguish Induction from the third figure of Syllogism, as this figure, with a definite predicate, will admit of universal as well as particular conclusions. Indeed, every Syllogism in this figure, in which the minor premise is collective, may be regarded as a logical Induction. In this point of view it is manifestly governed by the same laws as the syllogism, the affirmative moods by the Principle of Identity, and the negative by the Principle of Contradiction. The so-called *imperfect* Induction is altogether extralogical. The constituted whole can in thought be *identified* only with the sum total of its parts, not with a few representatives; and without such identification no inference can be necessitated by the laws of thought. The physical difficulty of adducing all the members of a given class is a purely material consideration, like that of the truth of the premises in a syllogism, and is assumed, not investigated, by the logician. But without such a preliminary datum, we have no

it is in many respects, has the merit of adhering accurately to the formal view of the process. And the admirable Article on Logic by Sir W. Hamilton, in No. 115 of the Edinburgh Review (reprinted in his *Discussions*), exhibits for the first time the logical character of Induction, divested of its material incumbrances and formal perversions.

[1] See Sir W. Hamilton, *Discussions*, p. 163.

materials for drawing a universal conclusion by logical Induction.

Thus far we have shown the several forms of mediate categorical reasoning to depend on two necessary laws of thought, the Principles of Identity and Contradiction. A separate examination is needed to ascertain the character of the Hypothetical Propositions and Syllogisms, which, as I am inclined to think, has not hitherto been accurately exhibited, even by the best logicians of the formal school.

By Kant and his followers, the Hypothetical Proposition is described as representing a form of judgment essentially distinct from the Categorical; the latter being thoroughly assertorial, the former problematical in its constituent parts, assertorial only as regards the relation between them. Two judgments, each in itself false, may thus be hypothetically combined into a single truth; and this combination cannot be reduced into categorical form.[1] The Hypothetical Syllogism, in like manner, is a form of reasoning distinct from the Categorical, and not reducible to it, being based on a different law of thought, namely, the logical Principle of Sufficient Reason, *a ratione ad rationatum, a negatione rationati ad negationem rationis valet consequentia.*[2]

Of this principle, as applied to judgments, I have before remarked, that it is not a law of thought, but only a statement of the necessity of some law or other. As applied to syllogisms, it has the same character. It states the fact, that whenever a condition, whether material cause of a fact or formal reason of a conclusion, exists, the conditioned fact or conclusion exists also. Thus viewed, it

[1] See Kant, *Logik*, § 25; Krug, *Logik*, § 57; Fries, *System der Logik*, § 32.
[2] Kant, § 76; Krug, § 82; Fries, § 58.

is not the law of any distinct reasoning process, but a statement of the conditions in which laws of nature or of thought are operative. When a material cause exists, its material effect follows, and the phenomenon indicates a law of nature; when a logical premise is given, its logical conclusion follows, and the result indicates a law of thought. *What law*, must in each case be determined by the particular features of the phenomenon or reasoning in question; but a statement of this kind is distinguished from laws of thought, properly so called, by the fact, that it cannot be expressed in a symbolical form: we require the introduction of a definite notion, *Cause*, *Reason*, *Condition*, or something of the kind, which is a special object of thought, not the general representative of all objects whatever. The principle in question is thus only a statement of the peculiar character of certain matters about which we may think, and not a law of the form of thought in general.

It is obvious that the relation of premises and conclusion in a syllogism may, like any other relation of condition and conditioned, be expressed in the form of a hypothetical proposition: "If all A is B, and all C is A, then all C is B;" and the actual assertion of the truth of these premises will furnish at once a so-called hypothetical syllogism: "But all A is B, and all C is A, therefore all C is B." This was observed by Fries, who hence rightly maintains that analytical hypothetical judgments are formal syllogisms.[1] It is strange that, after this, he should not have gone a step further, and discovered that synthetical hypothetical judgments are assertions of material consequences. The judgment, "If A is B, C is D," asserts the existence of a consequence necessitated by laws other

[1] *System der Logik*, § 44.

than those of thought, and consequently out of the province of Logic. The addition of a minor premise and conclusion in the so-called hypothetical syllogism, is merely the assertion that this general material consequence is verified in a particular case.

The distinction so much insisted on by the Kantians, of the *problematical* character of the two members of a hypothetical judgment, is, like the whole Kantian doctrine of modality, of no consequence in formal Logic. All formal thinking is, as regards the material character of its objects, problematical only. Formal Conception pronounces that certain objects of thought may possibly exist, leaving their actual existence to be determined by experience. Formal Judgment decides on the possible coëxistence of certain concepts; and Formal Reasoning, on the truth of a conclusion, subject to the hypothesis of the truth of its premises.

To state that this hypothesis is in a certain instance true, adds nothing to the *logical* part of the reasoning, but only verifies the empirical preliminaries which the logician in every case assumes as given. To exhibit a formal consequence hypothetically, is only a needless reässertion of the existence of data which the act of thought presupposes. To exhibit a material consequence hypothetically, is not to make it formal, but only to assert that, in a certain given instance, a consequence not cognizable by Logic takes place. The sequence of "C is D," from "A is B," is not one whit more logical than it was before; it is only stated to take place materially in the present case.

The omission of hypothetical syllogisms has frequently been deemed a defect in Aristotle's Organon; and his French translator takes some fruitless pains to strain his text, in order to make out that he does in fact treat of them.[1] If there is any truth in the preceding observations, it will follow, that Aristotle understood the limits of Logic better than his critics; and that his translator had better have allowed the omission as a merit than have attempted to deny it as a fault. When the hypothetical proposition states a formal consequence, the reasoning grounded upon it may always be reduced to categorical. When it states a material consequence, it states what the logician, as such, cannot take into account. Aristotle is therefore quite right in saying, that in this case the conclusion is not *proved*, but *conceded*.[2] Syllogism may be employed as a logical proof of the antecedent: the consequent is admitted to follow on grounds which the logician, as such, does not investigate, but which may be warranted by the principles of this or that material science.

The true character of hypothetical reasoning is lost sight of in the examples commonly selected by logicians, which have for their subject a *proper name*, and indicate, not a general relation of reason and consequent between two notions, but certain accidental circumstances in the history of an individual. The adoption of this type has led to the logical anomaly, that the propositions of a hypothetical syllogism are generally stated without any designate quantity; whereas it is obvious that, wherever *concepts* are compared together in any form of reasoning, two distinct conclusions may follow, according to the quantity assigned. For example, to the premise, "If men are wise, they will consult their permanent interests," we may supply two minors and conclusions, in the constructive form, according as we affirm the antecedent of *all* men or of *some*. It thus becomes necessary to distinguish

[1] St. Hilaire, *Logique d'Aristote Traduite en Français*, Preface, p. lx.
[2] *Anal. Prior.* i. 23, 11.

between two different kinds of apparently hypothetical syllogisms, — those in which the inference is from a general hypothesis to all or some of its special instances, and those in which a relation between two individual facts is assumed as a hypothesis leading to a singular conclusion. The former contain a general relation of determining and determined notion, which may always be expressed in three terms; the occasional employment of four being only an accidental variety of language. Thus the general assertion, "If any country is justly governed, the people are happy," is equivalent to, "If any country is justly governed, it has happy people." This we may apply to special instances; *all countries*, *some countries*, or *this country*, being asserted to be justly governed: and this is properly *hypothetical reasoning*. The latter denote only a material connection between two single facts, either of which may, to certain minds possessed of certain additional knowledge, be an indication of the other; but the true ground of the inference is contained in this additional knowledge, and not in the mere hypothetical coupling of the facts by a conjunction. This is not hypothetical reasoning; *i. e.*, it is not reasoning *from the hypothesis*, but from other circumstances not mentioned in the hypothesis at all.[1]

[1] This may be made clearer by an example. The following is cited by Fries as an instance of a hypothetical proposition not reducible to categorical form: "If Caius is free from business, he is writing poetry." This may be interpreted to mean either, generally, "Whenever Caius is disengaged, he writes poetry;" or, specially, "If he is now disengaged, he is now writing poetry." Under the former interpretation, it is a general hypothesis, which may be applied as a major premise to particular instances; but in this case the true form of the reasoning is, "All times when Caius is disengaged are times when he writes poetry; and the present is such a time." Under the latter interpretation, it is one of the cases

It thus appears that the only hypothetical judgment which can be employed as the real major premise of a syllogism may be expressed in the form, "If A is B, it is C," where A, B, and C, represent concepts, or general notions. The complete categorical equivalent to this is, "Every A which is B is C, because it is B," which admits of two interpretations, according as B stands for the physical cause of the fact, or for the logical reason of our knowing it. In the latter case, the judgment is analytical, and represents a disguised formal consequence, with B as a middle term; *e. g.*, "Every man who is learned has studied, because he is learned." Here the notion of study is implied in that of learning, and the major premise is, "All learned beings have studied." The hypothetical proposition thus becomes a complete syllogism, to which the subsequent consequence is related as an episyllogism.[1] In the former case, where B stands for a physical cause, the judgment is synthetical, and indicates a material consequence, which it requires some additional knowledge of facts to

of a material connection of two facts mentioned in the text. Now, in this last case, it is obvious that the inference is really made, not from the hypothesis, but from some circumstance known to the reasoner, but not appearing in the proposition. Any man being asked, "Why do you infer that Caius, being now disengaged, is writing poetry?" would reply, "Because he told me he should do so;" or something of the kind. Assuredly he would never dream of replying, "Because *if* he is now disengaged he is writing." In this case, then, he does not reason *from the hypothesis*, and the expressed propositions do not compose a syllogism.

[1] Thus:

Hypothetical Syllogism.	*Categorical Analysis.*
If any man is learned, he has studied:	All learned beings have studied:
Some men are learned;	All learned men are learned beings;
∴ Some men have studied.	∴ All learned men have studied:
	Some men are learned men;
	∴ Some men have studied.

reduce to formal; *e. g.*, "All wax exposed to the fire melts, because it is exposed." Here, on material grounds, we know that we cannot supply the premise, "All bodies exposed to the fire melt;" but only, "All bodies soluble by heat and exposed to the fire melt." In this case the consequence is extralogical, and requires additional data not given in the thought. But here, also, when the judgment in question is employed as the premise of a reasoning, the conclusion follows categorically; though the premise itself cannot, as it stands, be moved by a prosyllogism.[1]

The Disjunctive Judgment is usually described as representing a whole divided into two or more parts mutually exclusive of each other; and the Disjunctive Syllogism is supposed to proceed either from the affirmation of one member to the denial of the rest, or from the denial of all but one to the affirmation of that one, by the Principle of Excluded Middle.[2]

This can scarcely be regarded as a correct analysis of the process, unless the two members are *formally stated* as contradictory. The Principle of Excluded Middle asserts that everything is either A or not A; that of two contradictories, one must exist in every object; as the Principle of Contradiction asserts that they cannot both exist. But if the two members are not stated as contradictories, if my disjunctive premise is, "All C is either A

[1] The analysis in this case may be exhibited thus:

Hypothetical Syllogism.	*Categorical Equivalent.*
If any wax is exposed to the fire, it melts:	All wax exposed to the fire melts (because exposed):
This wax is exposed to the fire;	This wax is exposed to the fire;
∴ This wax melts.	∴ This wax melts.

The parenthesis indicates the material ground of the major premise.

[2] Kant, §§ 27-sqq., 77, 78; Krug, §§ 57, 84, 85; Fries, §§ 33, 59.

or B," I make the material assertion that All C which is not A is B. If then I reason, "This C is not A,[1] therefore it is B," I employ the Principle of Identity in addition to that of Excluded Middle. Again, if I maintain that No C can be both A and B, I make the material assertion that No C which is A is B; and from hence to reason, "This C is A, therefore it is not B," requires not the Principle of Excluded Middle, but that of Contradiction. In the first case, the Excluded Middle does not lead directly to the conclusion, but only to the contraposition of the minor premise. When we deny this C to be A, this principle enables us to assert that it is not-A, and hence to bring the reasoning under the Principle of Identity. But in the second case, in which one of the opposed members is *affirmed*, the ground on which we deny the other is not because both cannot be false, but because both cannot be true.

It may be questioned whether this second inference is warranted by the *form* of the disjunctive premise. Boethius calls it a *material consequence;*[2] and, in spite of the many eminent authorities on the other side, I am still disposed to think he is right. But let us grant for a moment the opposite view, and allow that the proposition, "All C is either A or B," implies, as a condition of its truth, "No C can be both."[3] Thus viewed, it is in reality a complex proposition, containing two distinct assertions, each of which may be the ground of two distinct processes of reasoning, governed by two opposite laws. Surely it is essential to all clear thinking that the two should be separated from each other, and not confounded under one form

[1] The indefinite minor, "But *it* is not A," is as objectionable in this syllogism as in the conditional.

[2] *De Syll. Hyp.* lib. i.; *Opera*, p. 616; Cf. Galen; *Isagoge Dial.* p. 11.

[3] Aquinas, Opusc. xlviii.; *De Enunciatione*, c. xiv.; Krug, *Logik*, § 86.

by assuming the Law of Excluded Middle to be, what it is not, a complex of those of Identity and Contradiction. Thus distinguished, the moods of the disjunctive syllogism are mere verbal variations from the categorical form, and may easily be brought under its laws.[1]

The preceding discussion may appear to some readers of trifling importance; and some apology for its length may be thought necessary. I believe nothing to be unimportant, in a logical work, which tends to mark out more accurately the nature of thought and its laws, to exhibit more precisely the formal character of logical processes, and to clear the subject from the remaining excrescences and inconsistencies with which, even in the writings of the best modern Logicians, it is still occasionally encumbered.[2] Either Logic is not worth studying at all, or it is worth studying in the utmost completeness and exactitude

1 Thus:

Modus tollendo ponens.	*Modus ponendo tollens.*
Every C which is not A is B.	No C which is A is B.
Every / Some / This } C is a C which is not A.	Every / Some / This } C is a C which is A.
∴ It is B.	∴ It is not B.

The first is governed by the Principle of Identity, and the second by the Principle of Contradiction.

2 For example: Fries, after expressly distinguishing the Principle of Sufficient Reason from the other Formulæ of Thought, as not being a principle of philosophical or formal Logic, places it in his next chapter in a coördinate position with them, as the distinctive law of hypothetical syllogisms. Krug describes it in one place as the highest principle of syllogism in general, and in another as the special principle of a single class of reasonings. It is proper to speak with respect even of the errors of the great philosopher of Königsburg; but perhaps even Kant was in some degree biassed, in his examination of logical processes, by an almost pedantic love of reproducing in every relation his four Functions of Judgment, and by the strange metaphysical theory which deduced the three Ideas of Pure Reason from the three kinds of dialectical syllogism.

of which it is susceptible. The length to which these remarks have run is justified, indeed demanded, by the eminence of the authors from whom the writer has ventured to dissent, — authors whose mere assertions in matters of logical science are not to be lightly regarded nor hastily departed from. Even if the views here advanced should be found, on examination, to be less tenable than the author believes them to be, they will not have been without their use, if, by calling the attention of others to one or two of the weaker defences of the received doctrines of Formal Logic, they should indirectly lead to a more satisfactory vindication of the positions assailed.

It only remains to sum up as briefly as possible the results of the present chapter. Formal or Logical Necessity is dependent on one negative condition, and on three positive laws. The negative condition, or *sine qua non* of thought in general, is contained in the Principle of Sufficient Reason, which, however, in this relation, belongs to Psychology, and not to Logic; being only a general statement of the conditions under which, in the existing constitution of man's mind, thought is possible; — its dependence, that is to say, on a higher thought, or on a fact of intuition. The three positive laws, or fundamental principles, assumed by Logic, as regulating all its actual processes, are those of Identity, of Contradiction, and of Excluded Middle; the last, however, operating in most cases in subordination to the other two. These three are the highest and simplest forms of identical judgments, to one of which all analytical thinking may ultimately be referred: and all pure thinking may be shown, on psychological grounds, to be of a strictly analytical character. The necessity arising from these laws is that of the harmony of thought with itself, — of its conformity to its own ruling principles; as the forms of necessity noticed in the previous chapters were those arising from the relation of thought to the laws and condition of intuition, — the requisite harmony of the several mental faculties one with another. These two harmonies constitute respectively Formal and Material Truth. Truth, relatively to man, cannot be defined as consisting in the conformity of knowledge with its object; for to man the object itself exists only as it is known by one faculty or another. Material Truth consists rather in the conformity of the object as represented in thought with the object as presented in intuition; and of this no general law or criterion can be given; its essence consisting in its adapting itself in every case to the diversities of this or that special presentation. But Logical Truth, which consists in the conformity of thought to its own laws, can be submitted to those laws as general and sufficient criteria; criteria, however, not of the real and existent, but of the thinkable and possible. Of actual truth it furnishes one element only, which becomes truth or not in combination, according as, upon further examination, it is found to be in conformity or at variance with the coördinate decisions of experience. By the same criteria we shall also be able to determine the logical or extralogical character of any portion of the contents of existing treatises on the science; according as it is a deduction of pure thinking from given materials, or a mixed process, combining the act of thought with the acquisition of further empirical data. On the distinction established between material and formal thinking, some further observations will be made in the next chapter.

CHAPTER VII.

ON THE MATTER AND FORM OF THOUGHT.

THE distinction adopted between Matter and Form in common language, relatively to works of Art, will serve to illustrate the character of the corresponding distinction in Thought. The term *Matter* is usually applied to whatever is given to the artist, and consequently, as given, does not come within the province of the art itself to supply. The *Form* is that which is given in and through the proper operation of the art. In Sculpture, for example, the Matter is the marble in its rough state as given to the sculptor; the Form is that which the sculptor, in the exercise of his art, communicates to it.[1] The distinction between Matter and Form in any mental operation is analogous to this. The former includes all that is given *to*, the latter all that is given *by*, the operation. In the division of notions, for example, whether performed by an act of pure thinking or not, the generic notion is that given to be divided; the addition of the difference in the act of division constitutes the species. And, accordingly, Genus is frequently designated by logicians the *material*, Difference, the *formal* part, or the Species. So, likewise, in any operation of pure thinking, the Matter will include all that is given to and out of the thought; the Form is what is conveyed in and by the thinking act itself.

[1] See Fries, *System der Logik*, § 19. His division corresponds to the above, though based on a somewhat different principle.

The same analogy may be carried on in relation to what are called *material* and *formal* processes of thinking. It may happen on certain occasions that the marble given to the sculptor is insufficient for the completion of the statue. It becomes necessary, therefore, to suspend the artistic process itself, in order to obtain additional material; and this provision of new material the artist does not undertake purely as a sculptor. So in relation to any process of thinking. The empirical data requisite for an act of conception, judgment, or reasoning, may be insufficient, and require the addition of fresh material not furnished by the mere act of thinking. The operation in this case is one of *mixed* or *material* thinking; *i.e.*, of thinking preceded by an appeal to experience for the provision of further data; and this appeal is no part of the duty of the logician, as such. Whereas, if the materials originally given are alone sufficient to necessitate, in obedience to the laws of thought, an act of conception, judgment, or reasoning, the process is properly distinguished as one of *pure* or *formal* thinking.

Notwithstanding this analogy, it is in many respects important that the matter and form of a thought should not be confounded with material and formal thinking respectively. Thinking is not always formal because its product has form, nor does the presence of a form in the antecedent of thought always necessitate a formal process in consequence. The sculptor, to continue our image, may ultimately complete his work with all the form and finish of art: it does not therefore follow that all his material must have been given to him at once in the first instance. Or he may have carved with exactness one subordinate figure of a group: it does not therefore follow that his material is sufficient to enable him to complete the whole.

The present chapter is intended to point out more clearly the distinction and relation between the form of thought and formal thinking.

The antithesis of matter and form, — the objective and the subjective, — the variable and the permanent, — the contingent and the necessary, runs through all the phenomena of consciousness. The manifold elements presented by any object of consciousness constitute the matter; the relations which the mind, acting by its own laws, institutes between the several elements as it combines them into an object, constitute the form.[1] In this point of view, Space and Time are called by Kant the Forms of the Sensibility in general, external or internal; the objects of the former being necessarily regarded by the mind as lying out of ourselves in Space, the objects of the latter, as succeeding one another in Time. These may thus be regarded as the subjective conditions under which sensibility in general is possible. The same antithesis may be carried through those special acts of consciousness, in which the understanding operates, whether in conjunction with the presentative faculties, as in an act of mixed thinking, or representatively, as in pure thinking. A savage, to adopt an illustration of Kant's,[2] sees a house in the distance, not knowing what it is. It is thus present to him only as an intuition in space. But the very same complex phenomenon is presented to a man who knows it to be a building designed for the habitation of men. To the same sensible data the understanding now adds its own contribution, by which the several presentations of sense are combined into one whole, under the general notion of

1 See Kant, *Kritik der r. V.* p. 32 (ed. Rosenkranz).

2 *Logik*, Einleitung v.

a house. The sensible attributes here constitute the matter; their union in a concept is the form.

In Thought, as in Intuition, there is thus a variable and a permanent, an objective and a subjective element, a matter given to the thinker, a form communicated by the thinking act. In respect to the matter, concepts differ one from another, as being composed of this or that variety of given attributes. In respect of the form, all agree, as being a collection of attributes constituting an object. The universal conditions under which attributes are conceived in this relation have been pointed out in the last chapter, as the Principles of Identity, Contradiction, and Excluded Middle. From these three laws we may deduce, with some amendment, the Forms which have been regarded by logical writers as distinctive of the Concept proper.[1] The concept is necessarily conceived as *one*, as *one out of many*, and *as constituting with the many a universe of all that is conceivable.* From the last of these three conditions it follows that the concept must possess a generic or universal feature, by which it is characterized as a concept in general, or a member of the conceivable universe. From the second it follows, that it must also possess a differential or peculiar feature, by which it is distinguished from all others. And from the first it follows, that these two features must be united in a single whole. Hence every concept, as such, must possess in some degree the attributes of *distinctness*, as having complex contents; of *clearness*, as being, by one portion of its contents, distinguishable from other notions; and of *relation to a possible object of intuition*, inasmuch as the unity of a complex

[1] See Kant, *Logik*, § 2; Fries, *System der Logik*, § 20. The former places the form of a concept in its universality; the latter adopts the same view, subdividing universality into extension and comprehension.

notion depends not on a mere juxtaposition of terms, but upon its being the representative of one object.[1] These three forms may be otherwise denominated (for the difference is merely verbal) *comprehension*, *limitation*, and *extension*. As having complex contents, every concept *comprehends* certain attributes; as distinguishable from others, it is *limited* by its specific difference; and, as representative of a class of possible objects, it has a certain field over which it is *extended*. The forms of the concept proper may thus be indifferently enumerated as Distinctness, Clearness, and Relation to an object; or as Comprehension, Limitation, and Extension.

The matter and form of Judgments may be distinguished in the same manner as those of Concepts. Omitting those judgments which involve merely the enumeration of the attributes comprehended in a concept (the *analytical* or *explicative* judgments of Kant), which may be more properly classed as acts of Conception; and confining ourselves to those in which the contents of the given concepts are distinct from each other (the *synthetical* or *ampliative* judgments of Kant), we may distinguish, as before, between the preëxisting materials, which must be given before the act of judging takes place, and the additions contributed by the act itself.

Thus, to take an example adduced in a former chapter: If I poise a piece of gold in my hand, in order to ascertain whether it is heavy, the presented phenomena belong to distinct acts of sensation. The evidence of sight attests

[1] Arist. *Metaph.* vi. 12. Ἐπὶ μὲν γὰρ τοῦ ἄνθρωπος καὶ λευκὸν πολλὰ μέν ἐστιν, ὅταν μὴ ὑπάρχῃ θατέρῳ θατέρον, ἓν δὲ, ὅταν ὑπάρχῃ καὶ πάθῃ τι τὸ ὑποκείμενον ὁ ἄνθρωπος· τότε γὰρ ἓν γίγνεται καὶ ἔστιν ὁ λευκὸς ἄνθρωπος. *Ibid.* vii. 6. Ὁ δ' ὁρισμὸς λόγος ἐστὶν εἷς οὐ συνδέσμῳ καθάπερ ἡ Ἰλιάς, ἀλλὰ τῷ ἑνὸς εἶναι.

the presence of a round, yellow, shining body; the evidence of touch, or rather of muscular pressure, attests its weight. To unite these attributes as belonging to one and the same thing, is an act, not of sensation, but of thought. The mere sensation, aided by the concepts, presents us with three things — the body which is seen, and a certain temporal and local juxtaposition of the two. To combine the present attributes as belonging to one thing — to pronounce that it is *the gold* which is heavy — is an act of thought constituting a judgment. Here, then, we have one form of the judgment expressed in the copula, "Gold *is* heavy:" this indicates the identification of the two concepts as related to a common object; an identification usually known as the *Quality* of the Judgment.

The same is the case with the *Quantity* of Judgments. I see a number of balls lying on a table, and pronounce at once that they are all white; I see another collection, and assert in like manner that some are white and some black. Here the senses, even when aided by the concepts in distinguishing the balls as such, yet present to us only individual objects. *This*, *this*, and *this*, are within their province; but they know nothing of *all* or *some*. It is by an act of thought that the several individuals are regarded as constituting a whole, and a judgment pronounced concerning that whole or a portion of it.

A third Form of the Judgment, as indeed of all thought, is *Limitation*. In predicating one notion of another, I at the same time necessarily exclude everything to which that predicate is opposed, and thereby limit the subject to one alone of those contradictory determinations which make up the universe of thought. In asserting, for example, that gold is heavy, I as much exclude it from the class of imponderables as I include it in that of bodies possessing weight. The canon that *predication is limitation* is now indeed generally admitted as an axiom in philosophy;[1] and the various metaphysical systems of modern Germany, since the days of Kant, may be briefly described as so many attempts to evade the consequences of this principle, by constructing a philosophy of the unlimited on a basis independent of logical predication.

The two forms of Quantity and Quality are generally recognized by logicians of the school of Kant. To these are added two others, *Relation* and *Modality*. The former of these includes the three subdivisions of Categorical, Hypothetical, and Disjunctive, and is necessarily included among the forms of thought by those who adopt Kant's theory of the nature of these three kinds of propositions. But the view which has been taken of these in the last chapter precludes the admission of Relation as a distinct form from Quantity and Quality. Disjunctive judgments have there been treated as reducible to Categorical forms; and Hypotheticals as containing, not a judgment, properly speaking, but a consequence, formal or material. In this case, the relation is not between the different parts of a single judgment, but between two judgments, one dependent on the other. The judgment proper being thus confined to the categorical form only, Relation becomes only a general expression for the connection of subject and predicate under certain conditions of quantity and quality, and thus is not a special form of judgment, but a term equivalent to Form in general.

[1] See for example, among others, Fichte, *Ueber den Grund unseres Glaubens an eine göttliche Weltregierung*, p. 16 (*Werke*, v. p. 187); *Gerichtliche Verantwortung*, p. 47 (*Werke*, v. p. 265); *Bestimmung des Menschen* (*Werke*, ii. p. 304); Hegel, *Logik*, P. i. b. ii. ch. 2, P. ii. ch. 2 (*Werke*, iv. p. 26, v. p. 70).

As regards Modality, judgments, according to Kant, are of three kinds: problematical, assertorial, and apodeictical. The first are accompanied by a consciousness of the bare possibility of the judgment; the second, by a consciousness of its reality; the third, by a consciousness of its necessity. Modality is thus dependent on the manner in which a certain relation between two concepts is maintained, and may vary according to the state of different minds; the given concepts, and consequently the matter of the judgment, remaining unaltered.[1] These grounds are fully sufficient to establish modality, in the extent to which it is acknowledged by Kant and by Aristotle,[2] as, in a psychological point of view, belonging to the *form*, not to the *matter*, of judgment. It is conveyed in the act of judging, not given in the preliminary materials, and affects the copula, not the predicate. But the forms cognizable by Psychology must not be confounded with the forms cognizable by Logic. The latter science is not concerned, as is sometimes maintained, with the Forms of Thought in general, but only with the Forms of Thought as related to pure or formal thinking. The meaning of this limitation will appear more clearly in the sequel. In this point of view, Modality stands on a very different footing from Quantity and Quality. In cases

[1] Kant, *Logik*, § 30.

[2] Aristotle, in the *De Interpretatione*, ch. 12, enumerates four modes of judgment: the necessary, the impossible, the contingent, and the possible. The addition of the true and the false is, I think, founded on a misinterpretation. These modes he reduces, *in the Prior Analytics*, i. 2, to the necessary and the contingent (τοῦ ἐξ ἀνάγκης ὑπάρχειν and τοῦ ἐνδέχεσθαι ὑπάρχειν). These, with the addition of the pure judgment (τοῦ ὑπάρχειν), correspond to the division of Kant. The spurious modes admitted in abundance by the scholastic logicians are not forms of the judgment, but modifications of one of its terms only. They affect, that is, the subject alone, or the predicate alone, not the relation between the two.

where a modal conclusion is drawn from modal premises, it is only the form of the conclusion *as a judgment* that differs from that of the pure syllogism: its relation to the premises *as a conclusion from them*, consequently the entire *form of the reasoning*, is the same in both. Whereas, by the substitution of a negative premise for an affirmative, or of a particular for a universal, the conclusiveness of the premises as necessitating a consequence, and hence the whole form of the reasoning, will, in most cases, vanish altogether. For this reason, Modality, though psychologically a form of judgment, is not one of those forms that properly fall within the province of Logic. This will be made clearer when we come to treat of the matter and form of syllogisms.[1]

As conception furnishes the material for an act of judgment, so judgment furnishes the material for an act of reasoning. The Matter of the inference consists in the several propositions of which it is composed, and which vary in every different instance: its Form appears in the manner in which those propositions are invariably thought as connected together as premises and conclusion. This connection consists in the recognition of a relation of identity or contradiction between the terms as given in the antecedent and those connected by the act of reasoning in the consequent. The Forms of the Syllogism may thus be determined by the following question: Given two judgments (no matter what may be their material signification), what relations must exist between them to warrant us in inferring a third judgment as their consequent?

In the first place, the premises and conclusion must stand to each other in the relation of condition and con-

[1] On the disputed question of the relation of Modals to Logic, some further remarks will be found in the *Appendix*, note H.

ditioned. As the predicate of a judgment limits and determines the subject, so the premises of a syllogism must limit and determine the conclusion. Limitation is thus a form of reasoning, as of all thinking; the act of reasoning being such as to determine the mind to one actual conclusion out of two contradictory possibilities.

In the second place, since the terms of the conclusion are not compared together directly, but through the medium of a third, it is necessary that this third concept should be compared with each of the others. This comparison, as we have seen in the last chapter, results in a relation either of identity or contradiction; the objects denoted by the two concepts being pronounced identical when the premise is affirmative, and contradictory when it is negative; and a similar relation being consequently inferred to exist between the concepts compared together in the conclusion. The Forms which the Syllogism exhibits in these relations are those of *Mood* and *Figure*, affirmative or negative, which show us what relations of identity or contradiction in the premises of a Syllogism may legitimately determine a similar relation in the conclusion.

Inferences, as well as judgments, are in some cases the result of an act of mixed thinking; of reasoning, that is, in conjunction with an appeal to experience. This is sometimes distinguished by logicians as *material consequence;* the strictly logical operation being designated *formal.* In the earlier portion of the present chapter it has been necessary to avoid this nomenclature; the object having been to show that in every act of thought, pure or mixed, the product exhibits the distinct features of a matter given *to*, and a form given *by*, the thinker. The matter and form of thought are thus by no means coëxtensive with material and formal thinking; and it becomes, therefore, necessary to examine separately the propriety of these last expressions, and to determine what is the exact sense in which Logic is defined to be a Formal Science.

The distinction between *formal* and *material*, or, as for the present it is better to term them, between *pure* and *mixed* thinking, has not in general been consistently followed out by logicians. They have allowed the existence of material consequences in which the conclusion does not follow from the given premises, but requires additional data from experience; and these they have rightly regarded as extralogical; but they have not observed that the same distinction is applicable to Apprehension and Judgment, as well as to reasoning; that there are pure and mixed concepts and judgments, as well as pure and mixed reasonings; and that in every case the province of Logic is with the first only. In consequence of this, the province of Logic has been by some too much widened, and by others too much narrowed. On the one side, we are told that it can remedy indistinctness of apprehension and falsity of judgment — a pretension which, announced without limitation, is perfectly absurd; and on the other side, it has been described as concerned with the operation of reasoning only; apprehension and judgment being considered only in subordination to this. Neither view has been consistently carried out. The advocates of the former ought to have included within the province of Logic, Induction, Analogy, and the whole field of probable reasoning; while the advocates of the latter ought to have extended the signification of the term *reasoning*, so as to include those forms of pure thinking which are governed by the same laws as the formal syllogism.

It would be more correct to distinguish, with regard to

all the three operations of the understanding, between those errors which arise from a defect in the thought itself, and those which arise from a defect in the corresponding experience. For example: my conception of a particular flower is *obscure*, when I have not noticed it so closely as to be able to distinguish it as a whole from certain others; it is *indistinct*, when I know it as a whole, but have not analyzed it so minutely as to be able to enumerate its botanical characteristics. In these cases the defect is empirical, and can only be remedied by closer attention to the individual flowers of that kind. But, on the other hand, my conception may be *obscure*, as containing attributes inconsistent with the existence of its object as an individual whole; or it may be *indistinct*, as containing attributes incapable of coëxisting with each other as parts of a whole. Thus we may be told to conceive a flower of no color at all, or a flower which shall be both red and white on the same part of the same leaf. In these cases the defect is in the thought itself; and, accordingly, Logic is competent to declare the supposed object inconceivable. Again, a judgment may be empirically false, as asserting a combination of attributes never actually found in experience; as if it is asserted that a horse has five legs. It may be logically false, as coupling together attributes which contradict each other; as if it is asserted that a quadruped has five legs. In the former case, I can contradict the assertion only by an appeal to the experience of all who are acquainted with the animal; in the latter, I can contradict it on logical grounds, as false in the thought itself. An inference, in like manner, may be empirically inconsequent, as grounded on a relation of phenomena not invariable in nature; it may be logically inconsequent, as deduced from premises not necessitating it by the laws of thought. Thus, if I am asked whether this particular fall of the barometer is a ground for asserting that it will rain within twelve hours, I can only reply, as a logician, that it is so, if all falls of the barometer are so; but whether this is the case in fact, cannot be decided by logic, but by experience. On the other hand, if it be expressly stated that some falls only of the barometer are indications of rain within twelve hours, I can at once decide that it is logically inconsequent to reason from a merely partial rule to any single instance: the rain may in this case be expected with more or less probability, but it cannot be inferred as a certainty.

It thus appears that, in all the three operations of the understanding, Logic is equally competent to detect their internal vices, as thoughts transgressing their own laws; and that in all it is equally incompetent to detect their external vices, as thoughts inconsistent with experience. It can detect the inconceivability of a notion, the self-contradiction of a judgment, the inconsequence of a conclusion, as not necessitated by given premises. It cannot supply the empirical deficiencies of a notion, nor determine the real existence of its object; it cannot ascertain the truth or falsehood of a judgment as a statement of a fact; it cannot decide as to the necessary sequence of a conclusion from understood premises, or the probability of its truth where the given premises are insufficient to necessitate it by the laws of thought. It remains to ascertain the exact meaning of the expressions *formal* and *material thinking*, as applied respectively to those operations which do or do not fall within the province of Logic.

Law and *Form*, though correlative terms, must not, in strict accuracy, be used as synonymous. The former is used properly with reference to an operation; the latter, with reference to its product. Conceiving, Judging, Reasoning, are subject to certain laws; Concepts, Judgments, Syllogisms, exhibit certain forms. But the laws of thought are not always competent to determine its form, as has been already shown in the case of all the products of mixed thinking. In a synthetical judgment, for example, the laws of thought can determine only its possible truth, which equally implies its possible falsehood; thus leaving it altogether undecided whether the form of the judgment should be affirmative or negative, universal or particular. The form in all these cases is determined by that universal tendency of the human mind, which has been noticed in a former chapter, the tendency to regard physical phenomena as indicating the existence of a substance or a cause similar to that of which we are directly conscious in our own mental states and operations. It is thus that, when experience presents certain phenomena in juxtaposition, the mind is invariably led to regard them as attributes of one and the same substance; and this constitutes the form of all mixed concepts and judgments. And in like manner, when one phenomenon is the invariable consequent of another, the mind is irresistibly led to regard them as respectively cause and effect; and this constitutes the form in all cases of mixed inference. The same tendencies which thus coöperate with the presentations of experience in the acts of mixed thinking, coöperate in like manner with the laws of thought in acts of pure thinking. In the former case, the attributes are given as empirically related as intuitions; in the latter, they are given as logically related as thoughts; and in both they are regarded as mutually related to some unknown *substance* or *cause.* But that these tendencies, however universal or irresistible, cannot properly be regarded as laws of thought or of intuition, is manifest from the fact, that they furnish no criterion for determining the legitimacy or illegitimacy of any product. Thoughts, whether empirically true or false, whether logically sound or unsound, in this respect present precisely the same features. An assertion, false in point of fact, or self-contradictory in point of thought, contains, as regards the supposed relation of attributes to a common substance, precisely the same form as one logically and empirically valid. The Principles of Substance and Causality are thus rather negative conditions than positive laws of thought. They have a psychological relation to thought as it actually exists, explaining and accounting for the fact of its invariably assuming a certain form; but they have no logical relation to thought as it ought to be, and furnish no criterion of its validity in any special instance.

Logical or pure thinking is not, therefore, called formal, because its product exhibits a form; for the coëxistence of matter and form is common to all thought, and to all spurious imitations of thought. But the justification of the terms *formal* and *material*, as applied to pure and mixed processes of thinking, is to be found in the circumstance, that in the former the act of thought is based on the form only of the preliminary data, without reference to the particular matter; while, on the other hand, matter is necessarily taken into account in every process of mixed thinking. To an act of logical conception, for example, it is not necessary to examine in any case the special character of the attributes, as having been actually combined in experience; but only that they should be compatible with the possible existence of an object in space or time. In an act of logical judgment, one of the given concepts being always comprehended in the other, it is indifferent of what special attributes either is composed, provided they possess sufficient clearness and distinctness to enable the mind to discern the relation between them. In an act of logical reasoning, the validity of the conclusion depends solely on the quantity and quality of the given premises, without any reference to the particular terms of which they are composed. In all, so long as the formal relation of the data remains the same, the matter may be changed as we please, without affecting the logical value of the thought. In mixed thinking, on the other hand, the matter is of principal importance. To determine that this or that object of conception actually exists, that this or that judgment is in accordance with experience, that this or that inference is sufficiently probable to furnish a reasonable motive to action, we require to be guided by a knowledge of the nature and circumstances of the particular object in question. And it is for this reason that all examples of logical thinking are better expressed by means of arbitrary symbols than of significant terms; not that it is in any case possible to think without some matter or other, but because it is wholly indifferent what matter we may at the time be thinking about; and, therefore, by employing an unmeaning sign, indifferently representative of any object of thought, we are enabled to clear the process from any accidental admixture of material knowledge, and to exhibit the form alone in its proper relation to the laws of thought.

In accordance with the view here given of Form and Formal Processes, it will be proper to modify slightly some of the definitions of Logic given by those philosophers whose views have been principally followed in the present work. Logic, to omit less accurate views of its nature, has been defined as the Science of the bare Form of Thought,[1] or as the Science of the Formal Laws of Thought;[2] — definitions which, though substantially approaching far nearer to the truth than any antagonist view, still leave something to desire in point of verbal accuracy. The term *formal* strictly belongs rather to the process of pure thinking than to the laws by which it is regulated, or to the science which takes cognizance of them; and Logic is not the science of the Forms of Thought in general, but only of such as are subservient to other processes of formal thinking. Other forms, such as modality, fall without the province of Logic, and within that of Psychology; to which latter science, indeed, all the forms and laws of thought belong in their relation to the constitution of the thinking subject. To Logic, on the other hand, belong the same forms and laws in relation to those acts and products of pure thinking which are suggested by the one and governed by the other. If, therefore, slightly altering the language of the above definitions, we define Logic as the Science of the Laws and Products of Pure or Formal Thinking,[3] we shall express with tolerable accuracy its character and province, according to the views advocated in the preceding pages.

1 Kant, *Logik*, Einleitung I.; Hoffbauer, *Logik*, § 17.

2 Sir W. Hamilton, *Discussions*, p. 119.

3 This coincides nearly with the definition given by Sir W. Hamilton (*Reid's Works*, p. 698), *The science of the laws of thought as thought.*

CHAPTER VIII.

ON POSITIVE AND NEGATIVE THOUGHT.

Logic has been described by Kant as the science of the necessary laws of the understanding and of the reason. Psychologically, the propriety of this division of the mental faculties has been called in question by eminent critics.[1] And in a logical point of view it is untenable, if, as I have endeavored to show, judgment and reasoning, in so far as they are logical processes, are both governed by the same laws, and must be referred to the same faculty. In the present chapter, however, it is proposed to examine another expression of the same definition, and to inquire in what sense the Laws of Thought can properly be called *necessary*. Kant employed this term to distinguish the laws of thought in general from those of thought as employed upon any definite class of objects; it being optional with every man, and therefore contingent, whether he shall exercise his understanding on one class of objects rather than another.[2] This distinction I have preferred to express in other words, by separating *pure* or *formal* from *mixed* or *material* thinking; but the Kantian phraseology may serve to introduce a subject, the right understanding of which is of considerable importance in Logic: the differ-

[1] Among others, by Sir William Hamilton (*Discussions*, p. 17), and by M. Cousin (*Leçons sur la philosophie de Kant*, L. vi.).

[2] Kant, *Logik*, Einleitung I.

ence, namely, between *positive* and *negative* thinking. The phrase *necessary laws of thought*, if such language is allowable, ought to imply that we cannot think at all except under their conditions; and yet it is notorious that such laws are daily transgressed, that nothing is more common than illogical reasoning. To reconcile the language with the fact is the object of the following observations.

Illogical reasoning may be of two very different kinds. It may violate the laws of thought in cases where they are applicable, or it may endeavor to extend them to cases where they are not applicable. The offence in the former case consists in attempting to draw a conclusion opposed to that which the laws require; in the latter, in attempting to draw a conclusion where none can be legitimately inferred. Thus we may, verbally at least, reason, "All A is B; all C is A; therefore no C is B." Or we may reason, "All A is B; some C is not A; therefore some C is not B." If the laws of thought are in the strict sense *necessary*, *i. e.*, obligatory upon every act of thinking, it will follow that these supposed reasonings are neither of them acts of thought at all.

It is, of course, always possible to compose a verbal representation of a thought in which the rules of Logic shall be violated, and to understand fully the meaning of each word of which it is composed. The test, however, of the reality of a thought does not lie in the possibility of *assertion*, but in the possibility of *conception*;[1] in the power, that is to say, of combining the given attributes in a single *image* representative of an individual object of intuition.[2]

[1] Οὐ γὰρ πρὸς τὸν ἔξω λόγον ἡ ἀπόδειξις, ἀλλὰ πρὸς τὸν ἐν τῇ ψυχῇ, ἐπεὶ οὐδὲ συλλογισμός. Ἀεὶ γὰρ ἔστιν ἐνστῆναι πρὸς τὸν ἔξω λόγον, ἀλλὰ πρὸς τὸν ἔσω λόγον οὐκ ἀεί. — Arist. *Anal. Post.* I. 10, 6.

[2] It will be necessary here to bear in mind what has been observed before,

I may make use of the words *a round square*, or *a bilinear figure;* but the terms imply no conception, because the attributes cannot be united in an image. These words, therefore, are not the signs of thought, but only express the negation of any object on which thought can be exercised.[1]

And such, in ultimate analysis, will be seen to be the case with all verbal combinations in which the laws of formal thinking are violated; whether directly, by denying their authority in cases to which they are applicable, or indirectly, by attempting to apply them to cases where they are not applicable. The only difference between these two offences is, that in the former case the product is no thought whatever; in the latter, it is not that kind of thought which it professes to be.

Let us suppose, for example, a syllogistic conclusion verbally asserted, the reverse of that which the laws of thought require; such as, "All A is B, all C is A, therefore some C is not B." This reasoning supposes the possibility of conceiving a C which shall at the same time be B and not B. Tried by this test, the form of words is ascertained to be representative of no thought at all.

On the other hand, in a case where the law of reasoning is not applicable, as in the apparent syllogism, "All Y is [some] Z, no X is [any] Y, therefore no X is [any] Z," the thought is annihilated as a syllogism only: as a mere judgment, the concluding proposition may or may not be true; and there is no impossibility in conceiving an X which is neither Y nor Z. But, as a syllogism, it maintains that X is not Z, *because it is not Y;* in other words, that nothing

that all conception implies imagination, though all imagination does not imply conception. See p. 33.

[1] See, on this subject, an excellent note in Sir W. Hamilton's edition of *Reid*, p. 377.

which is not Y can be Z, or that all Z is Y; — an assertion which again involves a contradiction of the major premise, which, in asserting that all Y is some Z only, implies at the same time that some Z is not Y. This contradiction is not so apparent in the ordinary form of the affirmative proposition, in which the predicate is *expressed* as indefinite, though *thought* as particular; and thus the elliptical and imperfect language of common Logic has caused to be overlooked the important truth, that *illogical thinking is in reality no thinking at all.*

The language of this chapter may recall to the mind of the reader a distinction made in an earlier portion of the present work, between positive and negative ideas. A comparison of the two cases will serve to show that the expression *negative thinking*, or *negation of thought*, is properly applicable to both, though in different relations and on different grounds. Positive thinking implies two conditions: firstly, the material condition, that certain attributes be given as united in a concept; secondly, the formal condition that the concept be capable of *individualization*, *i. e.*, that the attributes be such as can coëxist in an object perceived or imagined. If either of these conditions be wanting, we are deficient in the *sine qua non* of actual thought. A given form of words may thus in two different ways be void of a thought corresponding. We may be unable to conceive separately one or more of the attributes given, or we may be unable to conceive them in combination. The former is the case when we have never been personally conscious of the said attribute as *presented;* the latter is the case when the several presentations are incompatible with each other.

From defect in the first of these conditions, a man born blind may be said to have a negative idea of light, which he knows only as something different from darkness, and, consequently, of the various colors, which are different modifications of light; and any man, in like manner, has but a negative idea of a color which he has not actually seen.[1] The blind man may be able to distinguish a sphere from a cube, by touch; but if he is told that the ball which he has in his hand is white, he cannot connect the word with any sensation of which he has been at any time conscious. And in like manner, a man who has seen white objects only has no idea of red; he knows it only as some color which he has not seen. In this manner it is that we have negative ideas only of many of the objects on which men most boldly speculate. Such is the case with all our speculations on *causality*, as existing apart from the conscious exertion of power; on *substance*, other than as a conscious self; on *consciousness in general*, apart from the conditions of space and time. Of these we can only speak as a causality which is not our causality; as a substance different from our substance; as a consciousness unlike our consciousness.[2] The same is the case with all the speculations of our reason concerning infinity and infinite attributes as such. By removing the condition of limitation, we remove the only condition under which such attributes have ever been presented to our consciousness. Further speculation is not thought, but its negation.

[1] In the first of these instances the negative idea is so obscure as to be tantamount in its actual result to no idea at all. Still the corresponding state of mind is not one of pure quiescence, or mere absence of thought. A blind man who had lived all his life among a nation of blind men, and who had thus never been led to infer the existence of visible objects at all, would be in a different state from one who is continually told of things which he is unable to see, and whose mind is consequently roused to an effort, though an ineffectual one.

[2] Cf. Damiron, *Psychologie*, vol. ii. p. 221.

The second condition fails in cases of illogical thinking, all of which may be shown ultimately to annihilate themselves by involving a contradiction. And in these cases the attempt to individualize the thought furnishes at once a decisive criterion of its negative character. In the former instances, the thought is only ultimately discovered to be unattainable from the failure of every attempt to realize it; in the present case, the attributes can be immediately determined to be unthinkable, as mutually destroying one another. The former may be distinguished as *materially* or *relatively negative* from the absence of the requisite data for thinking; the latter are *formally* or *absolutely negative*, as containing data which offend against the universal laws of human thought. The former might become positive if man were furnished with a new sense, or any additional faculty of intuition; the latter could only become so by a complete inversion of the existing constitution of his mind. The negative character of the first is shown by Psychology, which ascertains empirically the limitations to which the mind is subject in the accumulation of materials for thinking; the negative character of the second is shown by Logic, which lays down *à priori* the conditions to which all materials, whencesoever derived, must be subjected in the formation of thought.

It is of the utmost importance to distinguish these two kinds of negative thinking, the material or psychological, and the formal or logical, from each other. No error in philosophy is more frequent in its occurrence, or more pernicious in its results, than a confusion on this point. Men are apt to mistake the absence of the materials for one thought for the presence of materials for its opposite; — to imagine that it is all one to be unable to think of an object as existing, and to be able to think of it as not existing; — to fancy that certain positions are condemned by the laws of the understanding, when the fact is only that their materials have not been given in an intuition; — to suppose that to be rejected by reason which in truth has never come in contact with reason at all.

To examine in detail the prominent instances of the above confusion, which are plentifully exhibited by some of the so-called philosophers of the present time, would require a work of a higher and more controversial character than the present. I shall content myself with selecting two examples, one ancient and one modern, as specimens of the confident manner in which men of all ages, and under all religious systems, have been prone to dogmatize upon the highest matters of speculation, upon no better basis than the absence of all materials for speculating at all.

Aristotle's well-known argument, to prove that the happiness of the gods consists in contemplation, is based on the ground that we cannot attribute to them moral attributes in the only way in which such attributes come within the sphere of human consciousness, viz., under the limitations and imperfections consequent upon human passion and human error. What scope, he asks, can there be for fortitude, where there is no pain to undergo; or for temperance, where there are no evil desires to keep in check?[1] But the reasoning is incomplete. Cotta, in Cicero, pursuing the same principle to its ultimate consequences, shows clearly that we must equally deny of the Deity the possession of any intellectual as well as of any moral quality. What is the object of reason and intelligence but to gain a knowledge of that which is obscure? What is the purpose of contemplation but to gain a closer insight into

[1] *Eth. Nic.* x. 8.

the nature of the things contemplated? Intellectual attainments have the same relation to human ignorance that moral virtues have to human frailty.[1]

The error of both these reasonings is the same: it consists in mistaking a psychological deficiency for a logical impossibility. To determine in thought that certain attributes *cannot exist* in any being except under given conditions of manifestation, it would be necessary that we should have had personal experience of the abrogation of those conditions, and of the absolute destruction of the attributes in consequence. But such an experience in the present case is, *ex hypothesi*, impossible; the conditions being those to which the universal human consciousness is subject. To pronounce how consciousness exists in beings of a different nature from ourselves, it would be necessary that we should be capable of possessing their nature and faculties, as well as our own, and of comparing the two together by the aid of a third power independent of either. To pronounce that certain modes of consciousness cannot exist save as they exist to us, it is necessary that we should have personally tried every other possible relation of modes of consciousness to a conscious subject. Until human experience has extended thus far, to limit the province of faith by that of reason, — to say that *what we cannot compass in thought we may not believe as existing*, — is to pass from criticism to dogmatism, a dogmatism resting its claims to dictation on a complete ignorance of the matter in which it dictates.

The modern Atheism of the German philosopher Feuerbach is based on a similar confusion. It assumes that the measure of what man is to believe is to be determined by what he can grasp in an act of positive thought; in other

[1] Cicero, *De Natura Deorum*, iii. 15.

words, that the mere absence of the necessary data for thinking at all is tantamount to a logical determination of the non-existence of a corresponding object. God, according to this system, is but humanity deified in its intellectual, or moral, or physical attributes, according to the varying condition, characters, and wants of this or that people; but in all, according to one form or another of Anthropomorphism.

Falsehood is only dangerous from its possessing a certain portion of a mutilated truth. The one element of truth which underlies the Atheism of the *Essence of Religion*,[1] is the fact, that finite thought can only be positively exercised on finite objects. Thought, on its positive side, is ultimately tested by the individualization of concepts. To effect this, they must be referred to the representative image of some actual state of consciousness, — sensation, volition, affection, etc. In attempting to grasp the Deity as an object of positive thought, to speculate beyond what is revealed to us of the divine attributes as manifested in relation and accommodation to human faculties, man can only bring God down to his own level, and exercise his reason on those analogous attributes of which he has had experience in his personal consciousness. The error consists in overlooking the religious feelings and affections, as a distinct class of psychological facts, coordinate with, not subordinate to, the thinking faculty. The history of mankind in general, as well as the consciousness of each individual, alike testify that religion is not a function of thought; and that the attempt to make

1 With this work, and others of the same author, I am acquainted through the French translation by M. Ewerbeck, entitled, *Qu'est-ce que la Religion d'après la nouvelle philosophie Allemande.*

it so, if consistently carried out, necessarily leads, firstly to Anthropomorphism, and ultimately to Atheism.

The incompetency of such reasoning to prove its conclusion is manifest from the fact, that the mental phenomena on which alone it rests, must, from the nature of the case, be precisely the same, whether that conclusion be true or false. If human thought is subject to laws and limitations, formal and material, the mode and the sphere of positive thinking must be such as those laws and limitations require, whether there exist objects beyond it or not. But the hypothesis, indispensable to the rationalist, that the sphere of thought and that of being are coëxtensive, fails altogether to account for the phenomenon of negative thinking; to explain, that is, how it can be that man, in the exercise of thought, ever finds himself encompassed with conditions and restrictions, which he is ever striving to pass, and ever failing in the effort; that he ever feels himself in the presence of yearnings unsatisfied and doubts unsolved; — yearnings which countless accessions to the domain of thought have left as vague and restless as before; — doubts which centuries of speculation have made no progress toward answering. These and such like humiliating truths, altogether inexplicable on the arrogant assumption of a human God contemplating the products of his creative intellect,[1] are the natural and necessary features of our position, if we believe that man, as individual

[1] "Ueber die Natur philosophiren," says Schelling, "heisst die Natur schaffen."

"Die Logik," says Hegel, "zeigt die Erhebung der Idee zu der Stufe von daraus sie die Schöpferin der Natur wird." In the same spirit, Logic is declared to be, "Die Darstellung Gottes, wie er in seinem ewigen Wesen vor der Erschaffung der Natur und eines endlichen Geistes ist."

The mock thunder of Salmoneus was modesty itself to this.

or as species, is but a lower intelligence in the midst of the works of a higher; a being of finite intuitions, surrounded by partial indications of the Unlimited, of finite thought, contemplating partial revelations of the Incomprehensible.

CHAPTER IX.

OF LOGIC AS RELATED TO OTHER MENTAL SCIENCES.

A DIVISION was early established in philosophy between the *Logica docens* and the *Logica utens*; the one concerned with the pure laws and forms of thought, the other with the application of thought to this or that object-matter. The relations of the latter it is not my present purpose to examine. Every art or science, in so far as it contains reasonings on its own special objects, may be regarded as furnishing an instance of the *Logica utens*; and in this point of view Logic has no special affinity with one branch of knowledge rather than another. But in relation to the *Logica docens*, there are three branches of science, real or apparent, which, from community of object and method, as well as from historical connection, demand a more special consideration.

The three sciences in question are Grammar, Psychology, and Metaphysics. Rhetoric, from an association with Logic and Grammar in the mediæval Trivium, might also be thought to have a special claim on our attention. But, in truth, Rhetoric is connected by community of object-matter rather with the art of Dialectic, as exhibited in the Topics of Aristotle and the Probable Syllogisms of the Scholastic Logic, than with the formal science as treated of in the present work. Its relation to the latter is only by way of application, inasmuch as logical forms may be applied in rhetorical exercises; a relation which reduces it to a level with any other employment of the *Logica utens.* With Psychology, indeed, its connection is far more intimate, but on the opposite side from that by which the same science is related to Logic. Logic, as the science of the laws and products of the understanding, is related to Psychology through the medium of the speculative and discursive faculties. Rhetoric, as concerned with the movement of the will, is related on the side of the emotional and practical faculties, and is thus correctly described by Aristotle as an offshoot of Dialectic and Moral Philosophy.

On the other hand, Psychology, Metaphysics, and Grammar, are intimately connected with the faculties, the laws, and the instruments of the universal process of thought, — a connection which has been recognized, with more or less clearness, from the origin of Logic to the present time. The Categories, from the days of Aristotle downwards, have been disputed ground between Logic and Metaphysics, and are treated of by the Stagirite himself in connection with both sciences. The treatise περὶ ἑρμηνείας, whose title, sorely misnomered by various translators, might be adequately expressed in English by, "Of Language as the interpretation of Thought,"[1] is, in the early portion, devoted to grammatical definitions and distinctions. Psychology also, though less prominently introduced, claims her share in the multifarious matter of the Organon; in the account of the processes of sensation, memory, and experience, as subsidiary to induction.

Were we indeed to start from the whole Organon of

[1] For various interpretations of *Interpretation*, see M. St. Hilaire, *De la Logique d'Aristote*, p. i. ch. 10. The version given in the text corresponds to that by Isidore of Seville: "Omnis elocutio conceptæ rei interpres est: inde perihermeniam nominant quam interpretationem nos appellamus."

Aristotle, as a uniform treatise on a single subject, it would be difficult to accommodate its contents to any modern classification of the mental sciences. But it may fairly be questioned whether even the authority of the philosopher himself can be adduced in support of such a proceeding. While we cannot help admitting, with Sir William Hamilton,[1] that the incorrect notions which have prevailed, and still prevail, in regard to the nature and province of Logic, are mainly to be attributed to the authority of the father of the science, it may be doubted how far that authority has been put to a legitimate use by his followers. The same eminent critic to whom we have just referred has observed, in another place, that there is required for the metaphysician not less imagination than for the poet; that it may, in fact, be doubted whether Homer or Aristotle possessed this faculty in greater vigor.[2] The two authors here placed in juxtaposition may be compared in more respects than that of their mental powers. The influence of Homer in Poetry has been similar to that of Aristotle in Philosophy; yet, while, from the Father of Criticism to the present day, there has never been wanting a champion to maintain against all impugners the unity of design of the Iliad, and its exact relation to a beginning, a middle, and an end, the primary argument of this "one entire and perfect chrysolite" has been almost as much disputed among critics as the question of the definition of Logic. Different portions of the poem have been pronounced genuine or spurious, according to this or that conception of the poet's design; and, finally, it has even been maintained that the model of all succeeding Epics is little more than a fortuitous concourse of atoms, the frag-

[1] *Discussions*, p. 141.

[2] *Reid's Works*, p. 99.

ments of distinct rhapsodists. The Organon of Aristotle has had a similar fate. Various have been the conjectures concerning its design and method. Portions have been at different times regarded as logical, as grammatical, as metaphysical; nor have there been wanting critics to deny the genuineness of this or that part. The parallel might be carried further. The different portions of the Iliad are said to have been collected and arranged in the time of Pisistratus, about three hundred and forty years after the date assigned by Herodotus (rightly or wrongly) to the birth of the poet; and the writings of Aristotle are generally supposed to have received their present form and arrangement at the hands of Andronicus of Rhodes, a philosopher who flourished about three centuries later than the Stagirite. I am not indeed aware that any critic has been bold enough to maintain a thoroughly Wolfian hypothesis of the origin of the Organon; and yet there are not wanting grounds on which a not very different theory might be supported; not indeed as regards the authorship, but certainly as regards the unity of design of the work. The title by which the collected treatises are known is undoubtedly of recent origin; it is not found in Aristotle himself, nor in any of his earlier commentators; and, as far as existing evidence can determine, it appears not to have been in common use before the fifteenth century.[1] The several treatises themselves are invariably mentioned by their author as distinct works under distinct titles; and even after the time of Andronicus, commentaries were generally written, not on the Organon as a whole, but separately on its constituent parts. If from the books we turn to the matters of which they treat, the result is the same. Logic, as the name of an Art or Science, does not once occur in the

[1] St. Hilaire, *De la Logique d'Aristote*, vol. i. p. 19.

writings of Aristotle; and the cognate adjective and adverb are used in a peculiar and much more restricted sense than that which has subsequently been given to them. The names sanctioned by the philosopher himself, such as Analytic and Dialectic, are commensurate with portions only of the Organon; the division of Philosophy into Logic, Physics, and Ethics, adopted by the Stoics, and sometimes attributed (on questionable grounds) to Plato, receives no sanction from the Stagirite; indeed, he adopts a classification in many respects at variance with it, distinguishing theoretical philosophy from practical and productive, and dividing the first into three branches, Physics, Mathematics, and Theology.[1]

Leaving, then, altogether the question of authority, and adopting the formal view of Logic taken in the preceding pages as the only one which promises to secure for the science what it has so long needed, an exact definition and a determined field of inquiry, I shall proceed to examine the relation in which Logic, as thus exhibited, stands towards the cognate sciences of Psychology, Grammar, and Metaphysics.

Of Psychology something has already been said in the earlier portion of the present Essay. Logic deals with the products of the several thinking acts, with concepts, with judgments, with reasonings, as, according to certain as-

[1] *Metaph.* v. 1. Mr. Karslake (*Aids*, p. 10) speaks of the Organon as presenting so coherent a system, that the assertion that it contains a few only of Aristotle's logical works is doubtful. To me there appears little more of coherence than may naturally be expected in distinct writings of the same author on any question of Grammar, Analytic, Dialectic, or Rhetoric. And, as far as we can conjecture from existing evidence, it is most probable that the several books were written in the reverse order of that in which they are now arranged. See Burgersdyck, *Inst. Log.* Præf.; Fries, *System der Logik*, p. 15.

sumed laws of thinking, they ought to be or not to be.[1] It is competent to test the validity of all such products in so far as they comply or not with the conditions of pure thought, leaving to this or that branch of material science to determine how far the same products of thought are guaranteed by the testimony of this or that special experience. Thus it accepts, as logically valid, all such concepts, judgments, and reasonings, as do not, directly or indirectly, imply contradictions; pronouncing them thus far to be legitimate as thoughts, that they do not in ultimate analysis destroy themselves. That they will be also accepted upon an appeal to experience, it does not decide; it only recommends them as qualified for further examination. It is thus competent to determine the *possible existence* of a class of objects corresponding to a given concept, the *necessary truth* of an analytical, and the *possible truth* of a synthetical judgment, the *formal validity* of a conclusion as necessarily following from certain assumed premises. Questions concerning the *real existence* of this or that class of objects, the *actual* truth of a synthetical judgment, or of a conclusion *out of relation to its given premises*, it sends up for judgment to the tribunal of Experience.

As Experience decides on the relations of any given product of thought to the actual phenomena presented by this or that object of intuition, so Psychology decides on its relations to the actual constitution of the human mind. Why it is that the laws of pure thinking extend thus far and no further; — what are the mental processes prelim-

[1] "Die ganze reine Logik hat es mit *Verhältnissen des Gedachten*, des Inhalts unserer Vorstellungen (obgleich nicht speciell mit diesem Inhalte selbst) zu thun; aber überall nirgends mit der *Thätigkeit des Denkens*, nirgends mit der psychologischen, also metaphysischen, Möglichkeit desselben." — Herbart, *Psychologie als Wissenchaft*. Th. II. § 119.

inary and subsidiary to thought, and the nature of the thinking act itself as giving rise to the logical products; — whence arises the phenomenon of illegitimate thinking; — the nature and origin of various impediments and errors to which thinking and other mental acts are subjected in mankind; — the relation of the several mental acts to one or more faculties of mind, and the value of such distinction as absolute or relative, implying a notional only, or an actual separability; — in short, all inquiries into the actual phenomena of man's mental constitution and their explanation, form the object-matter of Psychology.[1]

From this it appears that Psychology, as well as Physical Science, is, in the widest sense of the term, empirical. It inquires, that is to say, what are the actual phenomena of the several acts and states of the human mind, and the actual laws or conditions on which they depend; and in this sense the laws of thought themselves are empirical, and within the province of Psychology, inasmuch as it is a matter of fact and experience that men do reason according to them. Logic, on the other hand, can in no sense be called empirical, inasmuch as the actual constitution, whether of the world within, or of the world without, is assumed indeed and implied in its researches, but in no respect described or investigated. We are not to ascertain, as a matter of fact, that men do reason in this or that form, as governed by this or that law; but, on the assumption of certain laws, we are to determine *à priori* the forms which legitimate thinking ought to exhibit, whether mankind in general do comply with them or not.[2] Logic is

[1] Much of this is distinguished by Kant as *Applied Logic*, which however he allows to be more properly referred to Psychology.

[2] Kant, *Logik*, Einleitung II. 4; Drobisch, *Neue Darstellung der Logik*, § 9.

indeed ultimately to be referred to the test of experience; but only in respect of its conformity with facts without its province, not in respect of the coherence of its parts within. So far as it implies that, as a matter of fact, men do reason in syllogisms, so far its pretensions may be tested by reference to the empirical truths of Psychology. So far as it asserts that the legitimate forms of the syllogism are such and such, it is simply deductive *à priori*, and necessarily valid for any class of thinking beings whose laws are such as it presupposes. An empirical science may contain much partial truth, though omitting many important phenomena and erroneously accounting for many which it recognizes. It offers much, therefore, for enlarged experience gradually to supply and correct. An *à priori* Science, like Logic, is tested by experience only with reference to its fundamental hypotheses. If these are accepted, they carry with them the whole superstructure of details. If these are rejected, every portion of the science falls to the ground along with them.

But though Logic and Psychology have thus each their respective provinces and methods, it cannot be too often repeated that neither can be taught as a science, efficiently and satisfactorily, unless in connection with the other. We may learn by rote a multitude of logical rules, and fondly imagine that we are acquiring an art which will enable us to think; — a course of Logic being in fact about as necessary for making men thinkers as a course of Ethical Philosophy for making them honest, or a course of Optics for enabling them to see. Or we may analyze *in dictione* and *extra dictionem* all sorts of imaginary fallacies propounded by imaginary sophists, and dream that we are forging an impenetrable panoply against all the deceits of the world; — as if we could bind men down in heavy securities to lie and cheat by rule, in order that they may be detected in due course of art. Or we may draw up syllogisms in orthodox mood and figure, and babble about Laws of Thought, and never dream of asking what is the nature of Thought as a process, and with what elements does it combine in the actual formation of this or that compound. Or, on the other hand, starting from confused or erroneous notions of the nature and powers of the human mind, we may blame Logic for not accomplishing what no science can accomplish, and deem its whole contents a tissue of jargon and imposture, because it is neither able to open a Royal Road to the Encyclopædia, nor to convert natural folly into supernatural wisdom. It may safely be asserted that nine-tenths of the mistaken judgments to which Logic has been subjected on the part of friends and adversaries, unreasonable eulogy on the one hand, equally unreasonable abuse or contempt on the other, have been owing to its treatment out of relation to Psychology,—to its having been expounded and studied without any preliminary attempt to ascertain what are the nature and limits of the thinking faculty, and what character its laws and products ought to exhibit in conformity with the constitution of the human mind.

With Grammar Logic is connected through the medium of the universal instrument of thought, Language. The practical necessity of this instrument for the formation as well as for the communication of thought, has been noticed already; it remains to inquire in what different ways this their common object is dealt with by Logic and Grammar respectively. Universal Grammar, with which alone we are concerned (the history and idiomatic peculiarities of special languages being obviously unconnected with general Logic), has been happily defined as "The science of the relations which the constituent parts of speech bear to each other in significant combination."[1] It is thus concerned with Language primarily and essentially; Logic, secondarily and accidentally. The former has given certain articulate sounds, to find their relation to certain supposed counterparts in thought. The latter has given to determine the necessary relations of concepts to each other; but in so doing it is compelled secondarily to exhibit the corresponding relations of the sounds by which concepts are represented.

The two sciences differ also in the extent of their provinces. Logic considers language simply as the instrument and representative of thought. Grammar will include its relation to intuitions and emotions, and every state of consciousness which finds its expression in speech.[2] Logic considers language only in so far as it is indispensable to thought, and accordingly analyzes speech only to that point at which it is representative of the simplest element of thought, the concept. Any parts into which a concept may be divided, which are not themselves concepts, are beyond its province, as not being representative of a complete thought, nor competent instruments alone for the performance of an act of thinking. Hence all syncategorematic words, as not being *per se* significant, are not recognized by Logic.

In Grammar the unit of thought is a judgment, both terms being necessarily represented by words. Hence the unit of speech in Grammar is a proposition; the office of the subordinate parts of speech being to limit or connect

[1] Sir John Stoddart, *Philosophy of Language*, pt. i. p. 21. Universal Grammar is properly a science, particular Grammar an art, as is observed by Du Marsais, *Encyclopédie*, Art. *Grammaire*, p. 842.

[2] See Harris, Hermes, ch. iii.

the primary parts as subjects or predicates of a given assertion.[1] Such connections and limitations may be more conveniently effected by the invention of words expressive of relations between concepts, than by the use of distinct signs for every new concept resulting from such relations; this, however, is one of the luxuries only, not one of the necessaries of language, and, as such, is not noticed by Logic. Viewed simply as an element of thought, it is indifferent whether the same concept be expressed by a combination of substantive and adjective, as in the English "four-footed beast," or the German "vierfüssiges Thier," by the interposition of a preposition, as in the French "bête à quatre pieds," or by a single substantive, such as the classical equivalent, "quadruped."

In Logic the unit of thought is also a judgment, but not one which requires a verbal representative of both its constituent parts. Conception, the simplest act of thought, consists in the referring a given concept to possible objects as imagined. Here there is, in the psychological sense of the term, a *judgment; i. e.*, a consciousness of the presence of the objects in thought; but that consciousness does not form an additional concept, nor require as its necessary exponent a second verbal sign. Hence the unit of speech in Logic is a term; such being a sufficient verbal instrument for the performance of the first and the simplest act of thought.

With reference to the second operation of thought, judgment, wherein the two sciences come most nearly into contact, the following distinction is important. Grammar considers words objectively, as signs of things. Hence

[1] For a further illustration of this doctrine, not universally held by Grammarians, the reader is referred to an article by the present author, on the Philosophy of Language, in the *North British Review*, No. 27.

the distinction of *tenses*, according as the remote or represented object is considered as contemporaneous with, or distant in time from, the speaker. Logic considers words subjectively, as signs of thoughts. Hence the only logical tense is the present, the immediate or presented objects being necessarily contemporaneous with the act of consciousness by which they are now thought in conjunction.[1]

It is sometimes said that Logic recognizes two only of the grammatical parts of speech, the noun and the verb, forming the two terms of the proposition with and without time.[2] It would be more correct to say that Logic, viewing language in a different light from Grammar, and analyzing on a different principle, does not recognize the grammatical parts of speech at all. The simplest elements of a complete assertion in Grammar are the noun and the verb;[3] the latter being a combination of attribute and assertion. Hence the grammatical type of a proposition is that distinguished in scholastic language as *secundi adjacentis;* and to this form all varieties produced by

[1] See p. 71.

[2] "Grammatici enim, considerantes vocum figuras, octo orationis partes annumerant. Philosophi vero, quorum omnis de nomine verboque tractatus in significatione est constituta, duas tantum orationis partes esse docuerunt: quicquid plenam significationem tenet, siquidem sine tempore significat, nomen vocantes; verbum vero, si cum tempore." — Boethius, *Int. ad Syll.* p. 561. "Et sciendum est quod Dialecticus solum ponit duas partes orationis, scilicet nomen et verbum. Alias autem omnes appellat syncategorematicas, id est consignificativas." — Petr. Hisp. *Sum. Log.* Tr. i. Here, as in the *De Interpretatione* of Aristotle, the type of the logical proposition is the form distinguished as *secundi adjacentis*, the verb being neither the copula alone, nor the predicate alone, but the combination of the two, however expressed. A neglect of this has misled many commentators and critics on Aristotle, from Ammonius to the present day.

[3] "In all languages there are only *two* sorts of words which are *necessary* for the communication of our thoughts, the noun and the verb." — Tooke, *Div. of Purley*, ch. 3.

the accidents of particular languages must, in Universal Grammar, be virtually reduced.[1] In Logic, on the other hand, for the purposes of opposition and conversion, as well as from the necessity of assigning a quantity to both terms of the proposition, the type is required to be of the form *tertii adjacentis;* the subject and predicate being regarded as two given concepts, the objects of which are identified or distinguished by means of the copula. Hence, in every case in which the proposition is exhibited in its logical form, the grammatical verb will correspond not to any single word in the proposition, but to a combination formed of the copula and the quantified predicate, — to all, in short, that is asserted of the subject. The predicate concept may thus, in different points of view, answer to two distinct grammatical relations. Taken by itself, it is a noun, identified in certain respects with another noun as the subject. Taken in its predicate character, it forms a portion of the verb, the remainder being supplied by the copula. Those logicians who maintain the copula to be the logical verb, confound the accidents of particular languages with the essentials of language in general as a sign of thought. With them the verb is determined solely by the subordinate feature of its personal inflection, not by the primary characteristic of its signification.

With regard to the relation of Logic to Metaphysics, some preliminary verbal explanation is necessary, owing to

[1] Hence it follows that the copula is, grammatically speaking, no verb at all. It fulfils none of the functions of that part of speech; for it implies no attribute, and cannot, when united to a subject, form a complete assertion. In such a sentence as "The meadows are white with frost," the true verb is not the copula, but the copula with the adjective, *are white*, as may be seen by substituting the Latin, "prata canis *albicant* pruinis." Whether this can be expressed in one word or not, is an accident of this or that language, and is beyond the province of Universal Grammar.

the various senses in which the latter term has been used. Among modern philosophers, empirical psychology, which the ancients regarded as a branch of physics,[1] is frequently classified as metaphysical. Thus the contributions of Reid and Stewart to the inductive science of the human mind are not unfrequently spoken of as Scotch Metaphysics; a nomenclature which the latter of these philosophers has in some degree sanctioned by his own writings.[2] Such a classification is, however, inconsistent with the fundamental doctrines of the Scottish School. It has been before observed that one of their leading principles is, that, in the investigation of mind as well as of matter, phenomena alone are the legitimate objects of science; the substance and essential nature of both being beyond the reach of human faculties. Whereas Metaphysics has from the earliest days been distinguished as the Science of Being as Being, in opposition to all inquiries into the phenomena exhibited by this or that class of objects.[3] How far such a problem is capable of solution is another question; but the mere propounding of it implies an object totally distinct from that of an inquiry into the faculties and laws of the human mind.

The object of the older Metaphysics has been distin-

[1] See Hamilton on Reid, p. 216.

[2] For instance: "Nothing contributes so much to form this talent as the study of Metaphysics; not the absurd Metaphysics of the Schools, but that study which has the operations of the mind for its object."—*Elements*, vol. i. ch. 2. In other places Stewart has noticed this phraseology as a loose use of language, and has attempted to account for it. But the term ought never to have been used at all.

[3] Arist. *Metaph.* iii. 1. *Ἔστιν ἐπιστήμη τις ἣ θεωρεῖ τὸ ὂν ᾗ ὂν καὶ τὰ τούτῳ ὑπάρχοντα καθ' αὑτό.* The name Metaphysics is of much later date, but its object has always been regarded as identical with that distinguished by Aristotle as *First Philosophy*, or *Theology*. Cf. Wolf, *Ontologia*, § 1.

guished in all ages as the one and the real, in opposition to the many and the apparent.[1] Matter, for example, as perceived by the senses, is a combination of distinct and heterogeneous qualities, discernible, some by sight, some by smell, some by touch, some by hearing. What is the *thing itself*, the subject and owner of these several qualities, and yet not identical with any one of them? What is it by virtue of wh'ch these several attributes constitute or belong to one and the same thing? Mind, in like manner, presents to consciousness so many distinct states and operations and feelings. What is the nature of that one mind, of which all these are so many modifications? The inquiry may be carried higher still. Can we attain to any single conception of Being in general, to which both Mind and Matter are subordinate, and from which the essence of each may be deduced?[2]

Ontology, or Metaphysics proper, as thus explained, may be treated in two different methods, according as its exponent is a believer in τὸ ὄν or in τὰ ὄντα, in one or in many fundamental principles of things. In the former, all objects whatever are regarded as phenomenal modifications of one and the same Substance, or as self-determined effects of one and the same Cause. The necessary result of this method is to reduce all metaphysical philosophy to a Rational Theology, the one Substance or Cause being identified with the Absolute, or the Deity. According to the latter method, which professes to treat of different classes of Beings independently, Metaphysics will contain three coördinate branches of inquiry: Rational Cosmology, Rational Psychology, and Rational Theology.[3]

[1] Arist. *Metaph.* iii. 2.

[2] Wolf, *Phil. Rat. Disc. Prœl.* § 73; Herbart, *Allgemeine Metaphysik*, § 27.

[3] Herbart, *Lehrbuch zur Philosophie*, § 7; *Allgemeine Metaphysik*, § 31. Anm.

The first aims at a knowledge of the real essence, as distinguished from the phenomena, of the material world; the second discusses the nature and origin, as distinguished from the faculties and affections, of the human soul, and of other finite spirits;[1] the third aspires to comprehend God Himself, as cognizable *à priori* in his essential nature, apart from the indirect and relative indications furnished by his works, as in Natural Theology, or by his word, as in Revealed Religion. These three objects of metaphysical inquiry — God, the World, the Mind — correspond to Kant's three Ideas of the Pure Reason; and the object of his Critique is to show that, in relation to all three, the attainment of a system of speculative philosophy is impossible.

The former of these methods is the bolder and the more consequent; and, moreover, the only one which can be consistently followed by those who believe in the possibility of a Philosophy of the Absolute. For, a plurality of real objects being once admitted as the highest reach attainable by human faculties, these must necessarily be regarded as related to, and limited by, each other. Accordingly, this method has been followed by the hardiest and most consistent reasoners on metaphysical questions; by Spinoza, under the older form of Speculation, and by Hegel, after the Kantian revolution. But thus treated, metaphysical speculation necessarily leads to Pantheism;

1 "Man findet hier die Trennung der *empirischen* von der *rationalen* Psychologie; die erste durchlaüft die einzelnen sogenannten Seelenvermögen; die andre spricht über Natur und Ursprung der Seele, über Unsterblichkeit, Zustand nach dem Tode, Unterschied zwischen den Seelen der Menschen, der Thiere, und den höheren Geistern."— Herbart, *Allgemeine Metaphysik*, § 29. For a curious account of theories and theorists in rational psychology, see Burton, *Anatomy of Melancholy*, P. i. sect. i. Mem. 2, Subs. 9.

and Pantheism, at this elevation, is for all religious purposes equivalent to Atheism.[1] The method is thus condemned by its results; and the condemnation will not be retracted upon a psychological examination of its principles. Its fundamental conception is not thought, but its negation. The Thought which is identified with Being in general, is not my thought, nor any form of consciousness which I can personally realize.[2] My whole consciousness is subject to the conditions of limitation and relation of subject and object. A system which commences by denying this relation, starts with an assumption concerning the possible character of an intelligence other than human, and consequently incapable of verification by any human being. Yet the system is the product of a human thinker, and addressed to human disciples.

The second method of metaphysical inquiry is less presumptuous, though perhaps also less consistent. It starts with the assumption of a plurality of Beings, thus virtually abandoning the Philosophy of the Absolute. This plurality is primarily manifest in the contrast between the Subject and the Object of Consciousness, between *self* and

[1] It has of late been a favorite criticism of Spinoza to say, with Hegel, that his system is not Atheism, but Acosmism; and this is true in a speculative point of view. But if I allow of no God distinct from the aggregate of the Universe, myself included, what object have I of worship? Or if, according to the later manifestation of Pantheism, the Divine Mind is but the sum total of every finite consciousness, my own included, what religious relation between God and man is compatible with the theory? And, accordingly, the Pantheism of Hegel has found its natural development in the Atheism of Feuerbach.

[2] This is expressly stated by an eminent disciple of Hegel, who professes to discover in Aristotle's Metaphysics an anticipation of Hegelianism: "La pensée que nous venons de décrire est la pensée absolue. Il ne s'agit pas ici de la pensée subjective, qui est une fonction psychologique restreinte à l'âme humaine."—Michelet, *Examen de la Métaphysique d'Aristote*, p. 276.

not-self, as related to and limiting each other. But the consciousness of the relative and limited suggests by contrast the idea of the absolute and unlimited; and thus gives rise to three distinct branches of metaphysical speculation: the ego being identified with the substance of the human soul, as distinguished from its phenomenal modes; the non-ego being identified with the reality which underlies the phenomena of the sensible world; and the absolute or unconditioned with the Deity.[1] Of the last of these three branches, that commonly known as Rational Theology, which endeavors from the conception of God as an absolutely perfect Being to deduce the necessary attributes of the Divine Nature, I shall say nothing in this place. The question of the relation of the human mind to religious intuitions is one of the most delicate and the most difficult in Psychology, and to treat it adequately would require a separate volume. On the two latter branches of Metaphysics, which Kant regarded as equally unattainable with the first, something has been said in a former chapter. It was the opinion of Kant, as well as of Reid and Stewart, that the subject of mental as well as of bodily attributes is not an immediate object of consciousness; in other words, that in mind, as well as in body, Substance and Unity are not *presented*, but *represented.* Those who accept this doctrine are only consistent in regarding metaphysical inquiry in all its branches as a delusion. But a philosophical examination is incomplete unless it not only points out the truth, but likewise explains the cause of error. The weak point of the above doctrine is, that it fails in

[1] These three branches of Metaphysics have been considered somewhat more in detail, by the present author, in the Article *Metaphysics*, in the eighth edition of the *Encyclopædia Britannica*, vol. xiv. pp. 604 sqq., 615 sqq.

explaining, on psychological grounds, how the supposed delusion originated. Experience furnishes, if not the cause, at least the occasion of every object of our cognition; and, unless upon the supposition that a knowledge of Unity and Substance is immediately *given* in one phase at least of consciousness, it is impossible to account for its invention in any. The multifarious phenomena of internal as well as of external sense, present, on the opposite hypothesis, nothing in any respect analogous to the substance to which they are attributed, — nothing that can operate in any way even as the occasional cause from which the existence of such a substance could be suggested. Metaphysical philosophy may contain much that is groundless, much that is deceptive; but the whole analogy of deception and hypothesis in other branches of speculation leads to the conviction that it can only arise from rashly transferring to new relations ideas which are given in some relation or other.

Instead, therefore, of considering the whole of Metaphysics to be based on a delusion, and its ultimate destiny to be utter extinction, we shall probably come nearer to the truth if we regard its unsound portions as based on a perverted intuition, and anticipate that it will be finally absorbed in that science to which the intuition in its original relation properly belongs. If, for example, it should ultimately be made manifest that to the material world we have no relation except through the various phenomena of sense, but that in the mental world Self, as well as the phenomena of self, is an immediate presentation of consciousness, it will follow that in the former we have no ground for maintaining the existence of things other than the phenomena presented; and that consequently, in this department, Ontology, as distinct from Phenomenology, is occupied solely with chimeras of our own invention: whereas, Psychology, being called upon to extend its inquiries from the phenomena of self to that of which they are phenomena, will legitimately include the remaining portion of those problems which have hitherto been appropriated to Metaphysics.

But this question cannot be discussed here. My present concern is only with the relation supposed to exist between Metaphysics, as above described, and Logic. In the earlier form of Metaphysics, which prevailed from Aristotle to Kant, an intimate connection was supposed to exist between the two sciences. The Principles of Contradiction and Excluded Middle, which have been exhibited in a former chapter as Laws of Thought, are found in the metaphysical as well as in the logical writings of Aristotle;[1] and the former, together with that of Sufficient Reason, is placed by Wolf, the immediate predecessor of Kant, at the head of Ontology.[2] But, after the Kantian Critique, this association was no longer possible. Kant showed clearly that, without synthetical judgments *à priori*, Metaphysical science is impossible; and this at once put an end to all attempts which had hitherto been made to elicit a science of Being from the laws of formal thinking, which are the foundation of Logic. The two sciences, thus divorced, become apparently united again in the system of Hegel; but the union is apparent only. For the Hegelian Logic is

[1] For the principle of Contradiction see Arist. *Metaph.* iii. 3, x. 5; *Anal. Pr.* ii. 2; *Anal. Post.* i. 11. For that of Excluded Middle, see *Metaph.* iii. 7, ix. 4; *Anal. Pr.* i. 1; *Anal. Post.* i. 2, ii. 13. They may also be traced to Plato. See *Phædo,* p. 103; *Republic,* iv. p. 436; *Sophist,* pp. 250, 252. They are given more explicitly in the *Second Alcibiades,* p. 139; but this dialogue is generally considered spurious.

[2] Cf. Wolf, *Ontologia,* §§ 27, 29, 56, 71, 498.

based, not on an acknowledgment, but on a defiance of the Laws of Thought. It is a Logic of the Reason, of which the fundamental position is, that the Laws of the Understanding are applicable to finite objects only, and that Thought in relation to the infinite is free from their dominion. Logic thus returns, as regards its object, not to the Aristotelian Analytic, but to the Platonic Dialectic, as a science of the Real and the Absolute; though the method pursued is opposed to Plato as much as to Aristotle.[1] On the other hand, in proportion as we adhere more closely to the formal view of Logic, the separation of that science from Metaphysics becomes more complete. An eminent advocate of that view, who is far from adopting Kant's opinion of the impossibility of Metaphysics, expresses his conviction of the very different objects and methods of the two sciences, by likening the union of Metaphysics and Logic to a lecture on the Integral Calculus and the Rule of Three.[2] And there is much truth implied in this somewhat overstrained comparison. With formal Logic, Metaphysics stands rather in opposition than in connection. The former is the science of the ultimate laws of the thinking subject; the latter, of the ultimate realities of the objects about which we think.

Metaphysical inquiry, if capable of a successful prosecution, may furnish a criticism or explanation of certain forms of thought assumed by Logic; for a form of thought implies a certain relation between given objects, — a relation which might be further elucidated if the nature of objects in general could be satisfactorily determined. Thus we have seen that the form of logical judgments and rea-

[1] On the contrast between the methods of Plato and Hegel, see Trendelenburg, *Logische Untersuchungen*, i. p. 89.

[2] Herbart, *Lehrbuch zur Philosophie*, *Vorrede zur zweiten Ausgabe*.

sonings contains by implication those negative notions of substance and cause, the investigation of which is the special object of metaphysical inquiries. The science of Metaphysics, therefore, if it could be constructed on a solid basis, would furnish a criticism of those principles which are tacitly acknowledged in every mental process. But, for the purposes of formal Logic, such a criticism is not needed. It is sufficient for that science to accept the principles in the obscure form in which they are acknowledged by common thought and common language; especially as, being indifferently implied in sound and unsound thinking, they furnish no criterion by which we can distinguish the one from the other.

This view is confirmed by the history of philosophy down to the present time. While Logic, from the days of Aristotle, has been in possession of a scientific method and a definite contents, whose truth, whatever opinion may be entertained of their utility, no critic has succeeded in impugning; Metaphysics has, from the same period, been equally conspicuous as the changing Proteus of philosophy, whose concealed wisdom, sought after by ceaseless efforts of strength and countless varieties of artifice, has invariably eluded the inquiries of his worshippers. The union of the two, so far from contributing to the scientific completeness of the former, has only served to mar its beauty and simplicity by extralogical details, and to misrepresent its true purpose and value by obscure intimations of deeper mysteries lying hid beneath its apparent surface. On the other hand, in proportion as the true character of Logic as a science has become better known and appreciated, it has gradually been separated from Metaphysics, and been associated with Psychology. As the science of the laws of thought, it is absurd to expect that its object and character can be rightly estimated by those who are unacquainted with the nature and powers of the understanding itself, — with its relation to the cognate faculties and operations of the human mind, — with its legitimate province and duties. It is only in this connection that we can hope to see Logic finally freed from the unsightly excrescences with which it has hitherto been deformed, yet still retaining a clearly defined portion of valuable scientific truth, and cultivated in a spirit of enlightened appreciation and criticism, equally removed from the blind veneration of the idolater and the blind hostility of the iconoclast. It is only in this connection that the boundaries of the two sciences can be clearly marked out, and those portions of psychological matter and phraseology whose random introduction has contributed so much to deface and obscure the pages of logical treatises, can become of inestimable value as part and parcel of a cognate and complementary, but by no means identical study. And if, in this association, it becomes necessary to abase considerably the once towering ambition of the Art of Arts and Science of Sciences, the loss is more than compensated by the substitution of a humbler indeed, but more attainable and more serviceable aim, — the knowledge of the distinct provinces to be assigned to Thought and Experience respectively, of the true value of each within its province, and its worse than uselessness beyond; — the knowledge of ourselves and our faculties, of our true intellectual wealth, the nature of its tenure, and the conditions of its lawful increase. By such cultivation alone can we hope to see Logic finally exhibited in its true character, and estimated at its true value; neither encumbered with fictitious wealth by a spurious utilitarianism, nor unprofitably buried in the earth of an isolated and barren formalism.

APPENDIX.

APPENDIX.

Note A, p. 84.

It is much to be regretted that Dr. Whewell, who has made good use of Kantian principles in many parts of his "Philosophy of the Inductive Sciences," has not more accurately observed Kant's distinction between the necessary laws under which all men think, and the contingent laws under which certain men think of certain things. His neglect of this distinction has given a seeming advantage to the empirical arguments of his antagonist, Mr. Mill, who is thus enabled apparently to decide the question at issue by what is in reality no more than an *argumentum ad hominem*. Thus Dr. Whewell says, of certain discoveries of physical laws, "So complete has been the victory of truth in most of these instances, that at present we can hardly imagine the struggle to have been necessary. The very essence of these triumphs is that they lead us to regard the views we reject as not only false, but inconceivable." In this relation, it is obvious that the inconceivability is, with reference to the human mind, merely contingent, and relative to the particular studies of particular men. Before the days of Copernicus, men could not conceive the apparent motion of the sun on the heliocentric hypothesis: the progress of science has reversed the difficulty; but the progress of science itself is contingent on the will of certain men to apply themselves to it. By thus endeavoring to exalt inductive laws of matter into *à priori* laws of mind, Dr. Whewell has unintentionally contributed to give an undue plausibility to the opposite theory, which reduces all laws of mind into the mere associations of this or that material experience.

But, on psychological grounds, it would seem as if the point of separation between *à priori* principles and empirical generalizations ought not to be very difficult of determination. The difference is not one of degree, but of kind; and the separation between the two classes of truths is such that no conceivable progress of science can ever convert the one into the other.

That which is inconceivable, not accidentally from the peculiar circumstances of certain men, but universally to all, must be so in consequence of an original law of the human mind; that which is universally true within the field of experience indicates an original law of the material world. No transformation of the one into the other is possible, unless the progress of science can change mind to matter or matter to mind. It is therefore incumbent on the philosopher who would extend mathematical certainty to the domain of physical science, to confirm, in every instance, his theory by a psychological deduction of his principles, as Kant has done in the instances of Space and Time.

Dr. Whewell lays much stress on *clearness and distinctness of conceptions* as the basis of the axiomatic truths of physical science. But the clearness or distinctness of any conception can only enable us more accurately to unfold the virtual contents of the concept itself; it cannot enable us to add *à priori* any new attribute. In other words, the increased clearness and distinctness of a conception may enable us to multiply to any extent our analytical judgments, but cannot add a single synthetical one. Without something more than this, the philosopher has failed to meet the touchstone of the Kantian question: *How are synthetical judgments à priori possible?*

The spirit of Dr. Whewell's Philosophy of the Inductive Sciences is beyond all praise. In these days of Positivism and Empiricism it is refreshing to find a writer of such vast attainments in the details of physical science comprising them under such truly philosophical principles. But it is to be regretted that the accuracy of his theory has been in some instances vitiated by a stumble on the threshold of the Critical Philosophy. The distinction laid down by Kant between the synthetical, or, properly, geometrical, and the analytical or general axioms, seems to have been altogether overlooked. Thus, almost at the outset of the Philosophy of the Inductive Sciences, the analytical judgment, "If equals are added to equals, the wholes are equal," is given as a condition of the intuition of magnitudes;[1] and the same oversight runs through the Essay on Mathematical Reasoning, in which he speaks of "self-evident principles, not derived in any immediate manner from experiment, but involved in the *very nature of the conceptions* which we must possess, in order to reason upon such subjects at all." The very nature of the conceptions, however clearly apprehended, can give rise only to analytical judgments.

And such, I think, may be shown to be the character of all the mechanical axioms derived from the idea of *Force*. Of force, apart from the conscious exertion of will, we have no positive conception *per se;* we know

[1] Book ii. ch. ix.

it only by its effects. Of equal forces we have no positive conception beyond that of the production of equal effects. To assert, therefore, that equal forces will balance each other at the two extremities of a lever, is to assert no more than that effects universally equal will be equal in any particular case.[1]

But to establish Mechanics as an *à priori* science upon the idea of force, it will be necessary to commence with some axioms at least of a synthetical character, analogous to the geometrical principles, "Two straight lines cannot enclose a space;" or, "If a straight line meets two straight lines, so as to make the two interior angles on the same side together less than two right angles, the two straight lines will meet if produced."

As a matter of fact, I do not think that Dr. Whewell has hitherto succeeded in establishing, in the science of Mechanics, a system of *à priori* synthetical truths derived from the idea of force as distinct from those which are mere applications of the mathematical intuitions of time or space. But as regards mere hypothetical mechanics, such a system is not inconceivable. A more exact psychological analysis of the intuitive fac-

[1] We must distinguish between the general theoretical statement of this axiom and its practical application to any given object. In Geometry, the axiom, "If equals are added to equals the wholes are equal," is a mere analytical judgment derived from the principle of Identity; but to ascertain whether two given magnitudes are equal, is a question of experiment or observation. So in Mechanics, the axiom that bodies acting with equal forces to turn a lever in opposite directions will retain it in equilibrium, is analytical; and as thus stated, it is unnecessary to add either that the directions of both forces must be perpendicular, or the arms of the lever equal. But in any special application of the axiom there arises at once the question, How can we ascertain that any two given forces are equal *as forces acting upon the lever?* If the force, for example, be gravity, and two equal weights be suspended, one perpendicularly, the other obliquely, the whole weight of the latter does not act to turn the lever in opposition to the former, and the hypothesis of the axiom is violated; the forces not being in that relation equal. Or if both are suspended perpendicularly, but at unequal distances from the fulcrum, the moments, or forces in relation to the lever, are not equal. The axiom, as stated by Dr. Whewell, "If two equal forces act *perpendicularly* at the extremities of *equal* arms of a straight line," has the appearance of a synthetical judgment, by comprehending under one formula the mere analysis of the notion of equal forces, and the empirical determination of equality in any particular instance. If by *equal forces* is meant forces equal in effect on the lever, the axiom, as stated by Dr. Whewell, is tautological; if the meaning is, forces equal in their effects in *some other situation*, the axiom is empirical only, and not even universally true. But, except by its effect in *some situation or other*, what test have we of the magnitude of a force?

ulties may possibly establish the existence of other subjective conditions of intuition besides those of space and time, and, consequently, of other synthetical judgments *à priori* besides those of Geometry and Arithmetic.[1] But when the same theory comes to be applied, not to hypothetical rigid bodies without weight, but to the actual phenomena of natural agents, as in the "Demonstration that all matter is heavy," and, verbally at least, in speaking of the *inconceivability* of the pre-Copernican astronomy, we see at once that the boundary is overleaped which separates the necessary laws of thought from the generalized phenomena of matter. This absolute boundary is sufficiently marked. *No matter of fact can, in any possible state of human knowledge, be a matter of demonstration.*[2] Nay, even supposing such a demonstration possible, it would not add one tittle to the evidence of the fact, as such, in the eyes of any one but an egoist. By him it would be accepted as an additional proof that what are commonly considered as phenomena of the *non-ego*, are really only modifications of the percipient mind, and governed solely by mental laws. But to the Realist it would at most only suggest the possibility of a preëstablished harmony between the laws of mind and matter, — a suggestion which would require, in every special case, to be verified by the empirical examination of the latter. Mental laws, which alone determine conceivability, are primarily operative only on mental objects, and are applicable to external things only on the hypothesis of their conformity. This hypothesis can only be verified empirically. That every triangle, for example, has its angles equal to two right angles, is strictly true only of the perfect triangle as contemplated by the mind. That this bit of paper lying before me has its angles equal to two right angles, is only true on the supposition of its being a perfect triangle; and the truth of this supposition, in any possible state of perfection of human senses and instruments, can only be determined empirically. It remains always *conceivable* that there may be an error in the measurement, and that the paper may not have exactly two right angles. The probability of such an error may be diminished to any degree, according to the perfection of our means of measurement; but no approximation of this kind can ever become absolute certainty.

It is not without some hesitation that I have ventured thus far to criticize a work which I believe to be, in its whole spirit and conception, by far the most valuable contribution of modern times to the philosophy of the physical sciences. To those who would survey this branch of knowl-

1 *Personality* may perhaps be specified as another condition of this kind, and the *à priori* principles of morals as consequent upon it. On this I have remarked at greater length in the Bampton Lectures, Lects. III. and VII.

2 Compare Hume, *Essay on the Academical Philosophy*, Part ii.

edge in a sound philosophical spirit, alike removed from the idealism of Schelling and from the positivism of Comte, the writings of Dr. Whewell are especially valuable. To those who believe, with the present writer, that the future hopes of speculative philosophy rest on the possibility of a union of the critical principles of Kant with the sober practical spirit which is characteristic of English thinkers, the writings of the same author afford one of the most cheering assurances that the spirit of philosophy, under all its discouragements, is not yet extinct in this country. With this declaration, the spirit that has dictated the preceding criticism will not, I trust, be misunderstood.[1]

Note B, p. 128.

That Berkeley was fully aware of the inconsequence of the conclusions which Hume afterwards attempted to draw from his principles, is manifest from the third Dialogue between Hylas and Philonous, in which he meets by anticipation the argument of the skeptic,[2] by maintaining that we are directly conscious of our own being. He is wrong, indeed, in calling this consciousness *Reflection;* this term being properly applicable only to attention directed to our internal phenomena; — an attention which does not make known, but presupposes, the attending self. But when he asserts, "I know or am conscious of my own being; and that I myself am not my ideas, but somewhat else, a thinking, active principle, that perceives, knows, wills, and operates about ideas," he states the true ground on which we may refute the skeptical conclusions of Hume. Indeed, this part of the Dialogue wants little more than a more complete

1 The preceding note remains nearly as it appeared in the first edition of this work, published in 1851. Since that time, some additional remarks on the matter in question have appeared in Sir William Hamilton's *Discussions*, p. 323 (second edition, p. 335), in Dr. Whewell's *Letter to the Author of Prolegomena Logica*, and in the Author's pamphlet in reply, entitled, *The Limits of Demonstrative Science considered.* Sir W. Hamilton's view is substantially the same as my own; and I cannot help regarding this independent coïncidence as a confirmation of my original criticism. At the same time I feel bound to express my acknowledgments to Dr. Whewell for the instruction which his Letter has afforded me, and for the liberal and courteous tone in which his objections are urged.

2 This part of Berkeley's Dialogue is meant as an answer to Locke, *Essay*, B. II. ch. 23, § 5, but the same reasoning is also valid against Hume.

exposition of the nature of the will to anticipate in principle the position afterwards taken against the great skeptic by Maine de Biran.

The weak side of Berkeley's Idealism is not to be found in its relation to Hume, but in its relation to Fichte. The object proposed by Berkeley was to get rid of the contradictions and difficulties contained in the notion of matter as existing distinct from mind, and thus to leave the existence of minds, divine and human, beyond question. For this purpose he availed himself of two arguments, one of which was borrowed from the Cartesian philosophy, the other was added by himself.

The Cartesians, denying the possibility of any direct influence of matter upon mind or of mind upon matter, explained the phenomena of perception by the hypothesis of Divine Assistance and Occasional Causes. According to this theory, the mental phenomena of sensation are not produced by any direct action of body upon mind, but by the immediate agency of God, who produces certain sensations in the conscious mind, upon the occasion of certain corresponding movements in the bodily organism.[1] Berkeley, while denying the existence of matter, and therefore rejecting the supposition of a bodily occasional cause, retained the Cartesian theory so far as to maintain that the presence of ideas in the mind is caused by the direct agency of the Deity. Thus he says, "When in broad daylight I open my eyes, it is not in my power to choose whether I shall see or no, or to determine what particular objects shall present themselves to my view; and so likewise as to the hearing and other senses; the ideas imprinted on them are not creatures of my will. There is, *therefore, some other will or spirit* that *produces them.*"[2]

With this argument, which represents God as the efficient cause of our ideas, Berkeley combined another, in which the Deity is regarded as a constantly perceiving mind. Accepting, as allowed on all hands, the opinion that sensible qualities cannot subsist by themselves, and rejecting the ordinary hypothesis of their existence in an insensible substratum, he concluded that they must therefore exist in a mind which perceives them, and that they have no existence apart from being perceived. If, therefore,

1 This theory is hinted at by Descartes, *Principia*, l. ii. § 36, and more fully elaborated by De la Forge, *Traité de l'esprit de l'homme*, ch. xvi.; Malebranche, *Recherche de la Vérité*, l. vi. p. ii. ch. 3; *Entretiens sur la Metaphysique*, Ent. vii. Compare Laromiguière, *Leçons de Philosophie*, p. ii. l. 9, and Hamilton, *Lectures on Metaphysics*, p. 208.

2 *Principles of Human Knowledge*, § xxix. Compare §§ lvii. lxii. In § liii. he expressly refers to some modern philosophers, *i. e.*, the Cartesians, as agreeing with him in making God the immediate cause of all things.

they continue to exist when *we* do not perceive them (and that they do so is the irresistible conviction of all men), they must be perceived by some other mind. Hence the continuous duration of things implies the existence of a constantly percipient mind; that is, of God.[1]

The relation between the divine and the human mind, as thus conceived, may be adapted either to a *presentative* or to a *representative* theory of idealism. We may hold that the ideas perceived at any particular time by a given man are numerically one with those constantly perceived by the Divine Mind; or we may regard them as having only a specific identity, the former being the copy, and the latter the archetype. Under the first hypothesis, the divine ideas are *presented* to us as the direct objects of our perception; under the second, they are *represented* by similar ideas excited in ourselves. The former theory, though susceptible of various developments in detail, is in principle that of Vision in God, and is accordingly distinctly maintained by Malebranche, who asserts that a thousand men can see the same individual object, namely, the intelligible extension which is perceived in God.[2] Berkeley, by rejecting the theory of Malebranche, was logically driven to the representative hypothesis, though his language occasionally wavers between the two.[3]

But to make this hypothesis the foundation of a theistic argument, it is necessary to retain, as Berkeley in fact did retain, the supposition of a real distinction between the idea or object perceived and the mind perceiving. The idea, though existing only as perceived and in the act of perception, must yet not be identified with that act, nor regarded as a mere modification or mode of being of the percipient mind. If this simpler form of representationism be once adopted, the legitimate inference is not Theism, but Pantheism. The ideas of which I am conscious being admitted to exist only as modes of my own being, it is concluded, by parity of reasoning, that the archetypal world exists only in the form of various modes of the being of God.

1 *Principles of Human Knowledge*, §§ xc. xci.; *Second Dialogue between Hylas and Philonous*, *sub init.*

2 See his *Réponse au Livre des vraies et des fausses Idées*, ch. xiii.

3 I must acknowledge my obligations to Professor Webb, the author of "The Intellectualism of Locke," both for the instruction derived from his able and interesting work, and also for some unpublished communications on Berkeley's philosophy, of which I have availed myself in revising this note for the present edition. At the same time I am unable to agree with him in regarding Locke's and Berkeley's theory of ideas as identical with that of Arnauld, in which the representative idea is regarded as a modification of the mind. Indeed, in Berkeley's system the relation of substance and mode has properly no place.

And such is in fact the form which Idealism assumes in the hands of Fichte and Schelling. The theory of *perceptions essentially representative*, which virtually regards the act and its immediate object as produced by the inherent power of the mind itself, was not, in Arnauld's hands, carried into any consequences beyond those required by his controversy with Malebranche. But a similar theory in the hands of the German philosophers became the basis, first, of an absolute Egoism, and finally, of an absolute Pantheism. Consciousness being only possible in the form of this or that special modification, it is but one step further to regard the true substance as an unmodified substratum existing out of consciousness, though manifested only in the consciousness of its several modes. We have thus the Absolute Ego of Fichte, and, by a still further generalization, the Absolute Being of Schelling, which, as the one substance from which personal and impersonal phenomena alike proceed, may indifferently be called Ego or God; the conscious self and the objects of its consciousness being but opposite modes of the Divine One and All.

Nor will the Idealism of Berkeley, however opposed to these conclusions, offer any effectual barrier against them. The distinction between ideas existing as objects in the mind, and ideas existing as modes of the mind, is too slight to stand against that tendency to simplification which forms at once the chief virtue and the chief vice of philosophical speculation. The natural judgment of mankind, which affirms the knowledge of an external world existing independently of perception, being once abandoned, the only question which remains is, how to account for the phenomena on the simplest hypothesis. And the simplest hypothesis is that which postulates only one real existence underlying the multiplicity of phenomena, the hypothesis whose various subordinate theories all finally converge in Pantheism.

These consequences can only be avoided by abandoning the Idealistic theory, and substituting a Natural Realism, Dualism though it be. Admit, with Berkeley, that the real things are those very things which I see and feel and perceive by my senses; but deny his other main position, that the mind perceives only its own ideas. We may thus open the way for the direct recognition in consciousness, first of our own organism as extended, and secondly of an external world in relation to that organism.[1] On this theory we may get rid of the metaphysical distinction between *phenomena* and *noumena*, or between *representations* and *things in themselves*. The immediate object of perception is *the thing;* and the *representation* is not opposed to the unperceived *thing in itself*, but to the *presentation*, or thing as given in immediate relation to the conscious subject.

1 See Sir W. Hamilton's edition of *Reid's Works*, Notes D and D*.

Another weak point of Berkeley's philosophy is his theory of the nature of Belief. He considers that real things differ from chimeras in being more vivid and clear, and not dependent on the will. This accords with Hume's definition of Belief, "A lively idea, related to or associated with a present impression." But the will is completely inactive in a dream; and phantasms may be as lively and vivid when excited by a fiction as by a true relation. The truth is that Belief cannot be defined, being presupposed in all consciousness. Every act of consciousness is a judgment, and therefore a belief in the presence of its object: the question of reality or unreality depends upon *where* and *how* we judge it to be present. If an object present to the imagination is declared to be present to the sense, the judgment is false; but the object is *unreal* only if by *real* we mean *sensible*. All presentations, as such, may be called real relatively to their proper intuition, and unreal relatively to any other. The further question, which of our intuitions indicate the presence of external objects, and which are merely affections of the mind or the sensitive organism, is one which, however important on the realist hypothesis, is out of place in a system of idealism.[1]

Note C, p. 131.

The following is Sir William Hamilton's analysis of the causal judgment, as the result of the mental law of the conditioned. "The phenomenon is this: — When aware of a new appearance, we are *unable* to conceive that therein has originated any new existence, and are, therefore, *constrained* to think that what now appears to us under a new form had previously an existence under others, — others conceivable by us or not. These *others* (for they are always plural) are called its cause; and a cause (or, more properly, causes) we cannot but suppose; for a cause is simply every thing without which the effect would not result; and all such concurring, the effect cannot but result. We are utterly unable to construe it in thought as possible that the complement of existence has been either increased or diminished. We cannot conceive, either, on the one hand, nothing becoming something, or, on the other, something becoming nothing. When God is said to create the universe out of nothing, we think this by supposing that he evolves the universe out of nothing but himself; and, in

1 For some remarks on this question, see the Author's article *Metaphysics*, in the eighth edition of the *Encyclopædia Britannica*, p. 613.

like manner, we conceive annihilation only by conceiving the creator to withdraw his creation, by withdrawing his creative energy from actuality into power."

"Our judgment of causality," he continues, "simply is: — We necessarily deny, or, rather, are unable to affirm in thought, that the object which we apprehend as beginning to be, really so begins; but, on the contrary, affirm, as we must, the identity of its present sum of being with the sum of its past existence. And here it is not requisite for us to know, or even to be able to conceive, under what form or under what combination this quantum previously existed; in other words, it is unnecessary for us to recognize the particular causes of this particular effect. A discovery of the determinate antecedents into which a determinate consequent may be refunded, is merely contingent, — merely the result of experience; but the judgment that every event should have its causes, is necessary, and imposed on us as a condition of our human intelligence itself. *This necessity of so thinking is the only phenomenon to be explained.* The question of philosophy is not concerning *the* cause, but concerning *a* cause." [1]

Such is Sir W. Hamilton's statement of the phenomenon. The following is his explanation of it.

"The phenomenon of Causality seems nothing more than a corollary of the law of the Conditioned, in its application to a thing thought under the form or mental category of *Existence Relative in Time.* We cannot know, we cannot think a thing, except under the attribute of *Existence;* we cannot know or think a thing to exist, except as *in Time;* and we cannot know or think a thing to exist in Time, and think it *absolutely to commence or terminate.* Now this at once imposes on us the judgment of causality. Unable positively to think an absolute commencement, our impotence to this drives us backwards on the notion of *Cause;* unable positively to think an absolute termination, our impotence to this drives us forwards on the notion of *Effect.*" "We are compelled," he continues, "to believe that the object (that is, the certain *quale* and *quantum* of being whose *phenomenal* rise into existence we have witnessed) did *really* exist, prior to this rise, under other forms (and by *form,* be it observed, I mean any mode of existence, conceivable by us or not). But to say that a thing previously existed under different forms, is only to say in other words that *a thing had causes.* (It would be here out of place to refute the error of philosophers in supposing that anything can have a *single* cause; — meaning always by a cause that without which the effect would not have been. I speak of course only of second causes, for of the Divine causation we can pretend to no conception.") [2]

1 *Discussions*, pp. 609, 610 (2d edition). 2 *Discussions*, pp. 618, 621.

To these extracts from Sir W. Hamilton's *Discussions* may be added a short passage from the Appendix to his *Lectures on Metaphysics*, containing his latest explanation of his theory.[1] "Causation is, therefore, necessarily *within* existence; for we cannot think of a change either from non-existence to existence, or from existence to non-existence. The thought of power, therefore, always precedes that of creation, and follows that of annihilation; and as the thought of power always involves the thought of existence, therefore, in so far as the thoughts of creation and annihilation go, the necessity of thinking a cause for these changes exemplifies the facts, — that change is only from one form of existence to another, and that causation is simply our inability to think an absolute commencement or an absolute termination of being. The sum of being (actual and potential) now extant in the mental and material worlds, together with that in their Creator, and the sum of being (actual and potential) in the Creator alone, before and after those worlds existed, is necessarily thought as precisely the same. Take the instance of a neutral salt. This is an effect, the product of various causes, — and all are necessarily powers. We have here, 1. an acid involving its power (active or passive) of combining with the alkali; 2. an alkali, involving its power (active or passive) of combining with the acid; 3. (since, as the chemical brocard has it, 'Corpora non agunt nisi soluta') a fluid, say water, with its power of dissolving and holding in solution the acid and alkali; 4. a translative power, say the human hand, capable of bringing the acid, the alkali, and the water, into correlation, or within the sphere of mutual affinity. These (and they might be subdivided) are all causes of the effect; for, abstract any one, and the salt is not produced. It wants a coëfficient cause, and the concurrence of every cause is requisite for an effect."

In describing the above four conditions as all in different ways *causes* of the effect, Sir W. Hamilton will probably meet with the concurrence of most of his readers; but the further statement, that these causes are all forms under which the effect previously existed, will probably strike them as being at least verbally different from the common view. Most men would readily admit that the acid, and the alkali, and the portion of water necessary for combining them, are but previous forms of the salt itself; but they would hesitate to admit the hand or its action into the same list. In other words, they would allow that the earlier and the later substances are identical in the material particles of which they are composed; but they would insist on distinguishing these particles from the efficient cause by which the composition is effected. But when the identity is stated in this way, the judgment assumes a totally new character. Whether it be

[1] Page 690.

true or not that we cannot conceive the quantity of *existence* to be increased or diminished, there is at any rate no such inability as regards the quantity of *matter*. It may be true as a fact that no material atom has been added to the world since the first creation; but the assertion, however true, is certainly not necessary. The power which created once must be conceived as able to create again, whether that ability is actually exercised or not.

The same conclusion is still more evident when we proceed from the consideration of matter to that of mind. Of matter we maintain that the creation of new portions is perfectly conceivable, as a result at least, if not as a process; of mind we believe that such creation actually takes place. Every man who comes into the world comes into it as a distinct individual, having a personality and consciousness of his own; and that personality is a distinct accession to the number of persons previously existing. Whatever may be thought concerning the material particles of which my body is composed, it cannot be maintained that I, as a person, had a previous existence in the personality of my parents, however I may regard them as the causes of my being.

If, then, we are to identify the effect with the sum of its causes, we must rise above the conceptions of matter as matter and of mind as mind, and rise to the highest abstraction of existence in general, which is not any particular existence. "The sum of being (actual and potential) now extant in the mental and material worlds, together with that in their Creator, and the sum of being (actual and potential) in the Creator alone, before and after those worlds existed, is necessarily thought as precisely the same." This assertion involves a previous question: Is Being in this abstract form necessarily thought as a *sum* at all, or indeed necessarily thought in any way?

It is admitted that we not only can conceive, but actually know by experience, the origination of new *forms* of existence: it is questioned whether these forms are regarded as new existences. But strip off the form, and what is left to constitute the existence? The world, as a world, is not identical with its Creator; the Creator, as a Creator, is not identical with the world. The identity, if it is admitted at all, can only be admitted as regards an unmodified substratum of existence in general, which is no existence in particular. But existence, as an abstract substratum of this kind, is to human thought absolute zero: thus far the Hegelian paradox is true; pure being is pure nothing. When we have abstracted from the world all that distinguishes it as a world, and from the Creator all that distinguishes him as a Creator, we have nothing left to constitute the identity of existence. From the mere general statement that cause and effect both exist, we have no more right to say that they are the same existence, than, from the general statement that they both appear, we have a right to say that they are the same phenomenon.

Our conception of existence, as of appearance, is not singular, but plural. We are not conscious of existence in general, but of existing things; as we are not conscious of appearance in general, but of apparent objects. The two may not indeed be always regarded as coëxtensive. Diversity of phenomena does not always imply diversity of existence; but neither, on the other hand, does it always imply identity of existence. The primary fact of consciousness, the distinction between the *ego* and the *non-ego*, is a distinction, not of phenomena, but of realities. I know myself as a distinctly existing being; — indeed, it is probably from that knowledge that my conception of *being*, as distinguished from *appearance*, is derived; — and I know the external world as something different from myself. Arguing by analogy from this primary conviction, I believe every man to be a distinct being from every other man and from all the other objects around him; and I believe that every new person that comes into the world is, as a person, a new existence. How far the same distinction may be extended to impersonal objects is another question; for in these we have no immediate knowledge of any *principium individuationis*, constituting a single reality out of this or that aggregate of phenomena. But if we are unable to affirm the existence of such a principle, we are also unable to deny it; and hence we are not justified in asserting that all phenomena are but different modes of one and the same reality.

From this point of view, the conception of *potential existence*, on which Sir W. Hamilton's theory mainly depends, vanishes altogether. If our conception of existence, like all other conceptions, is subject to the conditions of plurality and difference, — if we have no conception of being at all except in the form of this being as distinguished from that, — it follows that, where the definite characteristics of this or that being are absent, the being itself has no existence in any form. The mere possibility of the existence of a man is not the existence of a man under another form; for the man, as such, has no existence except in the particular form by which he is actually constituted. To say that everything which begins had a previous existence in another form, is to say that the form is no part of the existence; — a position which necessarily leads us back to the Eleatic theory of the unity of all things, and identifies Existence with Indifference.

If these objections are tenable, the common statement of the causal judgment, in which the cause is regarded as something different from the effect, is more accurate, and more in accordance with the philosophy of the Conditioned, than that of Sir W. Hamilton, in which the cause is regarded as identical with the effect. Both statements equally repudiate the absurdity of supposing existence to have originated from absolute zero; for both alike suppose that nothing can begin to exist unless something had previously existed. The question between them is merely this: Is this *something* a different existence, or only the same existence in another form?

Neither on the one supposition nor on the other do we obtain any positive conception of the nature of Causation, beyond that which is furnished by, and limited to our own volitions. Mere temporal antecedence of one thing to another is not the whole of causation, any more than the mere antecedence of the same thing under other forms. We are compelled still to ask, what is that peculiar relation between antecedent and consequent, by which the one gives birth to the other, or is changed into the other? The origination of the consequent by the antecedent, and the evolution of the actual from the potential, alike require a further cause to account for them; and this causative energy, call it by what name you will, — *power, effort, tendency;* — still remains absolutely unknown, but is still supposed as absolutely indispensable.

NOTE D, p. 143.

The following is Mr. Mill's argument for the subjection of the human will to the law of physical causation: "To the universality which mankind are agreed in ascribing to the Law of Causation, there is one claim of exception, one disputed case, that of the Human Will; the determinations of which a large class of metaphysicians are not willing to regard as following the causes called motives, according to as strict laws as those which they suppose to exist in the world of mere matter. This controverted point will undergo a special examination when we come to treat particularly of the Logic of the Moral Sciences. In the mean time I may remark, that those metaphysicians who, it must be observed, ground the main part of their objection upon the supposed repugnance of the doctrine in question to our consciousness, seem to me to mistake the fact which consciousness testifies against. What is really in contradiction to consciousness, they would, I think, on strict self-examination, find to be the application to human actions and volitions of the ideas involved in the common use of the term Necessity; which I agree with them in thinking highly objectionable. But if they would consider that by saying that a man's actions *necessarily* follow from his character, all that is really meant (for no more is meant in any case whatever of causation) is that he invariably *does* act in conformity to his character, and that any one who thoroughly knew his character could certainly predict how he would act in any supposable case; they probably would not find this doctrine either contrary to their experience or revolting to their feelings. And no more than this is contended for by any one but an Asiatic fatalist."[1]

And no more than this, we might add, is needed to construct a system of fatalism as rigid as any Asiatic can desire. But we must proceed to Mr. Mill's further remarks in the Logic of the Moral Sciences. In this latter portion of his work, the author has done little more than repeat his belief that the law of causality applies in the same strict sense to human actions as to other phenomena, involving in both cases, not constraint, but "invariable, certain, and unconditional sequence;" so that, "given the motives which are present to an individual's mind, and given likewise the character and disposition of the individual, the manner in which he will act may be unerringly inferred: that if we knew the person thoroughly, and knew all the inducements which are acting upon him, we could foretell his conduct with as much certainty as we can predict any physical event." He adds a distinction, intended to rescue his theory from the charge of fatalism, as usually implied in the term Necessity. "That word, in its other acceptations, involves much more than mere uniformity of sequence; it implies irresistibleness. Applied to the will, it only means that the given cause will be followed by the effect, subject to all possibilities of counteraction by other causes; but in common use it stands for the operation of those causes exclusively which are supposed too powerful to be counteracted at all." "The causes, therefore," he continues, "on which action depends, are never uncontrollable; and any given effect is only necessary provided that the causes tending to produce it are not controlled. That whatever happens could not have happened otherwise, unless something had taken place which was capable of preventing it, no one surely needs hesitate to admit."[2]

That there is some fundamental weakness in the above theory, appears almost on the surface, from the fact that so acute a thinker as Mr. Mill can imagine that he has saved the principle of causality from the charge of fatalism by this concluding sentence. That whatever happens could not have happened otherwise, *unless something had taken place capable of preventing it*, is indeed in one sense a perfectly harmless position, but also a perfectly unproductive one. It is the mere truism of the Nursery Rhyme:

1 Mill's *Logic*, vol. i. p. 419. 2 Mill's *Logic*, book vi. chap. 2.

"There was an old woman lived under a hill,
And *if she 's not gone*, she lives there still."

Examine it closer, and the question at once arises, Whence is this counteracting *something* to come? If from *myself*, from a self-determined act of free will, this concedes the whole question at issue. If from an act of will determined by preëxisting causes, or altogether from without, I am still in the iron grasp of Necessity. If the preventing circumstance, come whence it may, comes as the certain sequence of antecedent phenomena, I am still the slave of circumstances; if otherwise, the whole resemblance between moral and physical causation vanishes.

But let us go up to the fundamental principle of the theory itself. The conduct of a man, we are told, is the invariable consequent of motives present to his mind; so that, given the motives and the man's character, we could certainly predict the action. *Character*, it must be observed, is not here to be understood in Aristotle's sense, as a disposition caused by a series of voluntary acts; it must be something coëval with the first act of so-called volition. At the earliest period at which I am capable of acting, I possess a character of some sort; and that character, together with the motives presented, determines certainly how I shall act.

The plausibility of the theory arises from an ambiguity in the term *motive*. In knowing the phenomena present to a man's mind at the moment of any act of volition, is it included that we are to know *their relation to his will?* If so, the supposed prediction is a mere begging of the question. When I know how he will be inclined to act, I know how he will act. If not, the advocate of the doctrine must succumb to the sophism of the *Assinus Buridani*, and concede that the unfortunate animal, between two bundles of hay exactly alike, must starve. The solution of this sophism, supposing, of course, that the ass in that instance represents a voluntary, and not merely a spontaneous agent, is likewise the solution of Mr. Mill's argument. What is meant by two bundles of hay exactly alike? They must be indistinguishable by sight, smell, touch, and so forth. But are objects exactly similar as regards the senses, therefore exactly similar as regards the will? A lump of salt and a lump of sugar may be similar to the eye: are they therefore similar to the palate? If taste is not dependent upon another sense, why may not will be independent of all the senses? If, on the other hand, the two bundles of hay are to be exactly similar, *as motives in relation to the will*, the argument amounts to the mere truism, that if the ass does not choose one he will choose neither.

Exactly the same fallacy runs through Mr. Mill's theory of the causality of actions. The so-called motives are either a set of phenomena viewed in their relation to the will, or viewed out of that relation. If the former, the argument has long ago been refuted by Reid.[1] The strongest motive prevails; but I only know the strength of motives in relation to the will by the test of ultimate prevalence; so that this means no more than that the prevailing motive prevails. I have no measure of strength but its effects. I only know certain things to be motives at all by the fact of their ultimate prevalence. If, on the other hand, the phenomena are considered out of their relation to the will, my consciousness testifies at once that my actions are not subject to the same invariable sequence as physical changes. I know, that is, whenever I lift my arm to my head, that it is at that moment in my power not to lift it; and that, the antecedent circumstances being precisely the same, I may decide not to do so at any future time. But, says Mr. Mill, this decision of the will is itself a new antecedent.[2] Certainly, a new antecedent *to the act;* but with what propriety can it be called a new antecedent *to itself?* The question is not whether the act of motion follows certainly upon that of volition, but whether the act of volition follows certainly upon antecedent circumstances. The former sequence depends on purely physical laws; and the preventing causes, such as a stroke of paralysis, are purely physical also. But if the latter sequence is invariable also, we admit, not one new phenomenon, but millions; since an opposite determination of the will can only come in with its determinant, and the determinant of that determinant, and so on, *ad infinitum.* For to suppose that two opposite volitions can follow from the same determinant is incompatible with the whole hypothesis of causality. If, on the other hand, the sequence of volition from given antecedents is variable, what becomes of the power of predicting a man's actions? The contingency of a single link affects all the subsequent portion of the chain.

In reply, then, to the question, Are our volitions, like other events, the result of causes? Certainly not, in the only intelligible senses of the term. I have only two positive notions of causation: one, the exertion of power by an intelligent being; the other, the uniform sequence of phenomenon B from A. (A may here stand for a single phenomenon, or a group; for that antecedent or sum of antecedents which constitutes the *Sufficient Reason.*) The former hypothesis is Fatalism. If my will results

1 *Active Powers*, Essay iv. ch. 4, p. 610, ed. Hamilton.

2 Mr. Mill says, "The *wish* is a new antecedent." If this term is meant to be synonymous with *will*, it would be an improvement in language to change it; if it is meant to be synonymous with desire, the confusion of desire with will vitiates his whole argument.

from the coercion of some other intelligence, I am the slave of Destiny. The latter hypothesis is Determinism, a necessity no less rigid than fatalism, besides being at variance with the whole testimony of consciousness and with the experience of every day. Besides these two, there is no alternative but to admit, in the fullest sense, the freedom of the will, by denying the applicability of the principle of causality to human actions.

"This objection, if not removed," says Mr. Mill, "would be fatal to the attempt to treat human conduct as a subject of science." Be it so. It is better to accept the consequence than to admit the alternative. But it is fatal only according to Mr. Mill's view of science. Ethology, as he conceives it, in relation to *individuals*, as the science of characters as they *must be* according to laws of physical and mental causation, I do believe to be, in its idea and pretensions, chimerical; but Ethics, as the science of such characters as they *ought to be* according to the laws of moral obligation, remains undisturbed, or, rather, more securely established. It seems to be forgotten by writers of this school that these two systems are absolutely exclusive of each other; that physical causation and moral obligation cannot in perfection exist side by side; and that where they do coëxist, each must be in the inverse ratio of the other. In proportion as we extend the domain of Necessity, we must diminish that of Duty; and Necessity, notwithstanding all that Mr. Mill has advanced, I still believe to be the inevitable result of subjecting moral acts to the laws of physical causation. But Ethology, in relation to *classes of men*, as affected by national, professional, educational, physiological, or even moral circumstances, may, notwithstanding, attain to a vast amount of important practical principles and rules, though still subject to the influence of individual contingency. The actuary of an insurance company, if he were to predict the duration of life of any one individual on the books of his office, would in all probability guess wrong; — as a matter of fact, it is true, mainly from his ignorance of physical circumstances; but as a matter of theory also, if we allow that the individual in question may falsify the prediction by a voluntary act of suicide. But if the same experiment is tried on a sufficiently large scale, opposite errors will counteract each other, and the general approximate result attains almost to a moral certainty. The general results of Ethology, as applied to classes, are dependent in a great degree on similar circumstances, and may attain to the same or a higher amount of practical utility.

In the course of the above remarks I have purposely avoided touching on a subject alluded to by Mr. Mill, the compatibility of man's free-will with God's foreknowledge. This question is insoluble, because we have nothing but negative notions to apply to it. To enable us to determine the exact manner in which an Infinite Intelligence contemplates succession in time, it would be necessary that our intelligence should be infinite also. In this, as in all other revelations of God's relation to man, we must be content to believe, without aspiring to comprehend. The fact of God's foreknowledge is all that is revealed to us: the manner He has left in darkness, and we cannot enlighten it. But we are not justified in rejecting what we can comprehend because we do not understand its possible relation to what we cannot.[1] That no conceivable amount of information could enable a being of human constitution to predict with certainty the acts of another, is established by the same evidence of consciousness by which we know that there is a human constitution at all. How far the same conclusion can be transferred to other orders of finite beings, still less to an Infinite Intelligence, we have no data for determining.

The Necessitarian theory has recently been stated anew, in two works, both of high ability and reputation, but written in very different spirits and with very different purposes. The author of the first of these works, while professedly writing in the name and in support of the principles of Necessitarianism, strenuously asserts, at the same time, the apparently opposite doctrine of the freedom of the will and the responsibility of man, and writes with the avowed purpose of reconciling these seemingly conflicting beliefs. The author of the second work pushes his principles to a conclusion which cannot be otherwise understood than as exonerating human actions from all voluntariness, and their agents from all responsibility. The former of these works, Dr. McCosh's "Method of the Divine Government," is one from which I cannot dissent without extreme reluc-

1 "Sed quia jam Deum agnoscentes, tam immensam in eo potestatem esse percipimus, ut nefas esse putemus existimare, aliquid unquam a nobis fieri posse, quod ante non ab ipso fuerit præordinatum; facile possumus nos ipsos magnis difficultatibus intricare, si hanc Dei præordinationem, cum arbitrii nostri libertate conciliare, atque utramque simul comprehendere conemur.

"Illis vero nos expediemus, si recordemur mentem nostram esse finitam; Dei autem potentiam, per quam non tantum omnia, quæ sunt aut esse possunt, ab æterno præscivit, sed etiam voluit ac præordinavit, esse infinitam: ideoque hanc qidem à nobis satis attingi, ut clare et distincte percipiamus ipsam in Deo esse; non autem satis comprehendi, ut videamus quo pacto liberas hominum actiones indeterminatas relinquat; libertatis autem et indifferentiæ quæ in nobis est, nos ita conscios esse, ut nihil sit, quod evidentius et perfectius comprehendamus. Absurdum enim esset, propterea quod non comprehendimus unam rem, quam scimus ex naturâ suâ nobis esse debere incomprehensibilem, de aliâ dubitare, quam intime comprehendimus, atque apud nosmet ipsos experimur." — Descartes, *Principia*, P. i. 40, 41.

tance, regarding it, as I do, as one of the most valuable contributions to Christian philosophy which the present age has produced. With many of the author's remarks on the present question I fully concur, and in others I am inclined to hope that the difference between us is more verbal than real. But there are some of his statements which, even if not substantially erroneous in themselves, may lead to error from their language and its associations.

Dr. McCosh takes his position, as a Necessitarian, on the ground "that the principle of cause and effect reigns in the domains of mind as in the territories of matter."[1] Thus he considers the doctrine of Necessity to be founded "on one of the very intellectual intuitions of man's mind, which leads us, in mental as in material phenomena, to anticipate the same effects to follow the same causes." Of this intellectual intuition he says, in another part of his work, "In regard to any one thought or feeling, we affirm that it must have had a cause in some property of the mind, or in some antecedent state of the mind, or in the two combined. It is by an intuition of our nature that we believe that this thought or feeling could not have been produced without a cause, and that this same cause will again and forever produce the same effects. And this intuitive principle leads us to expect the reign of causation, not only among the thoughts and feelings generally, but among the wishes and volitions of the soul."[2]

I cannot help thinking that what Dr. McCosh here describes as an intuitive principle of the mind, is in fact a combination of two principles, differing both in their nature and in their origin. That a given phenomenon, whether material or mental, "could not have been produced without a cause," is one assertion ; that "this same cause will again and forever produce the same effects," is another. Setting aside for the moment what we know empirically of the uniformity of nature, it is perfectly conceivable that the world might have been so constituted that there should be no regularity in the succession of events, but that the same cause which at one time is followed by a particular effect should at another have no such consequence. The latter portion, therefore, of Dr. McCosh's principle is not entitled to rank among the original intuitions of the mind, because, even if experience assures us that, as a matter of fact, it never *is* violated, we have no difficulty in conceiving that it *may be.*

But when the knowledge of the uniformity of nature is discarded, what remains to constitute the intuitive principle? How much or how little is implied in the mere conviction that every phenomenon must have *a cause* on the particular occasion of its occurrence, if we know nothing about

1 Appendix, p. 541. 2 p. 275.

similiarity of recurrence? In the first place, with regard to voluntary and involuntary phenomena alike, it is implied that some other phenomenon has immediately preceded. This is a necessary consequence of the subjection of our consciousness to the law of time. In the next place, with regard to voluntary actions alone, of which I am the cause, it is implied that, at the moment of doing them, I am conscious of being able to abstain from them; and this is an immediate consciousness of *power*, in the proper sense of the term. In the third place, with regard to involuntary occurrences, there is the assumption of an *unknown something* in the antecedent phenomenon analogous to the productive power in voluntary agents.[1] This unknown something, however, is not *power* in the only form in which we are conscious of it; nay, it is the direct negation of it; for power is positively conceived only in the form of ability to choose between two alternatives.[2]

It seems, then, that the apparent universality of the axiom, "Every event must have a cause," is partly due to the ambiguity of its terms. Define clearly what is meant by a *cause*, and the general axiom is at once divided into two special ones. I am the *cause* of my actions, inasmuch as I do them voluntarily, with a power at the same time to abstain from them. In this sense we cannot speak of *a cause* in relation to the phenomena of matter. It is not in this sense that the heat of the fire is *the cause* of the melting of the wax. On the other hand, in the sense in which Hume and Brown define a cause, it is applicable to material phenomena, but not to voluntary actions. *A cause*, in the sense of these philosophers, means some one invariable antecedent, or group of antecedents, the presence of which is always followed by the phenomenon in question. In this sense, it cannot be asserted that the determinations of the will have *a cause*, meaning that the will is always determined in a similar manner by the presence of similar antecedent circumstances. Or, thirdly, if we discard

1 See above, p. 134.

2 Dr. McCosh, p. 526, maintains that "power is implied in our very idea of substance," and that "this power, these properties of substances, are permanently in them, and ready to be exercised at all times." But power, in this sense, is not an idea distinct from the actual sequence of the effect; it is merely that sequence viewed hypothetically. When I speak of the *power* of fire to melt wax, that power not being in actual exercise, I mean no more than that the melting would follow if the wax were exposed to it. In this sense we know nothing of power or property except as the manifestation of an effect, hypothetical or actual. Moreover, power in this sense, as a permanent property, involves the empirical idea of the uniformity of nature as well as the mere conception of a substance as existing.

the conception of invariability, the axiom indeed becomes universal, but does not amount to an assertion of a *cause*. It then asserts positively no more than that every phenomenon has some other preceding it; *i. e.*, that no given phenomenon can be conceived as standing at the beginning of all time. The unknown something, which we term *power* in the cause to produce its effect, can neither be included in this universal assertion nor referred to an original intuition of the mind; for there can be no intuition of that which is unknown, and no universality in that which is denied of one class of actions in the only sense in which it is affirmed of another.

But it is urged on the other side that human actions can be calculated beforehand, and therefore are clearly subject to the operation of law. "We anticipate," says Dr. McCosh, "the voluntary actions of mankind, as we anticipate their judgments. No doubt we are at times mistaken in the one case as in the other in our anticipations, but we do not in these cases conclude that the voluntary actions of mankind have had no cause, any more than we infer that their judgments have had no cause; we conclude merely that we did not know the cause, and that if we had known the full cause, we could have certainly anticipated the result. There are statistics of the voluntary actions of mankind — as of crimes, for instance — which are as accurate as the laws of mortality."[1] This statement would be a sufficient answer to a theory of complete indifference, which regards the will as entirely uninfluenced by motives up to the time when its choice is made; but it does not meet the objections of those who, while fully allowing the influence of motives, yet maintain that that influence is different in its nature from any relation of material phenomena, and therefore should not be called by the same name. Doubtless there are general anticipations to be drawn from mental inclinations no less than from physical successions. If I throw a piece of wax into the fire, I expect that it will melt. If I offer money to an avaricious man, I expect that he will take it. The question is: Is the expectation in both cases equally certain? or is the difference only such as can be accounted for by our greater or less knowledge of circumstances? To assume this is to beg the entire question; and, on the strength of this assumption, to call both relations by the common name of *causation*, is only to confound together two different things under an ambiguity of language.[2]

[1] p. 276.

[2] "If in moral reasoning it be mere mockery to use the language of demonstration, and to build up systems by trains of *à priori* reasoning upon a single principle; it is assuredly not less absurd to affect the forms of inductive proof in political speculation. Every political as well as every moral principle practically involves the determination of the will, and thereby becomes at once sepa-

Dr. McCosh himself admits the existence of a *self-activity* of the will; which, if it means anything, means a power of resisting or yielding to the motives presented to it, and of resisting at one time and yielding at another, the concurrent circumstances being identical on both occasions. Is there anything similar to this in the relation of a physical cause to its effect? If not, why call two dissimilar things by the same name?[1]

In the other work to which I have above alluded, Mr. Buckle's "History of Civilization in England," the "statistics of the voluntary actions of mankind" are adduced to prove a further conclusion, which not merely subjects every moral agent to the law of causation, but apparently exempts him from all personal responsibility. Rejecting "the metaphysical dogma of free-will," as resting on the fallible testimony of consciousness, Mr. Buckle maintains that the actions of men "vary in obedience to the changes in the surrounding society;" and "that such variations are the result of large and general causes, which, working upon the aggregate of society, must produce certain consequences, without regard to the volition of those particular men of whom the society is composed."[2] And in applying this doctrine to particular cases, he carries it out so consistently as to maintain, "that suicide is merely the product of the general condi-

rated from that class of investigations in which we consider the immutable relations of physical phenomena. That the will is influenced by motives, no one pretends to deny; but to compare that influence to a physical cause, followed by an unvaried physical effect, is only to confound things essentially different, and must ever end in metaphysical paradox or practical folly." — Sedgwick, *Discourse on the Studies of the University of Cambridge*, p. 81, fifth edition.

1 The above remarks were written before the publication of Dr. McCosh's recent work on the "Intuitions of the Mind." I do not find any substantial difference between the author's view, as stated in this later work, and that previously given in the "Method;" though there are some expressions which tend to confirm my suspicion that the difference between us is more verbal than real. Thus he asserts (p. 472) that "causation in the will is entirely different from causation in other action;" a statement in which I fully concur, only doubting the propriety of calling the former by this name of *causation* at all. If there is a causation, though of a different kind, in moral as well as in physical action, the generic notion of *cause* should be the same in both, the specific features alone being different, as distinguishing this kind of cause from that. But can any univocal generic notion be pointed out, amounting to an adequate conception of causation as such? If not, the definition of causation, as a common genus, is not the same in both, and we have not the subdivisions of a generic notion, but only the different senses of an equivocal term.

2 p. 21.

tion of society, and that the individual felon only carries into effect what is a necessary consequence of preceding circumstances." "In a given state of society," he continues, "a certain number of persons must put an end to their own life. This is the general law; and the special question as to who shall commit the crime depends of course upon special laws, which, however, in their total action, must obey the large social law to which they are all subordinate. And the power of the larger law is so irresistible, that neither the love of life nor the fear of another world can avail anything towards even checking its operation."[1] This conclusion he endeavors to support by the evidence of statistics, "a branch of knowledge which, though still in its infancy, has already thrown more light on the study of human nature than all the sciences put together."[2]

It is surprising that this acute writer should not have seen that, in opposing the evidence of statistics to that of consciousness, he is comparing together two witnesses who are not speaking of the same thing. The fact to which consciousness bears witness is the freedom of our own personal actions. The fact which the statistical evidence is adduced to prove is the recurrence, within certain limits of greatest and least frequency, of actions distributed over an entire community. The former evidence tells us nothing directly concerning the actions of societies; the latter tells us nothing directly concerning the actions of individuals. Nay, it is precisely because the individual actions are not reducible to any fixed law, or capable of representation by any numerical calculation, that the statistical averages acquire their value as substitutes. No one dreams of applying statistical averages to calculate the period of the earth's rotation, by showing that four and twenty hours is the exact medium of time, comparing one month's or one year's revolutions with another's. It is only where the individual movements are irregular that it is necessary to aim at a proximate regularity by calculating in masses. To what cause the individual irregularity is due, whether to the complexity and minuteness of the physical conditions of the problem, or to the presence of moral conditions and free agency, — whether it indicates contingency in the facts themselves, or only a defect in our means of calculating, — this is a question which can only be answered by an acquaintance with the individual objects under examination, and which gains no elucidation from the statistics of large classes.[3]

1 pp. 25, 26. 2 p. 31.

3 Some good remarks on the fallacy of this kind of reasoning will be found in the Rev. W. B. Jones's Assize Sermon, *The Responsibility of Man to the Law of God.* Oxford, 1859, p. 15.

NOTE E, p. 145.

Sir W. Hamilton, in connection with his theory of the nature of the causal judgment, maintains that the schemes of liberty and necessity are both equally inconceivable; though for the fact of liberty we have, immediately or mediately, the testimony of consciousness. A free volition, he tells us, is inconceivable, because we cannot conceive an absolute commencement; a scheme of necessary determination is equally inconceivable, because we cannot conceive an infinite non-commencement. "As equally unthinkable," he says, "the two counter, the two one-sided, schemes are thus theoretically balanced. But, practically, our consciousness of the moral law, which, without a moral liberty in man would be a mendacious imperative, gives a decisive preponderance to the doctrine of freedom over the doctrine of fate. We are free in act, if we are accountable for our actions." [1]

This theory, though differing somewhat in the mode of reasoning, is in its conclusion similar to that previously arrived at by Kant. That philosopher, in his third Contradiction of Transcendental Ideas, arranges in parallel columns the opposite arguments in behalf of Liberty and Necessity, with the view of showing that each is irresistible in its attack upon the other. Kant, too, like Sir W. Hamilton, maintains that the fact of liberty is guaranteed by the testimony of the moral law, whose Categorical Imperative *thou shalt* necessarily implies a corresponding *thou canst*.[2] Kant, however, denies that the liberty as a fact can claim the direct testimony of consciousness; for consciousness in his philosophy is limited to the phenomena existing in space and time; whereas the freedom guaranteed by the moral law is a purely transcendental idea, subject to no conditions of time, and incapable of being presented in experience.[3] And this conclusion, so far as its negative result, the denial of a consciousness of freedom, is concerned, cannot be avoided, so long as we maintain, along with the universal authority of the principle of causality, the position that we are not directly conscious of self as a reality, but only of its several modes and affections. If my first consciousness relative to volition is not that of myself as willing, but only of will as a phenomenon, — if in the judgment "I will" there is no consciousness of *I*, but only of

[1] *Discussions*, pp. 624, 625. Compare *Reid's Works*, pp. 599, 602.

[2] See *Kritik der reinen Vernunft*, pp. 353, 429, 622; *Metaph. der Sitten*, p. 97; *Kr. der pr. V.* p. 139; *Religion innerhalb u. s. w.* p. 56, ed. Rosenkranz.

[3] *Kritik der r. V.* p. 414; *Metaph. der Sitten*, p. 92; *Kr. der pr. V.* p. 224.

will, — to this phenomenon of volition I am compelled by the principle of causality to suppose an antecedent determining phenomenon; and to that again another, and so on *ad infinitum*.

But this conclusion is no longer forced upon us, if we admit the existence of an immediate consciousness, not merely of the phenomena of mind, but of the personal self as actively and passively related to them. We thus obtain for the fact of liberty not merely the indirect testimony of consciousness through the medium of the moral law, but the direct testimony by the presence of the fact itself. I am conscious not merely of the phenomenon of volition, but of myself as producing it, and as producing it by choice, with a power to choose the opposite alternative. In this case I am not compelled to go back to any prior cause whatever. I need not suppose a prior intelligent cause; for my only positive notion of such a cause is *myself determining*, which does not imply *myself determined.* I need not suppose a prior phenomenal cause; for I am conscious of the influence of motives as inclining only, not as necessitating. The whole point at issue thus turns on the following question: Can the fact of consciousness expressed in the judgment *I will*, be analyzed into a relation of phenomena subject to the law of causality? Is the principle which we invariably apply to the sequence of one phenomenon on another also applicable to the relation of any phenomenon to the one given cause, *myself?*

Sir William Hamilton lays much stress on the impossibility of conceiving an absolute commencement. If by this is meant that I cannot conceive myself standing at the beginning of all time, out of all relation to any antecedent series of phenomena, it is undeniably true. But is such a conception needed to render the scheme of Liberty comprehensible? Is it not sufficient for me to know that none of the chronological antecedents stand to my volition in the particular relation of a determining cause? And this is the case if it is neither given as an active power coërcing, nor as a passive phenomenon invariably preceding. To say that some antecedent or other must go before my will, is only to say that I do not stand at the beginning of all time; but does this imply some *one* antecedent which is invariably followed by volition, or some active power, necessitating in each particular case? If, on the presence of the antecedent, or group of antecedents, A, my volition sometimes takes place one way, and sometimes another, it is not *determined* in the same manner as physical phenomena. If there is not always present some conscious being, exerting his power over my will, it is not *determined* in the same manner as it determines its own volitions. But, excepting these two senses, what is meant by *determining cause?*

Is there, then, extant any definition of will which does not imply another will preceding? Perhaps not; but the fault lies only in the authors of the definitions. To refute a given definition does not prove the non-existence of the thing defined. If liberty itself is a simple fact of consciousness, the error lies in the attempt to define it at all. The definition will necessarily involve a circle, and upon that circle, and not on the fact, the antagonist reasons. But, then, if the definition and the fact of consciousness are at issue, the former must give way, not the latter. Now, consciousness tells me not that *my will wills*, but that *I will*. Is it necessary to the conceivability of the fact that I should be able to analyze it into two constituent elements, — to place an abstract *I* on one side, and an abstract *will* on the other; thus literally fulfilling the satirical direction for the turbulent Puritan's burial, by laying John apart from Lilburn and Lilburn from John? Will any other state or act of mind bear a similar analysis? Can I in any case separate the state from the mind and the mind from the state; or give any definition which does not virtually repeat itself? But is it correct, on that account, to call states which I experience every day in consciousness *inconceivable?*

If, indeed, the freedom of the will be supposed to mean an absolute indifference to and independence of motives, such a liberty would be not only inconceivable as a fact, but worthless as a principle of moral action. But such is not the liberty to which consciousness bears witness; nor is such a liberty required as the only alternative against fatalism. The influence of motives on the will is not denied; only it is maintained that influence is not necessary determination; and that motives are not causes, in any proper sense of the latter term. Thus interpreted, I believe the scheme of liberty is inconceivable only if the determinist argument is unanswerable; and its answer is what I have attempted in this and the preceding note. If the attempt to establish a contradictory conclusion fails, liberty, though not definable, is surely as conceivable as any other simple datum of consciousness.

Note F, p. 146.

That our earliest notion of Causality arises from the fact given in the determination of our own volitions, is suggested by Locke, and established beyond all question by Maine de Biran. But then arises the question: By what process do we transcend our personal consciousness, and acknowledge, in relation to the changes of the sensible world, the operation of causes other than ourselves? This process is called by De Biran and Royer-Collard a *Natural Induction*, a term severely criticized by M. Cousin. Were the process really inductive, he argues, we must believe every cause in nature to be, like ourselves, voluntary, conscious, and free; and even then the belief in question might perhaps be regarded as universally true within the limits of experience, but could never rise to the character of a necessary truth. For a more satisfactory explanation, M. Cousin has recourse to the principle of causality, which he regards as a necessary law of the reason, by virtue of which it disengages, in the fact of consciousness, the necessary element of causal relation from the contingent element of my personal production of this or that particular movement. This necessity, which compels the reason to suppose a cause whenever the senses or the consciousness present a phenomenon, is the Principle of Causality.[1]

It is obvious to ask, What do we gain by the principle of causality thus supposed? Does it explain in any degree the nature of that *power* which we are supposed to attribute to inanimate objects? Does it explain how we divest our original notion of the attribute of personality, and what is left when we have done so? Does it furnish the slightest hint or help for investigating the true character of efficient causes? By no means. The principle itself is a mere statement of the fact, that we do invariably suppose a cause of physical changes, and that we cannot but do so. It offers no psychological explanation of the fact; it merely gives it the name of a principle of reason. It does not give us any positive notion of the cause in question; this remains, we know not what, — a something different from our own causality, and, as such, supposable perhaps, but inconceivable. It does not tell us how we can attain to a more positive knowledge. Not by the senses; for these present to us only successive phenomena. Not by the internal consciousness; for this informs us only of personal causation. Not by the reason; for this only tells us in general terms that there is a cause, but furnishes no means of observing and distinguishing its character and varieties. The cause of physical changes still remains, like the subject of physical attributes, a negative idea, a *je ne sais quoi*.

Nor does M. Cousin's theory, any more than that of De Biran, explain how we get rid of the personal element with which all intuitive causality is involved. It only says that we do so, and that we must do so. The term *Induction*, employed by De Biran and Royer-Collard, is indeed objectionable, whether it be taken in the Aristotelian or in the Baconian sense. The former is objectionable, inasmuch as our personal acts are not sup-

1 *Cours de Philosophie*, Leçon 19.

posed to constitute, or even adequately to represent, the whole body of causal relations. The latter is objectionable; for the same acts cannot be selected instances showing diverse operations of a law, but must, from the nature of the case, be all of one kind. But this objection affects only the language, and not the basis of the theory; indeed, the two philosophers in question have expressly stated that their natural induction must be carefully distinguished from that of physics.[1] But in point of language, the phrase *principle of reason* is equally objectionable; partly as tending to check all further psychological investigation into a point by no means as yet satisfactorily explained, and partly as opening the way to the thousand extravagances of ontological speculation, by concealing the purely negative character of the notion of physical power. On M. de Biran's theory, says M. Cousin, anthropomorphism becomes the universal and necessary law of thought.[2] It might be replied, that in all cases where the *presentation* is given by internal consciousness only, anthropomorphism is in fact the condition and the limit of all positive thinking.

I conceive, therefore, that there is nothing in M. Cousin's theory which dispenses with the obligation of a further psychological examination of the origin and character of the supposed principle of causality, such as I have attempted in the text of the present work. Whether that explanation itself be right or wrong, must be judged by others; but, whatever may be its fate in this respect, I shall deem its purpose sufficiently answered if it serves to call the attention of philosophers to a point hitherto too much neglected in speculation — the important distinction between positive and negative intuitions and thoughts.

Note G, p. 148.

In the controversy concerning the existence of a Moral Sense, the question at issue has suffered considerable misrepresentation from the want of an accurate distinction between intuitive or presentative consciousness, whose object is an individual thing, act, or state of mind, and reflective or representative consciousness, whose immediate object is a general notion or principle. Stewart, for example, in his Life of Adam Smith, observes:

1 *Œuvres de Maine de Biran*, vol. iv. p. 393; Jouffroy's *Reid*, vol. iv. pp. 383, 439.

2 *Œuvres de Maine de Biran*, vol. iv. Préface de l'Editeur, p. xxxvi.

"It was the opinion of Dr. Cudworth, and also of Dr. Clarke, that moral distinctions are perceived by that power of the mind which distinguishes truth from falsehood. This system it was one great object of Dr. Hutcheson's philosophy to refute, and in opposition to it, to show that the words *right* and *wrong* express certain agreeable and disagreeable qualities in actions, which it is not the province of reason, but of feeling, to perceive; and to that power of perception which renders us susceptible of pleasure or of pain from the view of virtue or of vice, he gave the name of the Moral Sense." The same philosopher, in his Philosophical Essays, endeavors to obviate Hume's deductions from Hutcheson's theory, by falling back, in some degree, upon the views of Cudworth and Clarke, and referring the origin of our notions of right and wrong to *reason* instead of *sense.* "Tastes and colors," said Hume, "and all other sensible qualities, lie not in the bodies, but merely in the senses. The case is the same with beauty and deformity, *virtue and vice.*" To this Stewart replies: "The decisions of the understanding, it must be owned, with respect to moral truth, differ from those which relate to a mathematical theorem, or to the result of a chemical experiment, inasmuch as they are always accompanied with some feeling or emotion of the heart; but on an accurate analysis of this *compounded sentiment* it will be found that it is the intellectual judgment which is the groundwork of the feeling, and not the feeling of the judgment."

In a Lecture on Moral Relations, by the late Professor Mills, the different opinions concerning our perception of Morality are summed up as follows:

"1. Some ascribe our apprehension of it, with Hutcheson, to a peculiar internal sense, similar in its operations to the external senses, and confound moral perception with taste; this is, strictly speaking, the theory of a moral sense.

"2. Others attribute moral perception, not to any peculiar sense, but yet to a peculiar faculty of the understanding distinct from its general powers, and they appear to identify conscience with the moral faculty.

"3. Many deny the existence of a peculiar moral faculty, and maintain that moral principles are apprehended by the same powers of the intellect which perceive other kinds of truth.

"4. The Utilitarian theory implies that moral relations are ascertained and embraced by the operations of the discursive faculty only."[1]

The whole controversy may be considerably cleared by distinguishing *Moral Facts from Moral Principles.* Facts of all kinds are *presented* to, and

[1] *Essays and Lectures by the late Rev. W. Mills*, p. 204.

perceived by, different faculties of intuition, similar in the manner of their operation to the perceptions of sense; and hence, with some allowance for metaphor, we may speak of internal or external *senses*.[1] Is it then asked whether we discern morality in *individual acts* by the same faculties by which we discern other qualities of individual objects presented to us? But, of these qualities, some are visible, some audible, and so on. Is it meant that an act can literally be *seen, heard, smelt, felt*, or *tasted*, to be virtuous or vicious? If not, the perception of the moral character of acts is a distinct *presentation*, and, as such, to be referred to a distinct faculty; though, being, as will appear, an object of internal, not of external perception, it is not, like the external senses, connected with a distinct bodily organ.

The question, whether right and wrong are apprehended by the same powers of the intellect which perceive other kinds of truth, is only applicable to the *general concepts* or *principles* through which morality is *represented* as an object of thought. Truth and Falsehood can be distinguished in representative knowledge only; and all such knowledge is most conveniently classified by reference to the single faculty of the Understanding. The same power of thought may inquire into the ground of various presentations; it may investigate, for example, why one object is white, why another is harmonious, why a third is sweet, why a fourth is beautiful, why a fifth is virtuous; but in all such investigations, the fact of a given object possessing a given quality must be presupposed as the groundwork of the investigation. The distinction between a true and a false theory of morals will be determined by the same test as that between truth and falsehood in any other inquiry — its agreement or not, with the facts as given in intuition.

It thus appears that a power of discerning right and wrong in individual acts must be allowed as the presentative basis, without which no system of Moral Philosophy is possible. Such a power, thus limited, it is

1 This has been observed by Aristotle, whose account of the Practical *Sense*, or *Intelligence*, is in this respect more accurate than that of modern philosophers. Καὶ γὰρ τῶν πρώτων ὅρων καὶ τῶν ἐσχάτων νοῦς ἐστὶ καὶ οὐ λόγος, καὶ ὁ μὲν κατὰ τὰς ἀποδείξεις τῶν ἀκινήτων ὅρων καὶ πρώτων, ὁ δ' ἐν ταῖς πρακτικαῖς τοῦ ἐσχάτου καὶ ἐνδεχομένου καὶ τῆς ἑτέρας προτάσεως· ἀρχαὶ γὰρ τοῦ οὗ ἕνεκα αὗται· ἐκ τῶν καθ' ἕκαστα γὰρ τὸ καθόλου. Τούτων οὖν ἔχειν δεῖ αἴσθησιν, αὕτη δ' ἐστὶ νοῦς. — *Eth. Nic.* vi. 11. Compare *Pol.* i. 2: Τοῦτο γὰρ πρὸς τἆλλα ζῷα τοῖς ἀνθρώποις ἴδιον, τὸ μόνον ἀγαθοῦ καὶ κακοῦ καὶ δικαίου καὶ ἀδίκου καὶ τῶν ἄλλων αἴσθησιν ἔχειν. These passages may serve as a qualification of Smith's assertion, that the word moral sense is of very late formation.

impossible for the Utilitarian to explain away by any theory of association or education. Education may corrupt and pervert our presented ideas, but it cannot originate them: it may teach me to regard an act as right which is really wrong, or *vice versa*, but it cannot *create* the original impression of either. To deny, with Locke and Paley, the existence of a moral sense, because one man holds to be wrong what another holds to be right, is like denying the existence of a faculty of sight, because a man with the jaundice sees all objects yellow. The existence of the faculty is shown by our approving or disapproving *at all;* it cannot therefore be disproved by the fact of our sometimes approving or disapproving wrongly. The opposite error of Hume, in holding that virtue and vice exist in the sense only, lies in a confusion of the subjective feeling of approbation with the objective quality which gives rise to it. The same confusion has taken place with regard to the secondary qualities of body. Heat and color, *as sensations*, exist only in a sentient being; but that such sensations originate from *nothing at all* in the bodies themselves, is an absurdity long ago exploded, if indeed ever seriously maintained.

This *presentation* of right and wrong, however, is by no means accurately exhibited in the account commonly given of moral sense. It is not correct to describe our perception of the moral character of actions in general as coördinate with or including the judgment of our own conduct in particular.[1] Right and wrong are not directly *presented* to me in any other actions than my own. If I see a murder committed in a puppet-show, I have all the same presented phenomena as if I see a murder committed by a man. I do not feel the same moral disapprobation, because I do not attribute to the puppet the same internal consciousness of obligation as to the man. But this consciousness is not *presented* except in the case of my own acts, and, from these, is transferred *representatively* to other men, whose mental constitution I believe to be in this respect similar to my own. The intuitive faculty is properly limited to the approbation or disapprobation of my personal acts; and to this personal consciousness must thus be traced the original notions of Right and Wrong, as of Cause, and of Substance, and of all internal phenomena. Hence, if the terms *Moral Sense* and *Conscience* be used according to the ordinary philosophical distinction, it will be more correct to describe Moral Sense as an extension of Conscience, than Conscience as a limitation of Moral Sense.[2]

1 As is done by Bishop Sanderson, in his *Prælectiones de Obligatione Conscientiæ*, as well as by Shaftesbury, Hutcheson, and most of the advocates of a moral sense, and still more by Smith, in his theory of Sympathy.

2 This is exactly the reverse of the theory of Adam Smith, who maintains that our judgments concerning the morality of our own acts is entirely derived from

Note H, p. 212.

The difference between the relations of the several Forms of Thought to Psychology and to Logic has not hitherto been accurately marked. Psychologically, all that is communicated by, not given to, the act of thinking, belongs to the form, not to the matter, of the product. But these psychological forms do not come within the province of Logic, unless some further process of pure or formal thinking is affected by them. In its psychological relation, modality is clearly one of the forms of judgment. The necessary judgment, "A *must be* B," expresses the existence of a law, of some kind or other, by which the attributes are inseparably connected; the contingent judgment, whose full expression is, "A *may or may not be* B," denies the existence of any law of the kind; while the pure judgment, "A *is* B," states the fact of an existing connection, without taking into account the question of law at all. The psychological question is this: "Is the presence or absence of a law connecting the terms of a judgment given *to* or *by* the act of judging? Is it part of the given phenomena, or a manner in which the mind regards them? In other words, Is modality an affection of the predicate, or of the copula? Do I in thought decide on the actual connection of A with a given *necessary-B*, or on the necessary connection of A with a given B? In the former case, the modality belongs to the matter of the judgment; in the latter, to the form.

The true answer to this question is sufficiently plain. If sensible experience is incompetent to furnish the notion of identity between two phenomena, it is equally incompetent to furnish that of necessary or contingent identity. These are additional products of the act of thought; experience having only presented the phenomena in a constant or variable juxtaposition. Nay, further, the hypothesis that modality is *given* in the predicate of a judgment, not *thought* in the copula, becomes, in ultimate analysis, destructive of itself. For, if in thought we connect A with what is *given* as necessarily B, this implies that B has previously been thought as necessarily connected with some subject or other. A *necessary-B* has no intelligible sense, except in relation to some previous judgment, "C *must be* B." The identification of A with B, then, takes place through the medium of C;

that which we pass on others. This theory he carries so far as to assert, "Were it possible that a human creature could grow up to manhood in some solitary place, without any communication with his own species, he could no more think of his own character, of the propriety or demerit of his own sentiments and conduct, of the beauty or deformity of his own mind, than of the beauty or deformity of his own face."

and the supposition that modality can be given as an affection of the predicate, implies that it has been previously thought as an affection of the copula. This is sufficient to establish the psychological position of modality as a form of the judgment. But, thus admitted, it is indispensable that it should be expressed in the copula, and not, as is frequently done, left to be gathered from our knowledge of the matter. A judgment of the form "A is B," whatever notions may be expressed by the terms, can never be thought as other than a pure or assertorial judgment. An apodeictical or problematical judgment requires a different statement of the copula relation, "A must be B," or "A may be B."

On the other hand, the criticism of Sir W. Hamilton, though accurately expressed in relation to one process of thought only, may be so extended as to be decisive as regards the exclusion of modality from Logic. "Necessity, Contingency, etc.," he says, "are circumstances which do not affect the logical copula or the logical inference. They do not relate to the connection of the subject and predicate, of the antecedent and consequent, as terms in thought, but as realities in existence; they are metaphysical, not logical conditions. The syllogistic inference is always necessary; is modified by no extraformal condition; is equally apodictic in contingent as in necessary matter."[1]

As regards the syllogistic inference, these remarks are strictly accurate, and would be conclusive against any modality proposed as a form of *reasoning*. Were a distinction, for example, set up between syllogisms in which the conclusion necessarily follows from the premises, and syllogisms in which it may be inferred with more or less probability, the latter would rightly be condemned as extralogical — the true syllogistic inference being always necessary. As regards the copula in judgments, the criticism cannot be accepted as verbally accurate unless we distinguish the logical copula from the psychological. That modality relates to realities in existence, is not conclusive; for quantity and quality, in all synthetical judgments, do the same in the same degree, and yet are rightly classed as forms of thought. But if we extend the distinction between formal and material thinking, so as to embrace judgment and conception, as well as reasoning, it is clear that the copula is always necessary in analytical or formal judging, as the inference is always necessary in formal reasoning. Material judgments, however, cannot be entirely excluded from Logic, in so far as they furnish data for formal reasoning. They are admissible, however, only in relation to this latter process; and hence those forms of judgment only are rightly to be regarded as logical which affect the formal inference derivable from them. This is the case with quantity and quality,

[1] *Discussions*, p. 146.

but not with modality: the latter affects the conclusion of a syllogism not as a conclusion, in its relation to the premises, but only in itself, as a proposition. For this reason, it is logically preferable to exclude modality as a form, and to treat it as if it affected the predicate only of the judgment. The *logical* copula thus becomes in every instance assertorial only; and if this be carefully distinguished from the *psychological* copula, the remarks of Sir W. Hamilton may be regarded as applicable to the whole of Logic, and to every process of thought.

THE END.

VALUABLE

LITERARY AND SCIENTIFIC WORKS,

PUBLISHED BY

GOULD AND LINCOLN,

59 WASHINGTON STREET, BOSTON.

ANNUAL OF SCIENTIFIC DISCOVERY FOR 1859; or, Year-Book of Facts in Science and Art, exhibiting the most important Discoveries and Improvements in Mechanics, Useful Arts, Natural Philosophy, Chemistry, Astronomy, Meteorology, Zoology, Botany, Mineralogy, Geology, Geography, Antiquities, &c., together with a list of recent Scientific Publications; a classified list of Patents; Obituaries of eminent Scientific Men; an Index of Important Papers in Scientific Journals, Reports, &c. Edited by DAVID A. WELLS, A. M. With a Portrait of Prof. O. M. Mitchell. 12mo, cloth, $1.25.

VOLUMES OF THE SAME WORK for years 1850 to 1858 inclusive. With Portraits of Professors Agassiz, Silliman, Henry, Bache, Maury, Hitchcock, Richard M. Hoe, Profs. Jeffries Wyman, and H. D. Rogers. Nine volumes, 12mo, cloth, $1.25 per vol.

This work, issued annually, contains all important facts discovered or announced during the year.

☞ Each volume is distinct in itself, and contains *entirely new matter.*

INFLUENCE OF THE HISTORY OF SCIENCE UPON INTELLECTUAL EDUCATION. By WILLIAM WHEWELL, D. D., of Trinity College, Eng., and the alleged author of "Plurality of Worlds." 12mo, cloth, 25 cts.

THE NATURAL HISTORY OF THE HUMAN SPECIES; Its Typical Forms and Primeval Distribution. By CHARLES HAMILTON SMITH. With an Introduction containing an Abstract of the views of Blumenbach, Prichard, Bachman, Agassiz, and other writers of repute. By SAMUEL KNEELAND, Jr., M. D. With elegant Illustrations. 12mo, cloth, $1.25.

"The marks of practical good sense, careful observation, and deep research, are displayed in every page. The introductory essay of some seventy or eighty pages forms a valuable addition to the work. It comprises an abstract of the opinions advocated by the most eminent writers on this subject. The statements are made with strict impartiality, and, without a comment, left to the judgment of the reader." — *Sartain's Magazine.*

KNOWLEDGE IS POWER. A View of the Productive Forces of Modern Society, and the Results of Labor, Capital, and Skill. By CHARLES KNIGHT. With numerous Illustrations. American Edition. Revised, with Additions, by DAVID A. WELLS, Editor of the "Annual of Scientific Discovery." 12mo, cloth, $1.25.

☞ This is emphatically *a book for the people.* It contains an immense amount of important information, which everybody ought to be in possession of; and the volume should be placed in every family, and in every School and Public Library in the land. The facts and illustrations are drawn from almost every branch of skilful industry, and it is a work which the mechanic and artisan of every description will be sure to read with a RELISH.

CHAMBERS' WORKS.

CHAMBERS' CYCLOPÆDIA OF ENGLISH LITERATURE. A Selection of the choicest productions of English Authors, from the earliest to the present time. Connected by a Critical and Biographical History. Forming two large imperial octavo volumes of 700 pages each, double column letter press; with upwards of 300 elegant Illustrations. Edited by ROBERT CHAMBERS. Cloth, $5.00; sheep, $6.00; full gilt, $7.50; half calf, $7.50; full calf, $10.00.

This work embraces about one thousand Authors, chronologically arranged, and classed as poets, historians, dramatists, philosophers, metaphysicians, divines, etc., with choice selections from their writings, connected by a Biographical, Historical, and Critical Narrative; thus presenting a complete view of English Literature from the earliest to the present time. Let the reader open where he will, he cannot fail to find matter for profit and delight. The selections are gems — infinite riches in a little room; in the language of another, "A WHOLE ENGLISH LIBRARY FUSED DOWN INTO ONE CHEAP BOOK!"

☞ THE AMERICAN edition of this valuable work is enriched by the addition of fine steel and mezzotint engravings of the heads of SHAKSPEARE, ADDISON, BYRON; a full-length portrait of DR. JOHNSON; and a beautiful scenic representation of OLIVER GOLDSMITH and DR. JOHNSON. These important and elegant additions, together with superior paper and binding, and other improvements, render the AMERICAN far superior to the English edition.

W. H. PRESCOTT, THE HISTORIAN, says, "Readers cannot fail to profit largely by the labors of the critic who has the talent and taste to separate what is really beautiful and worthy of their study from what is superfluous."

"I concur in the foregoing opinion of Mr. Prescott." — EDWARD EVERETT.

"A popular work, indispensable to the library of a student of English literature." — DR. WAYLAND.

"We hail with peculiar pleasure the appearance of this work." — *North American Review.*

CHAMBERS' MISCELLANY OF USEFUL AND ENTERTAINING KNOWLEDGE. Edited by WILLIAM CHAMBERS. With elegant Illustrative Engravings. Ten volumes. Cloth, $7.50; cloth, gilt, $10.00; library sheep, $10.00.

"It would be difficult to find any miscellany superior or even equal to it. It richly deserves the epithets 'useful and entertaining,' and I would recommend it very strongly, as extremely well adapted to form parts of a library for the young, or of a social or circulating library in town or country." — GEO. B. EMERSON, Esq. — *Chairman Boston School Book Committee.*

CHAMBERS' HOME BOOK; or, Pocket Miscellany, containing a Choice Selection of Interesting and Instructive Reading, for the Old and Young. Six volumes. 16mo, cloth, $3.00; library sheep, $4.00; half calf, $6.00.

This is considered fully equal, and in some respects superior, to either of the other works of the Chambers in interest; containing a vast fund of valuable information. It is admirably adapted to the School or Family Library, furnishing ample variety for every class of readers.

"The Chambers are confessedly the best caterers for popular and useful reading in the world." — *Willis' Home Journal.*

"A very entertaining, instructive, and popular work." — *N. Y. Commercial.*

"We do not know how it is possible to publish so much good reading matter at such a low price. We speak a good word for the literary excellence of the stories in this work; we hope our people will introduce it into all their families, in order to drive away the miserable flashy-trashy stuff so often found in the hands of our young people of both sexes." — *Scientific American.*

"Both an entertaining and instructive work, as it is certainly a very cheap one." — *Puritan Recorder.*

"If any person wishes to read for amusement or profit, to kill time or improve it, get 'Chambers' Home Book.'" — *Chicago Times.*

CHAMBERS' REPOSITORY OF INSTRUCTIVE AND AMUSING PAPERS. With Illustrations. A New Series, containing Original Articles. Two volumes. 16mo, cloth, $1.75.

THE SAME WORK, two volumes in one, cloth, gilt back, $1.50.

IMPORTANT WORKS.

A TREATISE ON THE COMPARATIVE ANATOMY OF THE ANIMAL KINGDOM. By Profs. C. TH. VON SIEBOLD and H. STANNIUS. Translated from the German, with Notes, Additions, &c. By WALDO I. BURNETT, M. D., Boston. One elegant octavo volume, cloth, $3.00.

This is believed to be incomparably the best and most complete work on the subject extant; and its appearance in an English dress, with the additions of the American Translator, is everywhere welcomed by men of science in this country.

UNITED STATES EXPLORING EXPEDITION; during the years 1838, 1839, 1840, 1841, 1842, under CHARLES WILKES, U. S. N. Vol. XII. MOLLUSCA AND SHELLS. By AUGUSTUS A. GOULD, M. D. Elegant quarto volume, cloth, $6.00.

THE LANDING AT CAPE ANNE; or, THE CHARTER OF THE FIRST PERMANENT COLONY ON THE TERRITORY OF THE MASSACHUSETTS COMPANY. Now discovered, and first published from the ORIGINAL MANUSCRIPT, with an inquiry into its authority, and a HISTORY OF THE COLONY, 1624—1628, Roger Conant, Governor. By J. WINGATE THORNTON. 8vo, cloth, $1.50.

☞ "A rare contribution to the early history of New England." — *Mercantile Journal.*

LAKE SUPERIOR; Its Physical Character, Vegetation, and Animals. By L. AGASSIZ and others. One volume octavo, elegantly Illustrated, cloth, $3.50.

THE HALLIG; OR, THE SHEEPFOLD IN THE WATERS. A Tale of Humble Life on the Coast of Schleswig. Translated from the German of BIERNATSKI, by Mrs. GEORGE P. MARSH. With a Biographical Sketch of the Author. 12mo, cloth, $1.00.

As a revelation of an entire new phase in human society, this work strongly reminds the reader of Miss Bremer's tales, In originality and brilliancy of imagination, it is not inferior to those; — its aim is far higher.

THE CRUISE OF THE NORTH STAR; A Narrative of the Excursion made by Mr. Vanderbilt's Party in the Steam Yacht, in her Voyage to England, Russia, Denmark, France, Spain, Italy, Malta, Turkey, Madeira, &c. By Rev. JOHN OVERTON CHOULES, D. D. With elegant Illustrations, &c. 12mo, cloth, gilt backs and sides, $1.50; cloth, gilt, $2.00; Turkey, gilt, $3.00.

ILGRIMAGE TO EGYPT; embracing a Diary of Explorations on the Nile, with Observations Illustrative of the Manners, Customs, and Institutions of the People, and of the present condition of the Antiquities and Ruins. By Hon. J. V. C. SMITH, late Mayor of the City of Boston. With numerous elegant Engravings. 12mo, cloth, $1.25.

POETICAL WORKS.

COMPLETE POETICAL WORKS OF WILLIAM COWPER; with a Life and Critical Notices of his Writings. Elegant Illustrations. 16mo, cloth, $1.00.

POETICAL WORKS OF SIR WALTER SCOTT. Life and Illustrations. 16mo, cloth, $1.00.

MILTON'S POETICAL WORKS. With a Life and elegant Illustrations. 16mo, cloth, $1.00.

☞ The above Poetical Works, by standard authors, are all of uniform size and style, printed on fine paper from clear, distinct type, with new and elegant illustrations, richly bound in full gilt, and plain.

GUYOT'S WORKS. VALUABLE MAPS.

THE EARTH AND MAN; Lectures on COMPARATIVE PHYSICAL GEOGRAPHY, in its relation to the History of Mankind. By ARNOLD GUYOT. With Illustrations. 12mo, cloth, $1.25.

Prof. LOUIS AGASSIZ, of Harvard University, says: "It will not only render the study of geography more attractive, but actually show it in its true light."

Hon. GEORGE S. HILLARD says: "The work is marked by learning, ability, and taste. His bold and comprehensive generalizations rest upon a careful foundation of facts."

"Those who have been accustomed to regard Geography as a merely descriptive branch of learning, drier than the remainder biscuit after a voyage, will be delighted to find this hitherto unattractive pursuit converted into a science, the principles of which are definite and the results conclusive." — *North American Review.*

"The grand idea of the work is happily expressed by the author, where he calls it the *geographical march of history.* Sometimes we feel as if we were studying a treatise on the exact sciences; at others, it strikes the ear like an epic poem. Now it reads like history, and now it sounds like prophecy. It will find readers in whatever language it may be published." — *Christian Examiner.*

"The work is one of high merit, exhibiting a wide range of knowledge, great research, and a philosophical spirit of investigation." — *Silliman's Journal.*

COMPARATIVE PHYSICAL AND HISTORICAL GEOGRAPHY; or, the Study of the Earth and Inhabitants. A Series of Graduated Courses, for the use of Schools. By ARNOLD GUYOT. *In preparation.*

GUYOT'S MURAL MAPS. A series of elegant Colored Maps, projected on a large scale for the Recitation Room, consisting of a Map of the World, North and South America, Geographical Elements, &c., exhibiting the Physical Phenomena of the Globe. By Professor ARNOLD GUYOT, viz.,

MAP OF THE WORLD, *mounted*, $10.00.
MAP OF NORTH AMERICA, *mounted*, $9.00.
MAP OF SOUTH AMERICA, *mounted*, $0.00.
MAP OF GEOGRAPHICAL ELEMENTS, *mounted*, $9.00.

☞ These elegant and entirely original Mural Maps are projected on a large scale, so that when suspended in the recitation room they may be seen from any point, and the delineations without difficulty traced distinctly with the eye. They are beautifully printed in colors, and neatly mounted for use.

GEOLOGICAL MAP OF THE UNITED STATES AND BRITISH PROVINCES OF NORTH AMERICA. With an Explanatory Text, Geological Sections, and Plates of the Fossils which characterize the Formations. By JULES MARCOU. Two volumes. Octavo, cloth, $3.00.

☞ The Map is elegantly colored, and done up with linen cloth back, and folded in octavo form, with thick cloth covers.

"The most complete Geological Map of the United States which has yet appeared. It is a work which all who take an interest in the geology of the United States would wish to possess; and we recommend it as extremely valuable, not only in a geological point of view, but as representing very fully the coal and copper regions of the country. The explanatory text presents a rapid sketch of the geological constilations of North America, and is rich in facts on the subjects. It is embellished with a number of beautiful plates of the fossils which characterize the formations, thus making, with the map, *a very complete, clear, and distinct outline of the geology of our country.*" — *Mining Magazine, N. Y.*

HALL'S GEOLOGICAL CHART; Giving an Ideal Section of the Successive Geological Formations, with an Actual Section from the Atlantic to the Pacific Oceans. By Prof. JAMES HALL, of Albany. *Mounted*, $9.00.

A KEY TO GEOLOGICAL CHART. By Prof. JAMES HALL. 18mo, 25 cts.

VALUABLE TEXT-BOOKS.

THE LECTURES OF SIR WILLIAM HAMILTON, BART., late Professor of Logic and Metaphysics, University of Edinburgh; embracing the METAPHYSICAL and LOGICAL COURSES; with Notes, from Original Materials, and an Appendix, containing the Author's Latest Development of his New Logical Theory. Edited by Rev. HENRY LONGUEVILLE MANSEL, B. D., Prof. of Moral and Metaphysical Philosophy in Magdalen College, Oxford, and JOHN VEITCH, M. A., of Edinburgh. In two royal octavo volumes, viz.,

I. METAPHYSICAL LECTURES (*now ready*). Royal octavo, cloth.

II. LOGICAL LECTURES (*in preparation*).

☞ G. & L., by a special arrangement with the family of the late Sir William Hamilton, are the Authorized American Publishers of this distinguished author's *matchless* LECTURES ON METAPHYSICS AND LOGIC, and they are permitted to print the same from advance sheets furnished them by the English publishers.

MENTAL PHILOSOPHY; Including the Intellect, the Sensibilities, and the Will. By JOSEPH HAVEN, Prof. of Intellectual and Moral Philosophy, Amherst College. Royal 12mo, cloth, embossed, $1.50.

It is believed this work will be found pre-eminently distinguished.

1. The COMPLETENESS with which it presents the whole subject. Text-books generally treat of only *one class* of faculties; this work includes the *whole*. 2. It is strictly and thoroughly SCIENTIFIC. 3. It presents a careful analysis of the mind, as a whole. 4. The history and literature of each topic. 5. The latest results of the science. 6. The chaste, yet attractive style. 7. The remarkable condensation of thought.

Prof. PARK, of Andover, says: "It is DISTINGUISHED for its clearness of style, perspicuity of method, candor of spirit, acumen and comprehensiveness of thought."

The work, though so recently published, has met with most remarkable success; having been already introduced into a large number of the leading colleges and schools in various parts of the country, and bids fair to take the place of every other work on the subject now before the public.

THESAURUS OF ENGLISH WORDS AND PHRASES, so classified and arranged as to facilitate the expression of ideas, and assist in literary composition. New and Improved Edition. By PETER MARK ROGET, late Secretary of the Royal Society, London, &c. Revised and edited, with a List of Foreign Words defined in English, and other additions, by BARNAS SEARS, D. D., President of Brown University. A NEW AMERICAN Edition, with ADDITIONS AND IMPROVEMENTS. 12mo, cloth, $1.50.

This edition is based on the London edition, recently issued. The first American Edition having been prepared by Dr. Sears for *strictly educational purposes*, those words and phrases properly termed "vulgar," incorporated in the original work, were omitted. These expurgated portions have, in the present edition, been *restored*, but by such an arrangement of the matter as not to interfere with the educational purposes of the American editor. Besides this, it contains important additions of words and phrases not in the English edition, making it in *all respects more full and perfect than the author's edition*. The work has already become one of standard authority, both in this country and in Great Britain.

PALEY'S NATURAL THEOLOGY. Illustrated by forty Plates, with Selections from the Notes of Dr. Paxton, and Additional Notes, Original and Selected, with a Vocabulary of Scientific Terms. Edited by JOHN WARE, M. D. Improved edition, with elegant newly engraved plates. 12mo, cloth, embossed, $1.25.

This work is very generally introduced into our best Schools and Colleges throughout the country. An entirely new and beautiful set of Illustrations has recently been procured, which, with other improvements, render it the best and most complete work of the kind extant.

VALUABLE TEXT-BOOKS.

PRINCIPLES OF ZOÖLOGY; Touching the Structure, Development, Distribution, and Natural Arrangement, of the RACES OF ANIMALS, living and extinct, with numerous Illustrations. For the use of Schools and Colleges. Part I. COMPARATIVE PHYSIOLOGY. By LOUIS AGASSIZ and AUGUSTUS A. GOULD. Revised edition, 12mo, cloth, $1.00.

"It is not a mere book, but a work — a real work in the form of a book. Zoölogy is an interesting science, and here is treated with a masterly hand. It is a work adapted to colleges and schools, and no young man should be without it." — *Scientific American.*

"This work places us in possession of information half a century in advance of all our elementary works on this subject. . . No work of the same dimensions has ever appeared in the English language containing so much new and valuable information."— PROF. JAMES HALL, *Albany.*

"The best book of the kind in our language."— *Christian Examiner.*

PRINCIPLES OF ZOÖLOGY, PART II. Systematic Zoölogy. *In preparation.*

THE ELEMENTS OF GEOLOGY; adapted to Schools and Colleges. With numerous Illustrations. By J. R. LOOMIS, President of Lewisburg University, Pa. 12mo, cloth, 75 cts.

"It is surpassed by no work before the American public." — *M. B. Anderson, LL. D., President Rochester University.*

"This is just such a work as is needed for our schools. We see no reason why it should not take its place as a text-book in all the schools in the land." — *N. Y. Observer.*

"Admirably adapted for use as a text-book in common schools and academies." — *Congregationalist, Boston.*

ELEMENTS OF MORAL SCIENCE. By FRANCIS WAYLAND, D. D., late President of Brown University. 12mo, cloth, $1.25.

MORAL SCIENCE ABRIDGED, and adapted to the use of Schools and Academies, by the Author. Half morocco, 50 cts.

The same, CHEAP SCHOOL EDITION, boards, 25 cts.

This work is used in the Boston Schools, and is exceedingly popular as a text-book wherever it has been adopted.

ELEMENTS OF POLITICAL ECONOMY. By FRANCIS WAYLAND, D. D. 12mo, cloth, $1.25.

POLITICAL ECONOMY ABRIDGED, and adapted to the use of Schools and Academies, by the Author. Half morocco, 50 cts.

"It deserves to be introduced into every private family, and to be studied by every man who has an interest in the wealth and prosperity of his country. It is a subject little understood, even practically, by thousands, and still less understood theoretically. It is to be hoped this will form a class book, and be faithfully studied in our academies, and that it will find its way into every family library; not there to be shut up unread, but to afford rich material for thought and discussion in the family circle." — *Puritan Recorder.*

All the above Works by Dr. Wayland are used as text-books in most of the colleges and higher schools throughout the Union, and are highly approved.

☞ *G. & L. keep, in addition to works published by themselves, an extensive assortment of works published by others, in all departments of trade, which they supply at publishers' prices. They invite the attention of Booksellers, Travelling Agents, Teachers, School Committees, Clergymen, and Professional men generally (to whom a liberal discount is uniformly made), to their extensive stock. Copies of Text-books for examination will be sent by mail or otherwise, to any one transmitting* ONE HALF *the price of the same.* ☞ *Orders from any part of the country promptly attended to with faithfulness and despatch.*

WORKS FOR BIBLE STUDENTS.

KITTO'S POPULAR CYCLOPÆDIA OF BIBLICAL LITERATURE. Condensed from the larger work. By the Author, John Kitto, D. D. Assisted by James Taylor, D. D., of Glasgow. With over five hundred Illustrations. One volume, octavo, 812 pp. Cloth, $3.00; sheep, $3.50; cloth, gilt, $4.00; half calf, $4.00.

A Dictionary of the Bible. Serving, also, as a Commentary, embodying the products of the best and most recent researches in biblical literature in which the scholars of Europe and America have been engaged. The work, the result of immense labor and research, and enriched by the contributions of writers of distinguished eminence in the various departments of sacred literature, has been, by universal consent, pronounced the best work of its class extant, and the one best suited to the advanced knowledge of the present day in all the studies connected with theological science. It is not only intended for ministers and theological students, but it is also particularly adapted to parents, Sabbath-school teachers, and the great body of the religious public.

THE HISTORY OF PALESTINE, from the Patriarchal Age to the Present Time; with Chapters on the Geography and Natural History of the Country, the Customs and Institutions of the Hebrews. By John Kitto, D. D. With upwards of two hundred Illustrations. 12mo, cloth, $1.25.

☞ A work admirably adapted to the Family, the Sabbath, and the week-day School Library.

ANALYTICAL CONCORDANCE TO THE HOLY SCRIPTURES; or, the Bible presented under Distinct and Classified Heads or Topics. By John Eadie, D. D., LL. D., Author of "Biblical Cyclopædia," "Ecclesiastical Cyclopædia," "Dictionary of the Bible," etc. One volume, octavo, 840 pp. Cloth, $3.00; sheep, $3.50; cloth, gilt, $4.00; half Turkey morocco, $4.00.

The object of this Concordance is to present the Scriptures entire, under certain classified and exhaustive heads. It differs from an ordinary Concordance, in that its arrangement depends not on words, but on subjects, and the verses *are printed in full.* Its plan does not bring it at all into competition with such limited works as those of Gaston and Warden; for they select *doctrinal* topics principally, and do not profess to comprehend as this the entire Bible. The work also contains a Synoptical Table of Contents of the whole work, presenting in brief a system of biblical antiquities and theology, with a very copious and accurate index.

The value of this work to ministers and Sabbath-school teachers can hardly be over-estimated; and it needs only to be examined, to secure the approval and patronage of every Bible student.

CRUDEN'S CONDENSED CONCORDANCE. A Complete Concordance to the Holy Scriptures. By Alexander Cruden. Revised and Re-edited by the Rev. David King, LL. D. Octavo, cloth backs, $1.25; sheep, $1.50.

The condensation of the quotations of Scripture, arranged under the most obvious heads, while it *diminishes the bulk* of the work, *greatly facilitates* the finding of any required passage.

"We have in this edition of Cruden the *best* made *better.* That is, the present is better adapted to the purposes of a Concordance, by the erasure of superfluous references, the omission of unnecessary explanations, and the contraction of quotations, &c. It is better as a manual, and is better adapted by its price to the means of many who need and ought to possess such a work, than the former large and expensive edition." — *Puritan Recorder.*

A COMMENTARY ON THE ORIGINAL TEXT OF THE ACTS OF THE APOSTLES. By Horatio B. Hackett, D. D., Prof. of Biblical Literature and Interpretation, in the Newton Theol. Inst. ☞ A new, revised, and enlarged edition. Royal octavo, cloth, $2.25.

☞ This most important and very popular work has been thoroughly revised; large portions entirely re-written, with the addition of *more than one hundred pages of new matter;* the result of the author's continued, laborious investigations and travels, since the publication of the first edition.

IMPORTANT NEW WORKS.

CYCLOPÆDIA OF ANECDOTES OF LITERATURE AND THE FINE ARTS. Containing a copious and choice Selection of Anecdotes of the various forms of Literature, of the Arts, of Architecture, Engravings, Music, Poetry, Painting, and Sculpture, and of the most celebrated Literary Characters and Artists of different Countries and Ages, &c. By KAZLITT ARVINE, A. M., author of "Cyclopædia of Moral and Religious Anecdotes." With numerous Illustrations. 725 pp. octavo. Cloth, $3.00 ; sheep, $3.50 ; cloth, gilt, $4.00 ; half calf, $4.00.

This is unquestionably the choicest collection of *Anecdotes* ever published. It contains *three thousand and forty Anecdotes:* and such is the wonderful variety, that it will be found an almost inexhaustible fund of interest for every class of readers. The elaborate classification and Indexes must commend it especially to public speakers, to the various classes of *literary and scientific men, to artists, mechanics,* and *others,* as a DICTIONARY *for reference,* in relation to facts on the numberless subjects and characters introduced. There are also more than *one hundred and fifty fine Illustrations.*

THE LIFE OF JOHN MILTON, Narrated in Connection with the POLITICAL, ECCLESIASTICAL, and LITERARY HISTORY OF HIS TIME. By DAVID MASSON, M.A., Professor of English Literature, University College, London. Vol. I., embracing the period from 1608 to 1639. With Portraits, and specimens of his handwriting at different periods. Royal octavo, cloth, $0.00.

This important work will embrace three royal octavo volumes. By special arrangement with Prof. Masson, the author, G. & L. are permitted to print from advance sheets furnished them, as the authorized American publishers of this magnificent and eagerly looked for work. Volumes *two* and *three* will follow in due time ; but, as each volume covers a definite period of time, and also embraces distinct topics of discussion or history, they will be published and sold independent of each other, or furnished in sets when the three volumes are completed.

THE GREYSON LETTERS. Selections from the Correspondence of R. E. H. GREYSON, Esq. Edited by HENRY ROGERS, author of "Eclipse of Faith." 12mo, cloth, $1.25.

"Mr. Greyson and Mr. Rogers are one and the same person. The whole work is from his pen, and every letter is radiant with the genius of the author. It discusses a wide range of subjects, in the most attractive manner. It abounds in the keenest wit and humor, satire and logic. It fairly entitles Mr. Rogers to rank with Sydney Smith and Charles Lamb as a wit and humorist, and with Bishop Butler as a reasoner. Mr. Rogers' name will share with those of Butler and Pascal, in the gratitude and veneration of posterity." — *London Quarterly.*

"A book not for one hour, but for all hours ; not for one mood, but for every mood ; to think over, to dream over, to laugh over." — *Boston Journal.*

"The Letters are intellectual gems, radiant with beauty, happily intermingling the grave and the gay. — *Christian Observer.*

ESSAYS IN BIOGRAPHY AND CRITICISM. By PETER BAYNE, M. A., author of "The Christian Life, Social and Individual." Arranged in two Series, or Parts. 12mo, cloth, each, $1.25.

These volumes have been prepared by the author exclusively for his American publishers, and are now published in uniform style. They include nineteen articles, viz. :

FIRST SERIES :— Thomas De Quincy. — Tennyson and his Teachers. — Mrs. Barrett Browning. — Recent Aspects of British Art. — John Ruskin. — Hugh Miller. — The Modern Novel ; Dickens, &c. — Ellis, Acton, and Currer Bell.

SECOND SERIES :— Charles Kingsley. — S. T. Coleridge. — T. B. Macaulay. — Alison. — Wellington. — Napoleon. — Plato. — Characteristics of Christian Civilization. — The Modern University. — The Pulpit and the Press. — Testimony of the Rocks : a Defence.

VISITS TO EUROPEAN CELEBRITIES. By the Rev. WILLIAM B. SPRAGUE, D. D. 12mo, cloth, $1.00 ; cloth, gilt, $1.50.

A series of graphic and life-like Personal Sketches of many of the most distinguished men and women of Europe, portrayed as the Author saw them in their own homes, and under the most advantageous circumstances. Besides these "pen and ink" sketches, the work contains the novel attraction of a *fac-simile of the signature* of each of the persons introduced.

VALUABLE WORKS

PUBLISHED BY

GOULD AND LINCOLN,

59 WASHINGTON STREET, BOSTON.

THE CHRISTIAN LIFE; Social and Individual. By Peter Bayne, M. A. 12mo, cloth, $1.25.

There is but one voice respecting this extraordinary book, — men of all denominations, in all quarters, agree in pronouncing it one of the most admirable works of the age.

MODERN ATHEISM; Under its forms of Pantheism, Materialism, Secularism, Development, and Natural Laws. By James Buchanan, D. D., L. L. D. 12mo, cloth, $1.25.

"The work is one of the most readable and solid which we have ever perused." — *Hugh Miller in the Witness.*

NEW ENGLAND THEOCRACY. From the German of Uhden's History of the Congregationalists of New England, with an Introduction by Neander. By Mrs. H. C. Conant, author of "The English Bible," etc. 12mo, cloth, $1.00.

A work of rare ability and interest, presenting the early religious and ecclesiastical history of New England, from authentic sources, with singular impartiality. The author evidently aimed throughout to do exact justice to the dominant party, and all their opponents of every name. The standpoint from which the whole subject is viewed is novel, and we have in this volume a new and most important contribution to Puritan History.

THE MISSION OF THE COMFORTER; with copious Notes. By Julius Charles Hare. With the Notes translated for the American Edition. 12mo, cloth, $1.25.

THE BETTER LAND; or, The Believer's Journey and Future Home. By the Rev. A. C. Thompson. 12mo, cloth, 85 cts.

A most charming and instructive book for all now journeying to the "Better Land."

THE EVENING OF LIFE; or, Light and Comfort amidst the Shadows of Declining Years. By Rev. Jeremiah Chaplin, D. D. A new Revised, and much enlarged edition. With an elegant Frontispiece on Steel. 12mo, cloth, $1.00.

☞ A most charming and appropriate work for the aged, — large type and open page. An admirable "Gift" for the child to present the parent.

THE STATE OF THE IMPENITENT DEAD. By Alvah Hovey, D. D., Prof. of Christian Theology in Newton Theol. Inst. 16mo, cloth, 50 cts.

A WREATH AROUND THE CROSS; or, Scripture Truths Illustrated. By the Rev. A. Morton Brown, D. D. Recommendatory Preface, by John Angell James. With a beautiful Frontispiece. 16mo, cloth, 60 cts.

"'Christ, and Him crucified' is presented in a new, striking, and matter-of-fact light. The style is simple, without being puerile, and the reasoning is of that truthful, persuasive kind that 'comes from the heart, and reaches the heart.'" — *N. Y. Observer.*

WORKS FOR CHURCH MEMBERS.

THE CHRISTIAN'S DAILY TREASURY; a Religious Exercise for every Day in the Year. By Rev. E. TEMPLE. A new and improved edition. 12mo, cloth, $1.00.

☞ A work for every Christian. It is indeed a " Treasury " of good things.

THE SCHOOL OF CHRIST; or, Christianity Viewed in its Leading Aspects. By the Rev. A. R. L. FOOTE, author of "Incidents in the Life of our Saviour," etc. 16mo, cloth, 50 cts.

THE CHRISTIAN PASTOR; His Work and the Needful Preparation. By ALVAH HOVEY, D. D., Prof. of Theology in the Newton Theol. Inst. 16mo, pp. 60; flexible cloth, 25 cents; paper covers, 12 cents.

APOLLOS; or, Directions to Persons just commencing a Religious Life. 32mo, paper covers, cheap, for distribution, per hundred, $6.00.

THE HARVEST AND THE REAPERS. Home Work for All, and how to do it. By Rev. HARVEY NEWCOMB. 16mo, cloth, 63 cts.

This work is dedicated to the converts of 1858. It shows what *may* be done, by showing what has been done. It shows how much there is NOW to be done at home. It shows HOW to do it. Every man interested in the work of saving men, every professing Christian, will find this work to be for him.

THE CHURCH-MEMBER'S MANUAL of Ecclesiastical Principles, Doctrines, and Discipline. By Rev. WILLIAM CROWELL, D. D. Introduction by H. J. RIPLEY, D. D. Second edition, revised and improved. 12mo, cloth, 75 cts.

THE CHURCH-MEMBER'S HAND-BOOK; a Plain Guide to the Doctrines and Practice of Baptist Churches. By the Rev. WILLIAM CROWELL, D. D. 18mo, cloth, 38 cts.

THE CHURCH-MEMBER'S GUIDE. By the Rev. JOHN A. JAMES. Edited by J. O. CHOULES, D. D. New edition. With Introductory Essay, by Rev. HUBBARD WINSLOW. Cloth, 33 cts.

" The spontaneous effusion of our heart, on laying the book down, was : 'May every church-member in our land possess this book, and be blessed with all the happiness which conformity to its evangelical sentiments and directions is calculated to confer.' " — *Christian Secretary.*

THE CHURCH IN EARNEST. By Rev. JOHN A. JAMES. 18mo, cloth, 40 cts.

"Its arguments and appeals are well adapted to prompt to action, and the times demand such a book. We trust it will be universally read." — *N. Y. Observer.*

" Those who have the means should purchase a number of copies of this work, and lend them to church-members, and keep them in circulation *till they are worn out!* " — *Mothers' Assistant.*

CHRISTIAN PROGRESS. A Sequel to the Anxious Inquirer. By JOHN ANGELL JAMES. 18mo, cloth, 31 cts.

☞ One of the best and most useful works of this popular author.

"It ought to be sold by hundreds of thousands, until every church-member in the land has bought, read, marked, learned, and inwardly digested a copy." — *Congregationalist.*

" So eminently is it adapted to do good, that we feel no surprise that it should make one of the publishers' excellent publications. It exhibits the whole subject of growth in grace with great simplicity and clearness." — *Puritan Recorder.*

VALUABLE NEW WORKS.

GOD REVEALED IN NATURE AND IN CHRIST; including a Refutation of the Development Theory contained in the "Vestiges of the Natural History of Creation." By Rev. JAMES B. WALKER, author of "THE PHILOSOPHY OF THE PLAN OF SALVATION." 12mo, cloth, $1.00.

PHILOSOPHY OF THE PLAN OF SALVATION; a Book for the Times. By an AMERICAN CITIZEN. With an Introductory Essay by CALVIN E. STOWE, D. D. ☞ New improved and enlarged edition. 12mo, cloth, 75 cts.

YAHVEH CHRIST; or, The Memorial Name. By ALEXANDER MACWHORTER. With an Introductory Letter by NATHANIEL W. TAYLOR, D. D., Dwight Professor in Yale Theol. Sem. 16mo, cloth, 60 cts.

SALVATION BY CHRIST. A Series of Discourses on some of the most Important Doctrines of the Gospel. By FRANCIS WAYLAND, D. D. 12mo, cloth, $1.00; cloth, gilt, $1.50.

CONTENTS. — Theoretical Atheism. — Practical Atheism. — The Moral Character of Man. — The Fall of Man. — Justification by Works Impossible. — Preparation for the Advent. — Work of the Messiah. — Justification by Faith. — Conversion. — Imitators of God. — Grieving the Spirit. — A Day in the Life of Jesus. — The Benevolence of the Gospel. — The Fall of Peter. — Character of Balaam. — Veracity. — The Church of Christ. — The Unity of the Church. — Duty of Obedience to the Civil Magistrate (three Sermons).

THE GREAT DAY OF ATONEMENT; or, Meditations and Prayers on the Last Twenty-four Hours of the Sufferings and Death of Our Lord and Saviour Jesus Christ. Translated from the German of CHARLOTTE ELIZABETH NEBELIN. Edited by MRS. COLIN MACKENZIE. Elegantly printed and bound. 16mo, cloth, 75 cts.

THE EXTENT OF THE ATONEMENT IN ITS RELATION TO GOD AND THE UNIVERSE. By Rev. THOMAS W. JENKYN, D. D., late President of Coward College, London. 12mo, cloth, $1.00.

This work was thoroughly revised by the author not long before his death, exclusively for the present publishers. It has long been a standard work, and without doubt presents the most complete discussion of the subject in the language.

"We consider this volume as setting the long and fiercely agitated question as to the extent of the Atonement completely at rest. Posterity will thank the author till the latest ages for his illustrious argument." — *New York Evangelist.*

THE SUFFERING SAVIOUR; or, Meditations on the Last Days of Christ. By FRED. W. KRUMMACHER, D. D., author of "Elijah the Tishbite." 12mo, cloth, $1.25.

"The narrative is given with thrilling vividness, and pathos, and beauty. Marking, as we proceeded, several passages for quotation, we found them in the end so numerous, that we must refer the reader to the work itself." — *News of the Churches (Scottish).*

THE IMITATION OF CHRIST. By THOMAS A KEMPIS. With an Introductory Essay, by THOMAS CHALMERS, D. D. Edited by HOWARD MALCOM, D. D. A new edition, with a LIFE OF THOMAS A KEMPIS, by Dr. C. ULLMANN, author of "Reformers before the Reformation." 12mo, cloth, 85 cts.

This may safely be pronounced the best Protestant edition extant of this ancient and celebrated work. It is reprinted from Payne's edition, collated with an ancient Latin copy. The peculiar feature of this new edition is the improved page, the elegant, large, clear type, and the NEW LIFE OF A KEMPIS, by Dr. Ullmann.

VALUABLE WORKS.

FOOTSTEPS OF OUR FOREFATHERS; What they suffered and what they sought. Describing Localities, and Portraying Personages and Events, conspicuous in the Struggles for Religious Liberty. By JAMES G. MIALL. Containing thirty-six Illustrations. 12mo, cloth, $1.00.

MEMORIALS OF EARLY CHRISTIANITY; Presenting, in a graphic, compact, and popular form, Memorable Events of Early Ecclesiastical History, &c. By Rev. J. G. MIALL, author of "Footsteps of our Forefathers." With numerous Illustrations. 12mo, cloth, $1.00.

☞ The above, by Miall, are both exceedingly interesting and instructive works.

REPUBLICAN CHRISTIANITY; or, True Liberty, as exhibited in the Life, Precepts, and early Disciples of the Great Redeemer. By the Rev. E. L. MAGOON, D. D., author of "Proverbs for the People," &c. Second edition. 12mo, cloth, $1.25.

"The author has at his command a rich store of learning, from which he skilfully draws abundant evidence for the support of the positions he assumes." — *Puritan Recorder.*

THE PERSON AND WORK OF CHRIST. By ERNEST SARTORIUS, D.D., Konigsberg, Prussia. Translated by Rev. OAKMAN S. STEARNS, A. M. 18mo, cloth, 42 cts.

"A work of much ability, and presenting the argument in a style that will be new to most of American readers. It will deservedly attract attention." — *New York Observer*

CHRISTIANITY DEMONSTRATED; in four distinct and independent series of proofs; with an Explanation of the Types and Prophecies concerning the Messiah. By Rev. HARVEY NEWCOMB. 12mo, cloth, 75 cts.

THE SAINT'S EVERLASTING REST. By RICHARD BAXTER 16mo, cloth, 50 cts.

THE RELIGIONS OF THE WORLD, and their Relations to Christianity. By FREDERICK DENISON MAURICE, A. M., Professor of Divinity in King's College, London. 16mo, cloth, 60 cts.

THE CHRISTIAN WORLD UNMASKED. By JOHN BERRIDGE, A M., Vicar of Everton, Bedfordshire. With a Life of the Author, by Rev. THOMAS GUTHRIE, D. D., Minister of Free St. John's, Edinburgh. 16mo, cloth, 50 cts.

"The book," says DR. GUTHRIE, in his Introduction, "which we introduce anew to the public, has survived the test of years, and still stands towering above things of inferior growth, like a cedar of Lebanon. Its subject is all-important; in doctrine it is sound to the core; it glows with fervent piety; it exhibits a most skilful and unsparing dissection of the dead professor; while its style is so remarkable that he who could *preach* as Berridge has *written* would hold any congregation by the ears."

THE IMITATION OF CHRIST. By THOMAS A KEMPIS. Introductory Essay, by T. CHALMERS, D. D. Edited by the REV. HOWARD MALCOM, D. D. *Cheap edition.* 18mo, cloth, 38 cts.

GUIDO AND JULIUS. THE DOCTRINE OF SIN AND THE PROPITIATOR; or, the True Consecration of the Doubter. Exhibited in the Correspondence of two Friends. By FREDERICK AUGUSTUS O. THOLUCK, D. D. Translated from the German, by JONATHAN EDWARDS RYLAND. With an introduction by JOHN PYE SMITH, D. D. 16mo, cloth, 60 cts.

DR. JOHN HARRIS' WORKS.

THE GREAT TEACHER; or, Characteristics of our Lord's Ministry. By JOHN HARRIS, D. D. With an Introductory Essay by H. HUMPHREY, D. D. Sixteenth thousand. 12mo, cloth, 85 cents.

"DR. HARRIS is one of the best writers of the age; and this volume will not in the least detract from his well-merited reputation." — *American Pulpit.*

THE GREAT COMMISSION; or, the Christian Church constituted and charged to convey the Gospel to the World. A Prize Essay. With an Introductory Essay by W. R. WILLIAMS, D. D. Eighth thousand. 12mo, cloth, $1.00.

"This volume will afford the reader an intellectual and spiritual banquet of the highest order." — *Philadelphia Ch. Observer.*

THE PRE-ADAMITE EARTH. Contributions to Theological Science. By JOHN HARRIS, D. D. New and revised edition. 12mo, cloth, $1.00.

MAN PRIMEVAL; or, the Constitution and Primitive Condition of the Human Being. With a finely engraved Portrait of the Author. 12mo, cloth, $1.25.

PATRIARCHY; or, the Family, its Constitution and Probation. 12mo, cloth, $1.25.

This is the last of Dr. Harris' series entitled "Contributions to Theological Science."

SERMONS, CHARGES, ADDRESSES, &c., delivered by Dr. HARRIS in various parts of the country, during the height of his reputation as a preacher. Two elegant volumes, octavo, cloth, each, $1.00.

The immense sale of all this author's Works attests their intrinsic worth and great popularity.

DR. WILLIAMS' WORKS.

LECTURES ON THE LORD'S PRAYER. By WILLIAM R. WILLIAMS, D. D. Third edition. 12mo, cloth, 85 cts.

"We are constantly reminded, in reading his eloquent pages, of the old English writers, whose vigorous thought, and gorgeous imagery, and varied learning, have made their writings an inexhaustible mine for the scholars of the present day." — *Ch. Observer.*

RELIGIOUS PROGRESS; Discourses on the Development of the Christian Character. By WILLIAM R. WILLIAMS, D. D. Third edition. 12mo, cloth, 85 cts.

"His power of apt and forcible illustration is without a parallel among modern writers. The mute pages spring into life beneath the magic of his radiant imagination. But this is never at the expense of solidity of thought, or strength of argument. It is seldom, indeed, that a mind of so much poetical invention yields such a willing homage to the logical element." — *Harper's Monthly Miscellany.*

MISCELLANIES. By WILLIAM R. WILLIAMS, D. D. New and improved edition. *Price Reduced.* 12mo, cloth, $1.25.

☞ "Dr. Williams is a profound scholar and a brilliant writer." — *N. Y. Evangelist.*

BUNGENER'S WORKS.

THE PREACHER AND THE KING; or, Bourdaloue in the Court of Louis XIV.; being an Account of the Pulpit Eloquence of that distinguished era. Translated from the French of L. F. BUNGENER, Paris. Introduction by the Rev. GEORGE POTTS, D. D. *A new, improved edition*, with a fine LIKENESS and a BIOGRAPHICAL SKETCH OF THE AUTHOR. 12mo, cloth, $1.25.

THE PRIEST AND THE HUGUENOT; or, Persecution in the Age of Louis XV Translated from the French of L. F. Bungener. Two vols. 12mo, cloth, $2.25.

☞ This is not only a work of thrilling interest, — no fiction could exceed it, — but, as a Protestant work, it is a masterly production.

BIOGRAPHIES AND WORKS ON MISSIONS.

THE MISSIONARY ENTERPRISE; a Collection of the most important Discourses in the language, on Christian Missions, by distinguished American Authors. Edited by BARON STOW, D. D. Second Thousand. 12mo, cloth, 85 cts.

"You here see the high talent of the American church. The discourses by Dr. Beecher, Dr. Wayland, and the Rev. Dr. Stone, are among the very highest exhibitions of logical correctness, and burning, popular fervor." — *New Englander.*

A HISTORY OF AMERICAN BAPTIST MISSIONS, in Asia, Africa, Europe, and North America, from their earliest commencement to the present time. Prepared under the direction of the American Baptist Missionary Union. By WILLIAM GAMMELL, Professor in Brown University. With seven Maps. 12mo, cloth, at the low price of 75 cts.

This work was prepared at the request of the Executive Committee of the Missionary Union; and the Committee appointed by the Union to examine the manuscript, consisting of Doctors Cone, Sharp, and Chase, say: "It exhibits gratifying evidence of research, fidelity, and skill. It sets before the reader, in a lucid manner, facts that should never be forgotten. Some of them, in power to awaken attention and touch the heart, could scarcely be surpassed by fiction."

Rev. E. Kincaid says: "As I have labored more or less at *all* the stations in Burmah, I could but admire the singular accuracy with which all the leading facts of these missions are detailed in Prof. Gammell's History of American Baptist Missions. I have not found a *single error* of any importance."

Rev. J. Wade says: "I can most cordially recommend it to the public as being a very truthful and well-written work."

DR. GRANT AND THE MOUNTAIN NESTORIANS. By Rev. THOMAS LAURIE, his surviving associate in that Mission. With a Likeness, Map of the Country, and numerous Illustrations. Third edition. Revised and improved. 12mo, cloth, $1.25.

☞ A most valuable Memoir of a *remarkable man.*

THE KAREN APOSTLE; or, Memoir of KO-THAH-BYU, the first Karen Convert. With notices concerning his Nation. By Rev. FRANCIS MASON, D. D., Missionary. Edited by Prof. H. J. RIPLEY. 18mo, cloth, 25 cts.

"This is a work of thrilling interest, containing the history of a remarkable man, and giving, also, much information respecting the Karens, a people until recently but little known."

MEMOIR OF ANN H. JUDSON, late Missionary to Burmah. By Rev. J. D. KNOWLES. A new edition. Fifty-seventh thousand. 18mo, cloth, 58 cts.

FINE EDITION, with plates, 16mo, cloth, gilt, 85 cts.

MEMOIR OF GEORGE DANA BOARDMAN, late Missionary to Burmah, containing much intelligence relative to the Burman Mission. By Rev. A. KING. With an Introductory Essay, by W. R. WILLIAMS, D. D. New edition, with beautiful frontispiece. 12mo, cloth, 75 cts.

"One of the brightest luminaries of Burmah is extinguished." — REV. DR. JUDSON.

☞ The introduction alone is worth the price of the book, says a distinguished reviewer.

MEMOIR OF HENRIETTA SHUCK, first female Missionary to China. By Rev. J. B. JETER, D. D. With a likeness. Fifth thousand. 12mo, cloth, 50 cts.

"We have seldom taken into our hands a more beautiful book than this. It will be extensively read, and eminently useful." — *Family Visitor.*

MEMOIR OF REV. WILLIAM G. CROCKER, late Missionary to West Africa, among the Bassas. Including a History of the Mission. By R. B. MEDBERY. With a likeness. 18mo, cloth, 63 cts.

"This work is commended to the attention of every lover of the liberties of man." — *Watchman and Reflector.*

VALUABLE WORKS.

THE LIMITS OF RELIGIOUS THOUGHT EXAMINED. By HENRY LONGUEVILLE MANSEL, B. D., Prof. of Moral and Metaphysical Philosophy, Magdalen College, Oxford, Editor of Sir William Hamilton's Lectures, etc. etc. With the COPIOUS NOTES of the volume translated for the American Edition. 12mo, cloth, $1.25.

☞ This is a *masterly* production, and may be safely said to be one of the most important works of the day.

FIRST THINGS; or, The Development of Church Life. By BARON STOW, D. D. 16mo, cloth, 75 cts.

HEAVEN. By JAMES WILLIAM KIMBALL. With an elegant vignette title-page. 12mo, cloth, $1.00.

"The book is full of beautiful ideas, consoling hopes, and brilliant representations of human destiny, all presented in a chaste, pleasing and very readable style." — *N. Y. Chronicle.*

THE PROGRESS OF BAPTIST PRINCIPLES IN THE LAST HUNDRED YEARS. By T. F. CURTIS, Professor of Theology in the Lewisburg University, Pa., and author of "Communion," &c. 12mo, cloth, $1.25.

Eminently worthy of the attention, not only of Baptists, *but of all other denominations.* In his preface the author declares that his aim has been to draw a wide distinction between *parties* and *opinions.* Hence the object of this volume is not to exhibit or defend the Baptists, *but their principles.* It is confidently pronounced the best exhibition of Baptist views and principles extant.

THOUGHTS ON THE PRESENT COLLEGIATE SYSTEM in the United States. By FRANCIS WAYLAND, D. D. 16mo, cloth, 50 cents.

SACRED RHETORIC; or, Composition and Delivery of Sermons. By H. J. RIPLEY, D. D., Prof. in Newton Theol. Inst. To which is added, DR. WARE'S HINTS ON EXTEMPORANEOUS PREACHING. Second thousand. 12mo, cloth, 75 cts.

THE PULPIT OF THE REVOLUTION; or, The Political Sermons of the Era of 1776. With an Introduction, Biographical Sketches of the Preachers and Historical Notes, etc. By JOHN WINGATE THORNTON, author of "The Landing at Cape Anne," etc. 12mo, cloth. *In press.*

THE EIGHTEEN CHRISTIAN CENTURIES. By the Rev. JAMES WHITE, author of "Landmarks of the History of England." 12mo, cloth. *In press.*

THE PLURALITY OF WORLDS. A NEW EDITION. With a SUPPLEMENTARY DIALOGUE, in which the author's Reviewers are reviewed. 12mo, cloth, $1.00.

This masterly production, which has excited so much interest in this country and in Europe, will now have an increased attraction in the addition of the Supplement, in which the author's reviewers are triumphantly reviewed.

THE CAMEL; His Organization, Habits, and Uses, considered with reference to his introduction into the United States. By GEORGE P. MARSH, late U. S. Minister at Constantinople. 12mo, cloth, 63 cts.

This book treats of a subject of great interest, especially at the present time. It furnishes a more complete and reliable account of the Camel than any other in the language; indeed, it is believed that there is no other. It is the result of long study, extensive research, and much personal observation, on the part of the author, and it has been prepared with special reference to the experiment of domesticating the Camel in this country, now going on under the auspices of the United States government. It is written in a style worthy of the distinguished author's reputation for great learning and fine scholarship.

VALUABLE BIOGRAPHIES.

EXTRACTS FROM THE DIARY AND CORRESPONDENCE OF THE LATE AMOS LAWRENCE. With a brief account of some Incidents in his Life. Edited by his son, WM. R. LAWRENCE, M. D. With elegant Portraits of Amos and Abbott Lawrence, an Engraving of their Birthplace, an Autograph page of Handwriting, and a copious Index. One large octavo volume, cloth, $1.50 ; royal 12mo, cloth, $1.00.

A MEMOIR OF THE LIFE AND TIMES OF ISAAC BACKUS. By ALVAH HOVEY, Professor of Ecclesiastical History in Newton Theological Institution. 12mo, cloth, $1.25.

This work gives an account of a remarkable man, and of a remarkable movement in the middle of the last century, resulting in the formation of what were called the "Separate" Churches. It supplies an important deficiency in the history of New England affairs. For every Baptist, especially, it is a necessary book.

LIFE OF JAMES MONTGOMERY. By Mrs. H. C. KNIGHT, author of "Lady Huntington and her Friends," &c. Likeness and elegant Illustrated Title-Page on steel. 12mo, cloth, $1.25.

This is an original biography, prepared from the abundant but ill-digested materials contained in the seven octavo volumes of the London edition. The Christian public in America will welcome such a memoir of a poet whose hymns and sacred melodies have been the delight of every household.

MEMOIR OF ROGER WILLIAMS, Founder of the State of Rhode Island. By Prof. WILLIAM GAMMELL, A. M. 16mo, cloth, 75 cts.

PHILIP DODDRIDGE. His Life and Labors. By JOHN STOUGHTON, D. D. With an Introductory Chapter, by Rev. JAMES G. MIALL, Author of "Footsteps of our Forefathers," &c. With beautiful Illustrated Title-page and Frontispiece. 16mo, cloth, 60 cents.

THE LIFE AND CORRESPONDENCE OF JOHN FOSTER. Edited by J. E. RYLAND, with notices of Mr. FOSTER, as a Preacher and a Companion. By JOHN SHEPPARD. A new edition, two volumes in one, 700 pages. 12mo, cloth, $1.25.

"In simplicity of language, in majesty of conception, his writings are unmatched." — *North British Review.*

THE LIFE OF GODFREY WILLIAM VON LEIBNITZ. By JOHN M. MACKIE, Esq. On the basis of the German work of Dr. G. E. GUHRAUER. 16mo, cloth, 75 cts.

"It merits the special notice of all who are interested in the business of education, and deserves a place by the side of Brewster's Life of Newton, in all the libraries of our schools, academies, and literary institutions." — *Watchman and Reflector.*

MEMORIES OF A GRANDMOTHER. By a Lady of Massachusetts. 16mo, cloth, 50 cts.

☞ "My path lies in a valley, which I have sought to adorn with flowers. Shadows from the hills cover it; but I make my own sunshine." — *Author's Preface.*

THE TEACHER'S LAST LESSON. A Memoir of MARTHA WHITING, late of the Charlestown Female Seminary, with Reminiscences and Suggestive Reflections. By CATHARINE N. BADGER, an Associate Teacher. With a Portrait, and an Engraving of the Seminary. 12mo, cloth, $1.00.

The subject of this Memoir was, for a quarter of a century, at the head of one of the most celebrated female seminaries in the country. During that period she educated more than *three thousand* young ladies. She was a kindred spirit to Mary Lyon.

VALUABLE WORKS.

SERVICE, THE END OF LIVING. An Address delivered before the Boston Young Men's Christian Association, at their Anniversary, on Monday evening, May 24, 1858. By ANDREW L. STONE, Pastor of Park-street Church, Boston. 16mo, flexible cloth covers, 20 cts.; paper covers, 12½ cts.

☞ An admirable work for circulation, especially among young men.

PERMANENT REALITIES OF RELIGION, AND THE PRESENT RELIGIOUS INTEREST. A Sermon preached in the Bedford-street Church, Boston, on the evening of Fast Day, April 15, 1858. By F. D. HUNTINGTON, D. D., Preacher to the University, Cambridge. Octavo pamphlet, 12½ cts.

CHRISTIAN CITIZENSHIP AND HONEST LEGISLATION. A Sermon delivered before the Legislature of Massachusetts, at the Annual Election, January 6, 1858, by F. D. HUNTINGTON, D. D., Preacher to the University, Cambridge. Octavo pamphlet, 12½ cts.

TRUTHS FOR THE TIMES. By NEHEMIAH ADAMS, D. D., Pastor of Essex-street Church, Boston. 12mo, paper covers.

This very useful and popular Series of publications comprises the following:

I. THE REASONABLENESS OF FUTURE ENDLESS PUNISHMENT, 10 cts.
II. INSTANTANEOUS CONVERSION AND ITS CONNECTION WITH PIETY, 10 cts.
III. JUSTIFICATION AND ITS CONSEQUENCES, 10 cts.
IV. GOD IS LOVE. A Supplement to the Author's Discourse on the "Reasonableness of Future Endless Punishment," with a brief notice of Rev. T. STARR KING'S Two Discourses in reply to the same, 20 cts.
V. OUR BIBLE, 20 cts.

EXCLUSIVENESS OF THE BAPTISTS; a Review of Dr. Albert Barnes' Pamphlet on "Exclusivism." By H. J. RIPLEY, Prof. Newton Theol. Inst. 16mo, printed cover, 10 cts.

A kind yet manly and most triumphant refutation of Dr. Barnes' serious charges of "*Exclusivism*," etc., against the Baptists.

REMARKS ON SOCIAL PRAYER-MEETINGS. By the Right Rev. ALEXANDER VIETS GRISWOLD, D. D., late Bishop of the Eastern Diocese. "He, being dead, yet speaketh."—Heb. xi. 4. Originally published in the Episcopal Register, for the years 1827–8. With an introductory statement by Rev. GEORGE D. WILDES, A. M. 12mo, cloth bound, 37½ cts.; cloth, flexible covers, 31 cts.; paper covers, 20 cts.

This admirable defence of social prayer-meetings, by one whose memory is still fragrant in the hearts of multitudes, is highly commended by Bishop Eastburn, and the Rev. John S. Stone, D. D.

THE INCARNATION; By ROLLIN H. NEALE, D. D. 32mo, gilt, 31 cts.

ANTIOCH; or, Increase of Moral Power in the Church of Christ. By P. CHURCH, D. D. With an Essay by BARON STOW, D. D. 18mo, cloth, 50 cts.

ONESIMUS; or, the Apostolic Directions to Christian Masters in reference to their Slaves considered. By EVANGELICUS. 18mo, cloth, 25 cts.

CHRISTIANITY AND SLAVERY. A REVIEW of Drs. Fuller and Wayland on Slavery. By WILLIAM HAGUE, D. D. 18mo, paper cover, 12½ cts.

CHRISTIANITY AND SLAVERY. STRICTURES on the Rev. Dr. Hague's Review of Drs. Fuller and Wayland on Domestic Slavery. By Rev. THOMAS MEREDITH, Raleigh, N. C. 18mo, paper, 12½ cts.

WORKS FOR BIBLE STUDENTS.

NOTES ON THE GOSPELS. Designed for Teachers in Sabbath Schools and Bible Classes, and as an Aid to Family Instruction. By HENRY J. RIPLEY, Prof. in Newton Theol. Inst. With Map of Canaan. Cloth, embossed, $1.25.

NOTES ON THE ACTS OF THE APOSTLES. With a beautiful Map, illustrating the Travels of the APOSTLE PAUL, with a track of his Voyage from Cesarea to Rome. By Prof. HENRY J. RIPLEY, D. D. 12mo, cloth, embossed, 75 cts.

NOTES ON THE EPISTLE OF PAUL TO THE ROMANS. Designed for Teachers in Sabbath Schools and Bible Classes, and as an aid to Family Instruction. By HENRY J. RIPLEY. 12mo, cloth, embossed, 67 cts.

The above works by Prof. Ripley should be in the hands of every student of the Bible, especially every Sabbath-school and Bible-class teacher. They are prepared with especial reference to this class of persons, and contain a mass of just the kind of information wanted.

MALCOM'S NEW BIBLE DICTIONARY of the most important Names, Objects, and Terms, found in the Holy Scriptures; intended principally for Sabbath-School Teachers and Bible Classes. By HOWARD MALCOM, D. D., late President of Lewisburg College, Pa. 16mo, cloth, embossed, 60 cts.

☞ The former Dictionary, of which more than *one hundred thousand copies* were sold, is made the basis of the present work; yet so revised, enlarged, and improved, by the addition of new material, a greatly increased number of articles, new illustrations, etc., as to render it essentially a NEW DICTIONARY.

THE EVIDENCES OF CHRISTIANITY, as exhibited in the writings of its apologists, down to Augustine. By W. J. BOLTON, of Gonville and Caius College, Cambridge. 12mo, cloth, 80 cts.

HARMONY QUESTIONS ON THE FOUR GOSPELS, for the use of Sabbath Schools. By Rev. S. B. SWAIM, D. D. Vol. I. 18mo, cloth backs, 12½ cts.

The plan differs from all others in this, that it is based upon a HARMONY of the gospels. Instead of taking one of the gospels, — that of Matthew, for instance, — and going through with it, the author takes from ALL of the gospels those parts relating to the same event, and brings them together in the same lesson.

SABBATH-SCHOOL CLASS BOOK; comprising copious Exercises on the Sacred Scriptures. By E. LINCOLN. Revised and Improved by REV. JOSEPH BANVARD, author of "Topical Question Book," etc. 18mo, 12½ cts.

United testimony of Dr. Malcom, author of "Bible Dictionary," Dr. Stow, "Doctrinal Question Book," Dr. Hague, "Guides to Conversations on New Testament":

"It gives us pleasure to express our satisfaction with its design and execution. We think the work is well adapted to the end designed, having avoided, in a great degree, the evils of extreme redundance or conciseness."

LINCOLN'S SCRIPTURE QUESTIONS; with answers, giving, in the language of Scripture, interesting portions of the History, Doctrines, and Duties, exhibited in the Bible. 8⅓ cts. per copy; $1.00 per dozen.

☞ Where Bibles cannot be furnished to each scholar, this work will be found an admirable substitute, as the text is furnished in connection with the questions.

THE SABBATH-SCHOOL HARMONY; containing appropriate Hymns and Music for Sabbath Schools, Juvenile Singing Schools, and Family Devotion. By NATHANIEL D. GOULD. 12½ cts.

VALUABLE WORKS.

MOTHERS OF THE WISE AND GOOD. By JABEZ BURNS, D. D. 16mo, cloth, 75 cts.; cloth, gilt, $1.25.

☞ A sketch of the mothers of many of the most eminent men of the world, and showing how much they were indebted to maternal influence for their greatness and excellence of character.

MY MOTHER; or, Recollections of Maternal Influence. By a New England Clergyman. With a beautiful Frontispiece. 12mo, cloth, 75 cts.; cloth, gilt, $1.25.

A writer of wide celebrity says of the book: "It is one of those rare pictures painted from life with the exquisite skill of one of the *Old Masters*, which so seldom present themselves to the amateur."

THE EXCELLENT WOMAN, as Described in the Book of Proverbs With an Introduction by Rev. W. B. SPRAGUE, D. D. Containing twenty-four splendid Illustrations. Third thousand. 12mo, cloth, $1.00; cloth, gilt, $1.75; extra Turkey, $2.50.

☞ This elegant volume is an appropriate and valuable "Gift Book" for the husband to present the wife, or the child the mother.

THE SIGNET RING, AND ITS HEAVENLY MOTTO. From the German. Illustrated. 16mo, cloth, gilt, 31 cts.

☞ Seldom within so small a compass has such weighty teaching been presented with such exquisite and charming skill.

THE MARRIAGE RING; or, How to Make Home Happy. From the writings of JOHN ANGELL JAMES. Beautifully Illustrated edition. 16mo, cloth, gilt, 75 cts.

WORKS BY DR. TWEEDIE.

GLAD TIDINGS; or, the Gospel of Peace. A Series of Daily Meditations for Christian Disciples. By Rev. W. K. TWEEDIE, D. D. With an elegant illustrated title-page. 16mo, cloth, 63 cts.; cloth, gilt, $1.00.

A LAMP TO THE PATH; or, the Bible in the Heart, the Home, and the Market-place. With an elegant illustrated title-page. 16mo, cloth, 63 cts.; clo. gilt, $1.00.

SEED-TIME AND HARVEST; or, Sow Well and Reap Well. A Book for the Young. With an elegant illustrated title-page. 16mo, cloth, 63 cts.; cloth, gilt, $1.00.

☞ The above interesting works, by Dr. Tweedie, are of uniform size and style, and well adapted for "gift books."

GATHERED LILIES; or, Little Children in Heaven. By Rev. A. C. THOMPSON, Author of "The Better Land." 18mo, flexible cloth, 25 cts.; flexible cloth, gilt, 31 cts.; and cloth, gilt, 42 cts.

"My beloved has gone down into his garden to gather lilies." — *Song of Solomon.*

"In almost every household such a little volume as this will meet a tender welcome." — *N. Y. Evangelist.*

OUR LITTLE ONES IN HEAVEN. Edited by the Author of "The Aimwell Stories," &c. 18mo, cloth, 50 cts.; cloth, gilt, 75 cts.

This little volume contains a choice collection of pieces, in verse and prose, on the death and future happiness of young children.

SAFE HOME; or, the Last Days and Happy Death of Fannie Kenyon. With an Introduction by Prof. J. L. Lincoln, of Brown University. 18mo, flexible cloth cover, 25 cts.; gilt, 31 cts.

This is a delightful narrative of a remarkable little girl, and is recommended to the attention, particularly, of Sabbath Schools.

www.ingramcontent.com/pod-product-compliance
Lightning Source LLC
LaVergne TN
LVHW020229110826
845151LV00003B/871

* 9 7 8 1 4 2 5 5 3 0 9 0 7 *